D1605892

"This book is a welcome addition to the literature on the social and cultural aspects of death and dying that I shall be recommending in my courses. It is perhaps the first sociologically relevant book-length treatment of popular media representations of death and is a significant advance on the current literature.

The argument moves us past tired old debates about media violence and into new territories that stress media as potentially community-building. It draws on contemporary media theory, a thorough analysis of media representations, and audience studies to present a narrative that is highly relevant to current thinking in thanatology. Expanding, too, into an analysis of the Internet and other new media in the final chapters, the book brings together hitherto diverse fields of scholarship in an exemplary fashion. I congratulate the author on his achievement."

Clive Seale, Professor of Sociology, Department of Human Sciences,
Brunel University, West London, and Author of
Constructing Death: The Sociology of Dying and Bereavement

"Charlton D. McIlwain's *When Death Goes Pop* is an ambitious and much-needed examination of the representation of death in contemporary popular culture. The book displays an impressive synthesis of media theory, rhetorical studies, and work in thanatology, and utilizes these various bodies of scholarship to render a lucid and provocative reading of contemporary popular culture.... *When Death Goes Pop* places representations of death within broader elements of culture, especially media technology, and, in so doing, provides an intelligible grid for thinking about death as a symbolic element in popular culture.

One of the most impressive elements of McIlwain's work is his integration of empirical observations with sweeping theoretical insights. This book is an excellent example of strong critical research and should be invaluable to anyone interested in the study of popular culture and media."

Kendall R. Phillips, Associate Professor of Communication
and Rhetorical Studies, Syracuse University, and Author of
Framing Public Memory: Rhetoric, Culture, and Social Critique

WHEN death GOES

PETER LANG
New York • Washington, D.C./Baltimore • Bern
Frankfurt am Main • Berlin • Brussels • Vienna • Oxford

CHARLTON D. McILWAIN

WHEN death GOES

POP

DEATH, MEDIA & THE
REMAKING OF COMMUNITY

PETER LANG
New York • Washington, D.C./Baltimore • Bern
Frankfurt am Main • Berlin • Brussels • Vienna • Oxford

Library of Congress Cataloging-in-Publication Data

McIlwain, Charlton D.
When death goes pop: death, media
& the remaking of community / Charlton D. McIlwain.
p. cm.
Includes bibliographical references and index.
1. Death on television. I. Title.
PN1992.8.D4M38   306.9—dc22   2003025197
ISBN 0-8204-7064-3

Bibliographic information published by **Die Deutsche Bibliothek**.
Die Deutsche Bibliothek lists this publication in the "Deutsche
Nationalbibliografie"; detailed bibliographic data is available
on the Internet at http://dnb.ddb.de/.

Cover design by Sophie Boorsch Appel

The paper in this book meets the guidelines for permanence and durability
of the Committee on Production Guidelines for Book Longevity
of the Council of Library Resources.

© 2005 Peter Lang Publishing, Inc., New York
275 Seventh Avenue, 28th Floor, New York, NY 10001
www.peterlangusa.com

Printed in the United States of America

To my mother and father, Annie and Ronald McIlwain

TABLE OF CONTENTS

FIGURES

ACKNOWLEDGMENTS

The idea for this book was hatched alone, but finishing it could not have been accomplished without the help of many.

While he cannot receive my thanks, I am grateful to Neil Postman, whose ideas helped me to think about the direction of this book, and who gave me encouragement in the beginning to pursue it.

I also need to thank my acquisitions editor at Peter Lang, Phyllis Korper, who helped me to focus the content of the book in a direction that I think has made it much better than originally conceived and written, and for her patience for the extended time it took for me to complete it.

I am indebted to my friend and colleague Phil Dalton, a former graduate student, Alexandra Ross, and friend Karen Philips, who read and gave invaluable feedback on several of the chapters included here.

Many thanks go out to the staff of Esperanto Café in New York City, where the majority of this book was written. Without the never-ending boosts of caffeine and an atmosphere conducive for writing, the book would not have turned out as well as I would have hoped.

Finally, I must thank many friends and colleagues—David Worth, Eric Kramer, Denise Scannell, Ted Magder, M. J. Robinson, Monique Mitchell, Sheridan Philips, Stephen and Jillian Maynard Caliendo, Siva Vaidhyanathan, and others that I may have neglected to mention—who helped me along the way by engaging me in helpful conversations, sharing their ideas, and providing much-needed encouragement.

INTRODUCTION

Permission to Speak the Discourse of Death

A few years ago I was sitting outside at a bar with several friends celebrating the end of another school semester. As time went on, my friends and I happened to make the acquaintance of a few strangers sitting near us, and, following a few minutes of small talk, the topic of conversation shifted to what my friends and I do for a living. When it was my turn to speak, I told them I am a researcher and writer, which immediately brought up the question of what exactly it is that I research and write about. Reluctant to break the norms of etiquette and describe in elaborate detail my thoughts about death and dying, I simply replied that I study the rituals surrounding death for some cultures in America. I was content to throw out that statement and move on to what might have been a more suitable topic of conversation.

As I made a gesture to politely signal my disinterest in continuing that line of discussion, I unexpectedly found myself listening to one of these strangers' stories about her mother who had recently passed away. She described many of the circumstances in elaborate detail, while the rest of us at the table listened with unremitting attention. The discussion (no doubt encouraged a little by several of the beverages we had consumed by this time) soon turned to each person explaining how they want to be eulogized when they die, how they want to be buried, what they want others to go through on their behalf, and what they want to leave behind. The question that emerged again and again, which acted as our transition into other parts of the conversation, was, "Why do you study death?" The answer I gave that particular night I cannot recall. I do, however, remember feeling as if none of my answers were sufficient. It is a question that I continue to ponder.

Why concern ourselves with death? It is meaningless to, as our positivist friends would, seek to understand death in order to mitigate its ultimate occurrence. While, undoubtedly, the scientists of our era and following will do all in their power to prove me wrong, all of our knowledge production about the phenomenon of death—from the empirical to the social—will not free us from the grip of the reaper. Why then do we take great pains to understand this inevitability? Why would we spend our time thinking about that thing which provides so much uncertainty for us? Why spend the time contemplating the dark regions of the dead—the nursing homes where the old go to decay and die; the hospital trauma wards where, despite the elaborate machinery and technology keeping a loved one "alive," the one in the bed already knows they are really dead; the cold morgues and funeral homes where quickly decaying flesh is poked at and sliced up, awaiting the filling of their cavities with fluid to mask death's sting; the frighteningly overgrown cemeteries where the dead are disposed of one beside (and often upon) the other; or the cemetery park where manicured lawns, high fences, and pavement conceal the dark lifelessness and isolation revealed by it? Are we masochists? Demented? Abnormal?

Despite all of its gruesomeness, humans from time immemorial have consumed themselves with deliberations about death. And, while we have, here in America, done well in masking this interest—though we have succeeded in convincing ourselves and others that the question of death really does not occupy a significant place in our thoughts and daily routines— beneath the façade, death permeates much more of our lives than we are most of the time willing to admit. That night at the bar, I probably would have been inclined to challenge this statement. I may have said that we have so many distractions that we rarely think about death, that life requires so much of us these days that we cannot afford to dwell on it too long. I might have even ventured that, in America, we have no time to die—that time thinking about death is time shamefully wasted.

Having delved into the phenomenon of death, and the variety of experiences surrounding it over the past few years, when I am now asked why I study death, I reply with the story of the person who asked the same question of me before them—the person who undoubtedly responded to my reply (which is always different) with a story—sometimes several stories—about how their mother died, about recently attending a funeral of a friend who died fifty years prematurely, about what they believe happens when they die or how they want to be treated at death. These stories, by people I have had the good fortune to interact with at one time or another, on an airplane, in a classroom, at a bar or a job interview, funeral home, or football game, demonstrated to me quite pointedly that, not only do Americans think often about death, but they are quite willing to talk about it. Why then does it seem we have no concern for it? I believe, precisely, because people need to be given a reason, or better yet, be given *permission* to speak about it. And, when given permission to do so, people rise to the challenge principally because it is meaningful for them to do so.

Meaning in Death: the Death of Ethics?

Death is life's only certainty. It is the only event of human existence not bound by time or space. In its universality it does not discriminate—affecting rich and poor, black and white, the "first world" and the "third world" alike. As the counter-pole of life, it is that which ultimately gives life its meaning. It is the one experience that, above others, begs to be made sense of. In light of this, it is no wonder that the human experience of death served as the initial impetus for what might be considered the first mass medium. From the time that human civilizations transitioned from nomadic life to permanent communal settlements, the meaningfulness of death was marked by the living. Whether a pile of rocks and sticks, vast pyramids, or large blocks of granite stone with linguistic inscriptions, people throughout time have erected mediums signifying the death of a member of the family, clan, or larger human community—a sign for all those who entered the space of the dead that this was sacred ground. Such mediums served a variety of functions. It was a place of contemplation for the living looking forward to their certain future, a place in which they could maintain a continuing connection with the ancestral community. It was also the center of religious and spiritual life. It was this function that marked such mediums, and the spaces they occupied, as the precursor to contemporary urban life. Lewis Mumford correctly made the point that the city of the dead antedates the city of the living.[1]

The primary purpose for permanence was our fore-parents' passion for their dead. People in these early times knew, seemingly instinctually, that it was important not only for their dead to be "properly" buried in the soil (or any other method deemed appropriate by a collective), but that their bodies were marked and recognizable—a visible sign of where "they" were. This is to say, the ancient cities of the dead were spaces for worship—of both deity and ancestry (which in some societies coincided). The germ of the modern city began in these cities of the dead as the central place for ceremony and ritual, a place where one could commune with ancestors, be enlightened, and be reinvigorated. It was a place where one could continually be reminded of the teachings of their relatives and contemplate one's own life and eventual death, where they would, in turn, take their place among those who had gone on before them to the mystery of the life following.

Given the depth of meaning associated with the experience of death, it is no wonder that the whole foundation of Western philosophy centered on existential contemplations about death, dying, and the afterlife. The questions philosophers pondered in this regard are significant, primarily because they provide some basis for ethical living. Plato's thoughts on this subject provide as good of a beginning to approach these ideas as any. Plato, it seems, was somewhat obsessed by death, but if obsession is too strong a description, he certainly believed that death, dying, and the afterlife were central to what it means to live—the manner of social organization we develop, our system of values and ethics, and our politics. His detailed attention to the subject is repeated throughout some of his most celebrated writings on government and democratic politics. Two examples of how Plato treated death are instructive for us here in understanding not only the role that death has played in the life of great thinkers throughout history, but also how it has provided a benchmark of sorts—showing how far we have come in terms of our relationship with death and the impact of this dissociation on our current cultural and political situation here in America.

Plato's interest in the experience of death lay in being able to establish some foundation for ethics—the pursuit of virtue that he considered central to the functioning of democratic government. The ethical basis he derived for his politics centered on what he believed was the irrefutable claim regarding the immortality of the soul. Plato argued that the soul was a separate and distinct entity from the physical body and, while various diseases of the flesh could corrupt and kill the body, he argued that the soul was inextinguishable, free from the corrupting powers of either external or internal corruption. That the soul lives—is immortal—meant that individuals themselves lived beyond the death of their bodies. Further, the individual soul after separation from the body incurred consequences. God (in whatever form so delineated) would mete out on each individual soul either reward or punishment, depending on how he or she lived. Only after a period of living with the recompense of their mortal deeds would these souls return to live among the living; the nature of their new life was theirs to choose. Plato's point was this: Individuals should seek virtue and justice, to strive to achieve as closely as possible a resemblance to God, the ideal soul—truth. They should do this because they would be spared suffering in the afterlife, reap its rewards, and be imbued with the wisdom necessary to choose prudently the course their mortal souls would take in their subsequent reincarnation. Plato reasoned that one could only attain truth through the soul's separation from the body, which is the source of all that impedes our ability to pursue truth. Knowledge of such expectations, he reasoned, should spur individuals to live ethically—and an ethical life was the hallmark of a free, just, and happy individual and collective state.

After telling Glaucon, in *The Republic,* the tale of how this transition from life to death, and the soul's transmigration, worked, Plato concluded his admonition saying,

> And thus, Glaucon, the tale has been saved and has not perished, and will save us if we are obedient to the word spoken; and we shall pass safely over the river of Forgetfulness, and our soul will not be defiled. Wherefore my counsel is that we hold fast ever to the heavenly way and follow after justice and virtue always, considering that the soul is immortal and able to endure every sort of good and every sort of evil. Thus shall we live dear to one another and to the gods, both while remaining here and when, like conquerors, in the games who go round to gather gifts, we receive our reward. And it shall be well with us both in this life and in the pilgrimage of a thousand years which we have been describing.[2]

This ethics—the pursuit of truth that can be approached through just and virtuous living without succumbing to the pleasures and corrupting appetites of the body—provides not only the mechanism for a just society, but allows one to place death in its proper perspective, the final attainment of that truth that was sought all along. His own death being imminent, Socrates stated that "True philosophers are ever studying death" because they know that death culminates their search for the true knowledge of the divine.[3] The extent to which philosophy has panted after death reveals a strange longing for it as something not to be feared but welcomed, a fitting culmination of a life spent in the virtuous pursuit of truth.

But not all philosophers share Plato's dogmatic claims of personal immortality and belief in an afterlife. Thus, the question becomes, is the belief in the soul's immortality a necessary condition for having some ethical foundation for civil, democratic life? Is one's longing for the rewards of death or fear of the punishment it may bring the only motivation for ethical behavior?

If we move to the other end of the spectrum—away from philosophers such as Plato and Immanuel Kant, and many modern philosophers and theologians between them and since—we get a sense that the answer to whether there can be ethics and morality without the expectation of the afterlife is absolutely, yes. Corliss Lamont was perhaps among the most formidable contemporary skeptics of the afterlife, and, in his *Illusion of Immortality,* he seeks not only to point out the failure of immortalists' claims about the afterlife, but offers some positive proof refuting all such notions. Lamont begins his questioning of the ethical arguments for the afterlife with Plato, noting that modern immortalists have both returned to, and departed from, his arguments for the immortality and transmigration of souls. Lamont argues that Plato's arguments were too ephemeral for modern thinkers and believers to grasp. "It is unlikely that the 'proofs' of immortality in the Phaedo, many of which subtly assume their conclusions from the start, never in themselves alone won anyone to a belief in an afterlife,"[4] Lamont is eager to point out.

For a more modern ground to cling to as a referent for his objections, Lamont turned to Kant, who, like Plato, reasoned that the soul's immortality can be inferred by a natural and instinctual human drive toward perfection and truth, found in our creator who is our ultimate ideal. Lamont quotes Kant's *Critique of Practical Reason* in this regard:

> Man, and indeed every rational being as such, exists as an end in himself, not merely as a means to be made use of by this or that will. ...The disposition it [the moral law] produces in him to promote the highest good that can be practically realized by us, presupposes at the very least that the highest good is possible. ...[This highest good] is the union of virtue and happiness in the same person, that is, in happiness exactly proportioned to morality.[5]

On this point Kant and Plato differed. That is, for Plato, virtue and morality are what the virtuous strive for because of the fact of immortality; for Kant, virtue and morality exist and are realized in light of the continuation of the soul. This is to say, this immortality is an *a priori* of sorts, a necessary condition for the possibility of living a virtuous life, which he reasons can only be accomplished through the inevitable perfect union of man with the greatest good, over the course of many lifetimes following our present corporeal existence.

This is significant for Lamont, as it shows the two extremes upon which many immortalists lie, in terms of the claims they offer for the afterlife. For some, knowledge of a hereafter filled with blessings or torments compels them to live virtuously; for others, the afterlife makes possible such living, but has little bearing on the condition of the life following since there is a universal predestination of the integration of all souls with the universal ideal, or God. One of the reasons that Lamont spends so much time making these distinctions is, in some respect, to highlight the motives of those who proffer arguments which are in between Plato and Kant's positions—namely, proponents of Christianity.

Lamont argues that Christians' belief in the afterlife was not originally predicated on compelling individuals to live ethically per se; nor were they interested in suggesting some universal ideal to which all are bound at some point in eternity. Rather, the Christian argument for the afterlife was a self-serving one. Their insistence on a final judgment where individuals' fates would be decided once and for all was a means of coercion whereby they could command and control the minds, hearts, and actions of their followers. Such behaviors were not engaged in out of a genuine longing to attain some godly state (though this is what Lamont would argue that church leaders would have followers believe), but in response to the will of spiritual leaders who could control their state of mind by reminding them of their doom or bliss, depending on whether they complied with what was right living as their leaders deemed it. Anyone who has had to endure growing up in a dogmatic, fundamentalist-Christian religion understands this clearly.

So it is by demonstrating not only the absurdity of reasoning that immortalists use to argue for the existence of the afterlife, but also its corrupting nature—the unethical use, we might say, of such arguments—that Lamont dismisses all such claims. But while Lamont does not explicitly address the question of whether there can be ethics without the expectation of the afterlife, one can infer from the body of literature he invokes to cast doubt on the existence of immortality that ethics and morality are not conditioned on a belief in the eternal, living soul or any element of human nature. After all, atheists do not disproportionately murder because they fear no eternal consequence, and even the most flagrant hedonists often draw the line as to what modicum of pleasure they derive at the expense of others of a given community. So, we must conclude, to some degree, the meaninglessness of the question of the afterlife insofar as it relates to our ability and propensity to act ethically, morally—with some regard for others of a particular community. One may do so irrespective of his or her belief in one position or the other. But I also maintain that there must be something more to hang our ethical hats on than the pure utilitarian self-interest that scholars such as Robert Putnam (whom I take up later in this chapter) offers.

By seeking some other ground, I believe that we can reconcile Platonic immortalists with those unbelievers in the afterlife, and those who locate rational self-interest as the foundation for ethical, communal living. This ground is identity. One may scarcely see the difference between what I offer and what I have previously referred to, yet I maintain that a drastic difference exists, primarily with respect to motivation. The Platonic idea of ethics and virtue is predicated on, and exists because of, the certainty of immortality; yet the nexus of its motivation is one of identity—with an ideal, with an ideal being, with a community of living beings who are reincarnations of who one was and whom one may someday become. Self-interest as an impetus for ethical community is also seen, in part, as an expression of identity: Do unto others, because they will do likewise unto you. However, this instrumental motivation is very different from one whose motivations stem from the dictum: Do unto others because others *are* me—a statement of identity that, I believe, must precede or provide the possibility for community.

What I suggest and explore throughout this book is that the experience of death provides motivation for ethical living and community, irrespective of the existence of an afterlife, and more efficacious than self-interest. Individual and collective contemplation of death provides an impetus for collective identity, despite the varieties of otherness we encounter. Perhaps Spinoza's view of death (which excluded the afterlife) provides a semblance of my contentions: "A free man," he said, "thinks of nothing less than of death, and his wisdom is not a meditation upon death, but upon life."[6] That death is a topic of public discourse engaged in by members of a given community is, I maintain, the most significant element of building and sustaining community itself. That is, our deliberations about death are more important than our knowing what follows; that we are able to speak about death supercedes our ability or need to provide an explanation for it.

Before providing a more explicit connection of this discussion about death and ethics to the primary thesis of this book, it is necessary to explore to some degree the state of denial and avoidance that exists in our culture, and the degree to which this avoidance has manifest itself in a culture of restraint (our reluctance to engage in public discourse on the subject) and restriction (systemic, compulsory barriers to our discussion of it) when it comes to public discourse about death and dying and the manner in which such constraints contribute to the decline of community.

Everybody Wants to Go to Heaven

Albert King, one of America's great bluesmen, summed up perfectly the pervading position of many Americans regarding death when he sang the words, "Everybody wants to go to heaven, but nobody wants to die." Indeed, in America, we have largely grown up, and have been taught to believe, that death is the ultimate fear. And while we can sometimes get a refund on our taxes, death is our deposit on life that we can never get back. While there are dynamic intersections between various aspects of the American way of death, they all seem to emanate from this general fear of death, this fear of the unknown—the unknowable. That which we fear, we tend not to want to think about, and it seems as though our public debates, politics, religious battles, technologies, bureaucracies—the very foundation of our society—are driven by this most pervasive fear. We have devised a complex set of relationships; an ecology of denial and fear helps us forget the fact that the day we must ourselves die will inevitably come, and that we will have to make the long journey into the great unknown—alone.

In 1955, Geoffrey Gorer compared death to pornography, saying that

> Traditionally, and in the lexicographic meaning of the term, pornography has been concerned with sexuality. For the greater part of the last two hundred years copulation and birth were the "unmentionables" of the triad of basic human experiences around which so much private fantasy and semi-clandestine pornography was erected. During this period death was no mystery, except in the sense that death is always a mystery. ...In the 20th century, however, there seems to have been an unremarked shift in prudery; whereas copulation has become more and more "mentionable," death has become more and more "unmentionable" *as a natural process* [emphasis given in original text].[7]

More than a half-century since Gorer's statements, is death, as most American writers on the subject still contend, our greatest taboo? Or is our fear of death a myth continually peddled by those who have something to gain by touting it as such? Are there those in our society who prosper by maintaining that death is hush-hush—not a topic for public discourse? I maintain that as we have gradually exceeded our prudery in sexual matters, so too have we begun a process of dragging death out of the mire of fear, denial, and privacy. Throughout this book I argue that the transformation of death from taboo to "pop" has been a gradual one, beginning to firmly take hold only within the past couple of years. I further argue that perpetuating the "death-taboo" myth—as it is done by scholars, death-care professionals, journalists, government bureaucrats, and others—serves only to stifle public involvement in public discourse about death and dying and all the trappings surrounding it for those of us who remain alive to die another day.

However, while they may not be definitive characteristics, fear and denial, no doubt, still pervade much of our collective attitude about death and dying. One does not have to look far for evidence of this fact. For example, shortly following the horrible events of September 11, 2001, it was almost no time, in the broader scope of things, that former New York City Mayor Rudy Giuliani urged New Yorkers to "get back to work." Go out and shop. Spend money. Engage in your favorite hobby. Indulge in your favorite form of entertainment—anything and everything you can do to keep your eyes and minds away from the carnage that lies all about you! Giuliani told New Yorkers to "Stop being afraid. That doesn't mean getting rid of your emotions, but overcoming them.... You can go back to your normal way of life. You would honor the people who died to protect your normal way of life," (which, apparently does not include death) he said. "Those who want to help, come to New York and spend money." Even former President Bill Clinton, who rarely agrees with the mayor, gave similar exhortations for people to start shopping and flying again shortly after the attacks. Psychologists and medical professionals also chimed in, urging parents not to belabor discussions with their children over what had happened or spend too much time trying to explain the graphic scenes of death their children were exposed to on television. How soon we were all urged to forget. How soon we were all expected to turn our eyes toward other things—the bastards who perpetrated this horrible tragedy, our government's response, or to look for answers.

Hospitals used to be places where people went to be made well; now we have created places where people go to die—out of sight and out of mind. The old and infirm are not seen, not heard from, and have few rights. Why? Because we who are young do not want to be reminded of where we are headed. We prefer to remain blind, deaf, and dumb to the mirror images that stare us in the face—the image of a wrinkled grandmother or grandfather suffering with Alzheimer's, who does not know who we are, or perhaps a brother who no longer resembles the lifelong friend we once knew. When one goes in to see a dying person these days, doctors are apt to tell you to leave the room when the one who is dying is writhing in pain—seeking to shield our eyes and emotions from such torture. When the person is alert and awake, hospital personnel urge visitors gathered not to speak of death—not while in earshot of the one who lies there on the brink.

Perhaps nothing is more telling an example than the way in which physicians themselves view and deal with death and the dying. It seems almost common knowledge in our society that doctors shy away from death as much as possible; they are reluctant—if not fearful—to engage their dying patients on such matters. However, a good part of the reason for this is that they simply are not trained to do so. A study in 1998 by the Association of American Medical Colleges (AAMC) found that almost a third of graduating medical school students expressed that their instruction on issues of death and dying was inadequate; this is especially seen in the list of courses on the topic that are and are not required by most medical schools.[8] This was the case, despite the fact that Dr. Jordan Cohen, former president of the AAMC, stated shortly after the study's publication that "today's medical students and residents are being much better prepared to take on this important job. Indeed, around the country, future physicians begin to hone these and other communications skills at the earliest stages of the medical education process." Cohen added to her contention the fact that at the time (1999) virtually all medical schools in the United States offered some course that addresses issues of death and dying.[9] While strides are being made in this arena, it is still evident that many doctors lack the skills to deal with death and dying, their dying patients, and/or their families.[10]

The way we deal with death on a general, public scale, the manner in which we treat the dying, and the practice of avoidance among physicians when dealing with the dying are but a few examples of how our fear and denial of death seep into everyday life.

The core foundation for this fear and denial is the pervasiveness of religious belief in American culture. In 1980, the Gallup public opinion polling organization decided to devote the entirety of its resources to studying American public attitudes about death, dying, and the afterlife. The study reported that most Americans believe in an afterlife, and that the majority of them believe in hell, a place of eternal suffering. From the fifties until the eighties, the number of people saying they believe in hell steadily increased and remained well above 50 percent, stretching well into the 70th percentile for certain sectors of the population. As well, the United States, in 1980, ranked at the top of the list among people around the world who say they believe in hell.[11] Almost twenty years later, the Gallup organization, in cooperation with the Nathan Cummings Foundation and the Fetzer Institute, conducted the most far-reaching survey of attitudes about death and spirituality.

The following summarizes the study's findings regarding Americans' belief in certain spiritual matters:

- Most Americans believe they will exist in some form after death; the experience will be positive; they will be on a journey of some kind; they will experience spiritual growth; and the quality of existence will depend on things done in one's life and one's spiritual state at the time of death.

- Seven in ten believe in heaven, and most believe their chances of going there are excellent or good.

- Fifty-six percent believe in hell, with 4 percent believing their chances of going to hell are excellent or good.

This pervasive belief in hell is revealing in that it provides an underlying motive for this general fear of death. First, we fear the unknown. When we compound this with a belief or faith in the existence of a place where people go after death where they will suffer for all eternity, it helps one understand why people may not be so eager to die, or think about it. What is also telling is that most people who claim to have been privy to some awareness of, or glimpse into, the afterlife—either in near-death or temporary-death experiences—return with positive stories.[12] These stories are usually couched in theological language as people say they experience going to "heaven," or have met Jesus Christ. In any case, they describe their experience as positive—that they were reunited with loved ones, felt emotional peace, experienced mental clarity, and were destined to live in a beautiful place of eternal bliss.

The point here is that for a culture with a general fear of the unknown, coupled with an overwhelmingly belief in a place called hell where they might go to when they do die, it is no surprise that there arises an overwhelming need to pacify these fears with such projections of positive images of the afterlife—such imaginings that pervade other areas of the culture—allowing us, on the one hand, to put out of our mind the inevitability of death, and on the other, to provide an assurance that when death does come, everything will be alright. What seems to be a contradiction, however, is that for all those who share such spiritual beliefs, there seems to be equal, if not much more, anxiety expressed about the issue of death. This is seen in the

Gallup Organization's recommendations to the public, given the findings of their most recent study. Members of the Gallup study wrote that many members of our society should take steps "to help overcome the dire and all-too-common situation of people dying alone, feeling unloved, unforgiven by God, with little hope, and in physical, emotional, psychological, and spiritual pain."[13]

Returning to my original contention that the "taboo" characterization of death is a myth, I do not maintain that death and fear are not conjoined in the collective American psyche. It seems that we are, as it were, schizophrenic in regards to death. At one and the same time we fear it, but nevertheless we crave it. We do not crave death itself, but death's attention—our giving it attention. We seem to want to keep it close at hand so that every now and then, and more and more, we take a peek into its dark shadows, hoping to fulfill some expectation about what it is like. Why this is, is, in part, the subject of this book. I offer the explanation that this curiosity about death is, to some degree, a manifestation of the desire and need to belong, to feel connected to a community of others.

Dying Alone

This crisis of dissociation that makes the possibility of dying alone so frightening was cited early in the last century by cultural philosopher Jean Gebser, and more recently addressed in Robert Putnam's popular book *Bowling Alone*. Both of these scholars differently characterize this problem of rampant disconnection between individuals and to society as a whole, yet they similarly offer little in the way of a prescription for our contemporary predicament. Putnam's analysis rather narrowly focuses on what are only symptoms of the problem. In the language of political economy, he identifies our current quandary as stemming from our general loss of what he calls "social capital." The decreasing sense of connection we have with one another, evidenced by a widespread lack of civil engagement by Americans, Putnam argues, has diminished the scope and veracity of externalities that follow from being engaged in social networks. This, in his view, has produced a vicious circle whereby individuals disengage from the network(s), thereby contributing to a general cultural attitude that pursues rational self-interest at the expense of collectivistic best practices.

But again, Putnam focuses primarily on the symptom: the mutually defining fact that we do feel disconnected, and are consequently disengaged. Gebser provides a better explanation of the essential elements of this disconnect by citing a complete shift of awareness—a different form of cultural sense-making—as the defining aspect of our contemporary circumstances. Gebser views our dilemma as the necessary manifestation of a cultural attitude that privileges rationality over other modes of awareness, namely magic and myth. He argues that the modern, hyper-rational world is forced to, in the face of the ever-expansion of space (nature), emphasize the "I" or the individual. He argues that the expanding discovery of space creates conditions favorable for collectivism in that the "I" is disintegrated in the expanse.[14] However, he also argues that this creates a vital need for the individual to preserve himself or herself—to fight against losing one's individual identity. In doing so, the individual is apt to assert his or her perspective, his or her individuality, to the point that he or she loses sight of all other horizons—resulting in a condition of extreme isolation for the individual, which itself has problematic consequences not only for the individual, but for the larger society as well.

Though we have an adequate understanding of the problem, in the final analysis we are left with either inadequate or improbable alternatives: We can attempt to reengineer community and the collectivism of bygone days in accordance with contemporary social institutions and values, as Putnam offers; or we need to experience a revolutionary shift in consciousness such that the relevance of magic and myth are resurrected and integrated with our hypermodern sensibilities. This is Gebser's suggestion. The question left begging by both Gebser and Putnam is this: If rampant individualism and dissociation expressed in the decline of social engagement is the manifestation of the perspectival privileging of rationality, then what provides us the impetus or motivation to reawaken the mythical and magical sense of collective identity and connection? I believe the experience of death provides such.

The longing to know death is, to some degree, an expression of our will to conquer it. But beyond this, it is an expression, a longing, a crying out for and seeking connection and community—what one needs to make the isolation of life, and the individuality of death, more bearable. What I am saying then is that beyond reengineering institutions, in order to create community, we must reinvigorate a different conception of (life)-(time)—our connection between birth and eventual death—such that death is allowed to play a prominent role in moderating our public values, discourses, and politics. In short, we must resurrect death from the sphere of privacy it has long occupied.

Competing Interests and the Myth of Privacy

Perhaps no other case in recent memory better illustrates the crisis of disconnection as it relates to death and dying—particularly the manner and consequences of death's relegation to the private sphere—than the case of Ray Brent Marsh and the Tri-State Crematory in rural Georgia (still ongoing at the time of this writing).[15] One might think the case was ripped straight from the pages of a macabre Stephen King novel. It was a gruesome scene: a large acreage overgrown by brush and unmanicured trees, covered in debris—and among it, the dead, decayed, and disfigured bodies of 339 men, women, and children who were brought there to be cremated. But for reasons as yet unknown, Ray Brent Marsh, a seemingly upstanding, well-liked, and longtime citizen of the small, southern, rural community, did not fulfill his professional and sacred obligation.

Instead of cremating the remains, Marsh disposed of these once soulful beings in whatever manner he saw fit. When Environmental Protection Agency officials, and later other state and federal law enforcement, finally initiated their search of the crematory property and Marsh's practices (beginning on February 18, 2002), they found body upon body, in varying stages of decomposition, stored in dilapidated hearses, buried in shabby, hollow graves, and stacked one on top of another in tightly packed concrete vaults. Some were simply lying unhidden in the brush, others in a lake; some were still in their caskets, adorned with the clothing they came in following their funerals, while still others were positioned so as to be deliberately disguised. The dead were sent to Marsh by funeral home operators, hospitals, and nursing homes with the expectation of sacred, reverent, and professional care; but instead of receiving the remains of their loved ones, unbeknownst to them, family members were sent away with urns filled with concrete, gardening soil, wood chips and a variety of crushed bone fragments.

No one really knows why Marsh did what he did. Some speculate his was the work of a man severely depressed, others of a pathological hoarder, and others of someone simply unorganized beyond belief. Without shifting blame for these horrible acts from the one most culpable, we can point to other aspects of this case that made what Marsh did more of a probability.

Such enabling mechanisms demonstrate the degree of dissociation that exists between the living and the dead as a result of death residing largely in the private domain, and the resulting deleterious effects it has on the continuance of community.

First, this case manifests a sharp division between rational ideals codified in law that refer to the dead as essentially property, and the emotional reactions of citizens that belie such designations. When all was said and done, Ray Brent Marsh was charged with 334 counts of "theft by deception"—a designation that hardly seems appropriate for the horrific acts described earlier. It was not until charges began to be filed that law enforcement officials became aware that Georgia had no law regarding the mistreatment or abuse of human remains, or unburied corpses. In Georgia, as it was in many states at the time, the corpse was legally simply a piece of property. While legal statutes maintained this perspective of Marsh's acts, others held a vastly different view.

It is more than clear from public reaction to the case that the families of the deceased who were found on the Marsh property, if not most people, regard the dead as much more than a piece of property. Even in death—perhaps especially in death—the living and the dead maintain a magical relationship, a continuing sense of connection with each other through the medium of the corpse.[16] There is an evident disconnect between how an impersonal system of law treats the dead as inscribed in various federal and state statutes and regulations, and how people connected with the deceased feel about the physical remains of their loved ones. The question is, if law is supposed to be an expression of community values, and communities obviously place significant value on the sanctity with which their dead should be treated, why does the law not reflect this overwhelming sentiment?

A second idea exemplified in the Georgia case that demonstrates the atmosphere of privacy that surrounds issues of death is that of trust. The discourse among professionals within the funeral industry and otherwise, following the Georgia case, centered largely on this idea of a trust that was violated by Marsh. Tom Baxter, a reporter covering the case for the *Atlanta Journal Constitution,* framed the case saying, "The breach of trust [is] at the heart of the story."[17] These people are correct in their assessment of the issue. Trust was breached. But the question is why we would treat this kind of financial transaction differently than we would any other commercial business matter—that is, with some modicum of skepticism? Why is it that we should implicitly trust the agents of this form of financial endeavor when we implicitly (and sometimes explicitly) distrust those who would sell us a car, or someone we wouldd pay to build us a house, or otherwise?

A third revelation made by this case, insofar as how we conceptualize and communicate about issues of death in the public arena, is demonstrated by the question asked by Dana Tofig, another *Atlanta Journal Constitution* reporter: "How come nobody noticed?"[18] This is perhaps the most troubling question of them all. A total of 338 bodies were improperly disposed of. Some were left in plain sight; some were hidden over the course of two to three years—on private property, but not out of the reach of neighbors, and not invisible to the hundreds who delivered the bodies and other goods and services to the Marsh acreage. And no one noticed? That no one noticed is not a precise statement of the facts, actually. Twice before, as far back as the year 2000, a delivery driver had noticed and reported the scene to authorities. The local sheriff's office twice shrugged it off without investigation, saying simply that it was a regulatory issue. The EPA disregarded the notices as the ramblings of gossiping busybodies out to settle a beef. So the question why no one noticed is perhaps not as relevant as the question why no one seemingly cared.

No one knew or cared that the laws operating at the time made it hardly criminal to abuse a corpse. No one knew or cared that a state legislator twice made the Tri-State crematory exempt from licensure and mandatory inspection (Georgia only began regulating crematories in 1990). To federal regulators and bureaucrats, it was purely a state issue that warranted little intervention and no financial assistance in dealing with the aftermath of the incident.[19] It seems we were all strangely, blissfully ignorant of all such circumstances of how and why such things could and did happen—until they did. Only then was there an outcry about the failures of the law. Only then were lawmakers pressured to close the loopholes complicit in Marsh's crimes. Only then did federal elected officials begin to inquire about these and other such circumstances and commence suggesting ways to further prevent them from occurring. And even these inquiries and new prescriptions lie abandoned now more than two years following the incident.[20]

Why do the laws that govern our actions not reflect our true beliefs and feelings regarding the dead? Why is there an implicit expectation of trust by all parties in our financial dealings regarding the deceased? And how can our underlying regard and sympathies for the dead be violated literally right under our noses, and for years at a time without notice? There is a simple and singular explanation: Through our years of fear and denial of death we have erected an almost impenetrable wall of privacy around the issue of death. That is, we have not only made known our fear of the issue itself, we have expressed through both action and inaction the sentiment that when death does occur among our own ranks or to others, it is none of our business.

When we first handed over our dead to be dealt with by a professional class of handlers so that our eyes no longer had to witness that which repelled us; when we washed our hands of the stench, degradation, and coldness of deceased bodies, no longer using those hands to directly care for them; we began to view death as something to be managed only by those whose job it is to do so. We created and prepared the foundation for incidents such as these to occur in the manner in which it did. Politicians can make deals in smoke-filled back rooms not in accordance with our true values because it is not really our business. We should not busy ourselves with the circumstances of desecration that happen across the country or to the family down the street because it is none of our business; we say they should be left to deal with such ineffable circumstances in private. The federal government, which has an interest in legislating morality and conduct in virtually every other circumstance—whose very involvement in such issues signals our national priorities—willingly passes issues of the treatment of the dead off to individual states free to act on whatever whims they so choose, saying, in effect, "it is none of our business."

The subject of death has long been seen as a private affair, the manifestations of which demonstrate how disconnected we have become from each other, and our unwillingness to fully participate in civic life. Yet, what the Georgia case and many others that have to deal with this subject of death and dying illustrate is that there are two sides of this prism of privacy that death and the dead occupy. On the one hand, we have sealed ourselves off from death and the dead personally. On the other hand, when we look at the question of interests—who has them, who does not, and why—we begin to see that death is, in reality, anything but a private affair.

When Death Meets Popular Culture

To wholly assert that death remains taboo ignores the manner in which public fascination, concern, and contemplation of death and dying have continually increased over the past three to four decades. This is to say, the growing attention given to this topic, especially in mass entertainment, is significant in terms of what we as Americans think and believe about death and dying, and how these sentiments influence human behavior and the broader American culture in our search for community.

Proof of this rising trend in the degree to which death has invaded public discourse is evident in a variety of forms. Over the past five decades there has been an increase in the number of popular and academic writings about the subject. In the 1950s, only nineteen books on the subject were published (zero books were published in the years 1951 to 1953, and 1958). As we get into the 1960s, the number increases to 120 books; at least two books each year, with most coming at the end of the decade. The greatest increase in number comes between the 1960s and 1970s. In the 1970s, 714 recorded books were on the market, followed by virtually the same number (699) in the 1980s. The second major increase between decades was between the 1980s and 1990s, which brought the American public 1,123 books on the topic of death and dying.

The increasing degree to which the subject of death and dying has crept into public discourse is also seen in the degree to which "life and death" social issues and debates have skyrocketed over the past four decades. Spurred by technological advances that have given humans increased power over life and death, debates increased over issues we are all too familiar with in today's society—abortion, euthanasia, cloning, stem-cell research, and others. A Lexis-Nexis search of international and U.S. newspapers, magazines, newsletters, and journal documents reveals the increase in discourse about such topics in print media. The number of articles for euthanasia increased from just five articles in the decade of the 1960s, to 354 between 1970 and 1980, 5,752 during the 1980s, and soaring to over 26,000 from 1990 to 2000.[21]

Where one comes down on the moral and ethical side of any of these issues is not of importance here. What is significant is the interrelationship between the heightened frequency in which death became a part of public discourse in this limited arena and the rise of technologies, which generally gave us the ability to lengthen life and decide when it should begin or end. Intertwined with this are the various moral and religious values from which debates over these newfound powers emanate, and the influence all of them have had on how we generally treat the dead and the dying. Increasingly, because of our technologies which extend the average life, those who do most of the dying are the elderly. Dissociated from family and friends, these people more and more are placed in nursing homes which, unlike hospitals,

are places where people go to die, rather than to receive maintenance or bet-
terment of one's health. Yet, the pervasiveness of these issues in public discourse has raised awareness and public discussion about the moral and
ethical implications of such practices. This leads us to turn our attention to
the arena I believe provides the greatest evidence of our culture's increasing
fascination with, attention to, and concern with death and dying—television.

"Mortality as home entertainment? This cannot be the future—can it?"
Tom Cruise's character in the recent movie *Vanilla Sky* asked this rhetorical
question when he came to the startling realization that he had, while in the
depths of despair, arranged to have his body frozen at death, discontinuing
the life he would have had, and replacing it with a "perpetual dream"—a life
spawned by his own private fantasies. There is perhaps no better way to state
one of the most important questions of this book. Should we turn to entertainment media as a vehicle to lift death's discourse out of the mire of private
fascination?

The question of popular, or "pop," culture is generally of worth to those
who own its commodities. For all others, the accepted notion is that when
some form of cultural expression reaches the level of mass appeal, much is
lost—creativity, artistic value, self-reflection, and dialogue, to name a few.
Noted scholars, from critical theorist Theodor Adorno[22] to hermeneutician
Hans Georg Gadamer,[23] have, along with practitioners of various art forms,
defined art in terms of its ability to stimulate self-reflection—that the work
of art exists independent of its creator, containing in it the power to arouse
the subjective gaze of the individual, transforming both the person and the
work. Yet, without getting into the variety of class debates between "high"
and "low" art and culture, it is evident that in the subjecting of any form of
artistic expression to the mass capitalist market—in which the breadth of
appeal and the construction of capital becomes the prime motivation for the
form—virtually all semblance of art is stripped away.

When death, with all of its seriousness, fear, and denial, is brought face-
to-face with the "pariah" that seems to characterize popular culture (exhibited in the medium of television, film, and recently, the Internet, among others), we are behooved to confront the question that, I believe, was moot until
fairly recently: What will be the likely result when these two cultural contexts confront each other? The purpose of this book is to explore various fac-
ets of this question. Until this point I have made the effort to provide a partial
view of the larger ecology of death and various forms of expression which
point to a move away from fear and denial, to making death increasingly a

part of public discourse. The remainder of this book seeks to provide arguments regarding how the intersection of death and popular media may impact not only the ecology of media, but, more importantly, the larger ecology of death in American culture.

The Book

In light of this introduction, the purpose of this book is to demonstrate how the increase in public discourse about death and dying can contribute to the remaking and reshaping of community. I argue in the remaining chapters that there is a positive link between the degree to which death is a part of everyday life that permeates public discourse and the development of community. I also argue that the growth of death-related programming and the use of new technologies in the service of extending our individual and collective memory of the dead not only express our desire to deliberate about death more openly, but also aid in the broadening of death's discourse. To this end, in the next two chapters I consider the normative manner that death has typically been represented on television, and what I see as the departure from this standard form.

In chapter 1 I argue that the degree to which we have come, and continue to be, motivated by denial and fear in terms of death and dying is due, in large part, to a failure of public education to prepare young people (who later become adults) to deal with such issues. I also argue that complicit with this failure is our reticence to recognize or appeal to entertainment media as a means by which to educate ourselves about, or use as a tool for, reflecting on death-related issues. In advancing these arguments I deconstruct the literature and critiques of media violence (and death) as being counterproductive to developing a mature orientation toward death and dying.

Chapter 2 is based on a content analysis of television programming in genres most apt to feature issues of death and dying—daytime soap operas and prime-time medical dramas. The entire series of episodes from two major programs in each genre, from 1970 to 2000, are analyzed for the frequency that death occurred, those whose deaths were depicted, their causes of death, and the depiction of other contextual circumstances surrounding it such as displays of grief, funerals, or other forms of memorials. The results of this analysis form the basis for my argument that over the last three decades television programming has represented issues of death and dying with increasing sophistication, openness, and depth.

Chapter 3 is the first of three chapters focused on what I believe represents a defining break with stock ways of representing death and dying in television programming—the airing of HBO's *Six Feet Under*. This chapter begins my study of this program by advancing a reading of the characters of the show and their role, not only in the general narrative of the television series, but the more substantive message it presents about our culture's way of dealing with death, accepted forms of emotional expression, and the commercial practices of disposing of the dead.

Following in chapter 4, I continue this analysis by elucidating the rhetorical nature of *Six Feet Under*. By offering an interpretation of the dominant images in the show, its structural form, its characters and narrative, and the overall plot, I demonstrate the way in which the show constructs specific arguments about how we deal with death and dying and the function of both rational and emotional appeals to support its arguments, and explain the connection of the arguments to a larger body of discourse about death and dying expressed in other forms of media.

Chapter 5 connects the arguments made in chapter 1 with my interpretation of *Six Feet Under* in chapters 3 and 4, by retelling and analyzing viewers' reactions to various aspects of the show. One set of responses is derived from a group of teenagers who express in their own words their viewing of the show, in light of previous experiences they have or have not had with death and dying, and with their perceptions of traditional ways that the media depict death and dying. The second group of responses stem from HBO's *Six Feet Under* online fan community. What individuals in each of these groups express is that this show stimulates critical examination about death and dying, educates about the variety of circumstances associated with it, provides a foundation upon which to connect and build community with other viewers, and motivates individuals toward personal and collective discussion about challenging aspects of our contemporary death culture.

Chapter 6 is one of two chapters that assert that while new forms of programming about death and dying are patently different than those which came before, sophisticated treatment of, and advisement regarding, death and dying have not been absent in the media landscape, especially within the genre of science fiction. Chapter 6 provides a reading of the dominant tropes of time, space, discovery, and death within the narrative structure and content of *The Twilight Zone,* uncovering the way in which the show depicts death and dying as an experience of new possibilities of existence and discovery to be welcomed, rather than a finite end to be feared.

To the same end as the previous chapter, chapter 7 illustrates what Heidegger and Gadamer have referred to as the "hermeneutic circle." The chapter interprets the message of *The X-Files* in relation to *The Twilight Zone*, demonstrating their similar interpretive purpose to offer a perspective about death and dying contrary to the prevailing attitudes that similarly existed at and between the disparate time in which the two programs aired. While *The Twilight Zone* draws on tropes of time, space, and discovery to articulate its message, *The X-Files* utilizes the tropes of truth and its pursuit, and the symbol "X" as a representation of the unknown but possible, to construct a message about death as a return to origin, as a mode of understanding the self and relating to the Other, and as the domain of infinite possibility.

Chapter 8 takes a look at the popular Sci-Fi Network series, *Crossing Over with John Edward,* in which Edward, a psychic medium, purports to relay messages of the dead to the living. In this chapter I argue first that American audiences have been primed for the acceptance of, belief in, and curiosity surrounding what is popularly referred to as paranormal phenomenon. I argue that the basis for this priming lies not in the acceptance or rejection of "science," but in the failure of religion to provide the required assurance and comfort regarding the meaning and nature of death (specifically what happens after). Second, I argue that the significance of *Crossing*'s host, psychic medium John Edward, lies not in his credibility in practicing his craft, but the nature of his interpersonal interaction with members of both his immediate and mediated audience. Third, I argue that *Crossing* is important in that it forces the private experience and conversation about death and dying into the public sphere, and that participants and viewers in the public sphere provide the much needed impetus to explore death and the validation of our fears surrounding it.

The purpose of chapters 9 and 10 (meant to be ready together) is twofold: to describe and analyze the specific ways in which innovations in technological use shape the way in which we think about, orient ourselves toward, or otherwise interact with each other given the experience and prospects of death and dying; and to speculate more generally about the implications the use of technology in this realm may have on the future of American death culture. This is accomplished, in part, by focusing on the origins and services offered by Forever Enterprises, Inc. (FEI).

My analyses are categorized into two separate areas. The first area (chapter 9) deals with what I call the empirical domain, dealing with the temporal, spatial, and visual implications of technology on death attitudes and practices. The second area (chapter 10) focuses on what I call the social realm of influence, and includes critiques of the theatrical, relational, political, and commercial implications of technology used in the sphere of death and dying. These various areas of analysis lead to the general conclusion of these two chapters—the way that the use of video and computer technologies are helping the public to gain greater access to the memories of the dead, transform the spaces of public memory, and equalize the relationship between consumers and providers of death-related goods and services.

NOTES

[1]   Lewis Mumford, *The City in History: Its Origins, Its Transformations, and Its Prospects* (New York: Harcourt, Brace & World, 1961), 6–10.

[2]   Plato, "The Republic: Book X," in *The Essential Plato* trans. Benjamin Jowett (The Book–of–the–Month–Club, Inc., 1999), 416.

[3]   Plato, "Phaedo," in *The Essential Plato*, trans. Benjamin Jowett (The Book–of–the–Month–Club, Inc., 1999), 605.

[4]   Corliss Lamont, *The Illusion of Immortality* (1935; Fifth Edition: Continuum, 1990).

[5]   Immanuel Kant, *Critique of Practical Reason* (New York: Liberal Arts Press, 1956), Quoted in Lamont, p.1.

[6]   Benedictus de Spinoza, *The Ethics and Selected Letters* (Indianapolis: Hackett Publishing, 1982).

[7]   Geoffrey Gorer, "The Pornography of Death," *Encounters* 1955, 50.

[8]   See Hellen Gelband, "Professional Education in Palliative and End–of–Life Care for Physicians, Nurses and Social Worlers," in *Improving Palliative Care for Cancer*, eds. Kathleen Foley and Hellen Gelband (Washington, DC: National Academy Press, 2001), 277–310; and Association of American Medical Colleges 2000–2001 report, "Number of U.S. Medical Schools Teaching Selected Topics," extracted from the report by the Liaison Committee on Medical Education Part II Annual Medical School Questionnaire for 2000–2001.

[9]   Jordan Cohen, M.D., "Doctors Are Now Taught How to Deliver Bad News," *The Boston Globe* 16 August 1999, sec. A, p. 14.

[10] Martin Miller, "When a Doctor Must Say the Worst," *Los Angeles Times* 26 January 2004, sec. F, p. 1.

[11] George Gallup, Jr. *Adventures in Immortality* (New York: McGraw–Hill, 1982).

[12] Ibid., pp. 1–17.

[13] The George H. Gallup International Institute, "Spiritual Beliefs and the Dying Process: A Report on a National Survey" (Nathan Cummings Foundation and the Fetzer Institute, 1997), available at http://www.ncf.org/reports/rpt_fetzer_contents.html.

[14] A recent article in *Time* magazine reveals scientists' newfound understanding of the expansiveness and continued expansion of what we know as "outer space" and discusses what this means in terms of the significance of human beings and our time spent here on earth. See William Underhill, "A Universe of Riddles," *Newsweek,* 20 October 2003, 68.

[15] The summary of this case was derived from a collection of stories compiled by the *Atlanta Journal Constitution* from the initiation of the findings of Tri–State from February 17, 2002 through July of 2003. The AJC provided the most in–depth and continuous coverage of the event, and specific references are used hereafter when direct quotes are taken from the reports. As well, Marsh's trial date has been set for mid–October, 2004.

[16] The significance of the corpse as the primary medium of connection between the dead and the living is seen as a universal principle throughout history. For a more thorough discussion of this subject see Christine Quigley, *The Corpse: A History* (Asheville, NC: McFarlane, 1996).

[17] Tom Baxter, "Capitol Feels Effects of Tri–State Debacle," *Atlanta Journal Constitution,* 1 March 2002, sec. D, p. 3.

[18] Dana Tofig, "Crematory Owners: Everyone Knew the Marshes, or So They Thought," *Atlanta Journal Constitution,* 22 February 2002, sec. A, p. 1.

[19] The Governor of Georgia petitioned the federal government, through the Federal Emergency Management Agency, for emergency disaster relief aid. Joe Albaugh, the head of FEMA, ruled that the situation did not constitute an "emergency" and therefore was not eligible to receive funding.

[20] On February 26, 2002, Senator Chris Dodd (D–CT) wrote a letter to Mr. David Walker, chief administrator of the General Accounting Office, requesting the office to examine the practices of the funeral industry and to ascertain whether such practices warrant further federal involvement in regulating the industry. Legislation resulting from this inquiry was proposed at the end of the 107th Congress, but has not been considered since. The resulting GAO report can be found online at http://www.gao.gov/archive/1999/gg99156.pdf.

[21] While the numbers during the sixties are assuredly low, the numbers presented here for that decade may be lower than the actual numbers because of the limitations of the data-

base in surveying media outlets from that time period. The increasing number of media outlets over the decades would also contribute to the increase in trends.

22   Theodor Adorno, *The Culture Industry: Selected Essays on Mass Culture* (London: Routledge, 1991).

23   Hans Georg Gadamer, *Truth and Method* (New York: Seabury Press, 1975).

CHAPTER ONE

Amusing Ourselves about Death
Violent Media and Death Education

For many social critics who lament the bygone days when teaching was unencumbered by the trappings of technology, entertainment and education are mutually exclusive. For others who have embraced entertainment and its media to service educational endeavors, some topics simply are not meant to be dealt with in this regard; chief among these are the concomitant subjects of death and violence. As such, this chapter examines, in part, the intersection of entertainment and education as it relates to the topic of death and dying, particularly in regard to those in our society who have generally been ignored and silenced in their experiences of death—children and young people.

The argument that runs throughout this book is that entertainment media can be "educational," or produce what is commonly referred to by political economists as "positive externalities." I enclose the former descriptor in quotes because what counts as "education" is highly contestable. The quotations around the latter term qualifies that, unlike many such phenomenon dealt with by political economists (from whom the term is borrowed here), I do not (and probably could not) generate any quantitative, measurable effects of death-related media (which generally underlie the argument that other such externalities exist). In any case, I argue here and throughout the remainder of the book that television programming about death and dying, in the variety of forms that they frequently appear, can benefit individuals and our society as a whole in terms of how we view death, as well as how we respond to its occurrence. I proceed to this end in the following manner. First, I interrogate critics' writing on the subject of television violence—a topic discussed more often than death on television and one that is obviously closely related to how death is depicted on the small screen. Second, I deconstruct the popular conceptualization of "education" to counter television violence critics' assertions that depictions of violence and death are a primary causal component of aggressive behavior and heightened anxiety which precludes it from being, in any form, educational. I argue that violent media is only a symptom, rather than a root, of the real problem. Third, I argue that our culture's failure at general education regarding death and dying, particularly among the young, is the missing link in such discussions that mitigate, in part, how media representations of death and dying under any circumstances will affect us. Before getting to these three areas, let us briefly trace the terrain of television criticism more generally and its relationship in general to young viewers and the topic of death and dying.

The Television Critics' Obsession(s)

According to many television critics, three conclusions circulate as generally accepted truths that characterize our current death culture and media ecology: Television can do no good; death is not for children; and God forbid that the former can have anything to do with playing a positive role in dealing with the problem of the latter. When television first appeared on the scene of American life, it not only produced great wonder regarding the newfound ability to place the images of real people and objects into a little electronic box. Beyond this technological wonder lay a host of useful possibilities for the new medium. For those in the arts, particularly theater, the new invention held the promise of broadening the audience for the art form, allowing more people outside the local geographic specificity of its actual performance to take advantage of "high" cultural forms. For the politically minded, the new mechanism held the potential to increase the political sophistication of the masses—an aid to democracy itself—by creating a more informed, enlightened, and involved electorate. These are but a couple of the hopes creators, purveyors, and proprietors had for the new medium.

It is no secret what turned the tide of American sentiment in regard to television, shattering the hopes and dreams of many—commercial advertising.[1] Almost overnight the medium of television was transformed from an instrument of good to a tool of evil. This evil, in the minds of many social critics, was television's relegation as a tool to further capitalist, materialist purposes. In other words, the medium which was originally conceived as a technology *of* the people, *by* the people, and *for* the people was now to be used in the service of an invisible structure predicated on commodification, the creation and sustenance of insatiable material appetites, exploitation, and, above all, the creation and concentration of wealth in the hands of a few members of a powerful and elite class.

This argument regarding the transformation of television has dominated social criticism since the day the first commercial spot hit the small screen (July 1, 1941), altering the way in which television programming would be created, produced, and controlled. "Air time" became the hottest commodity for the marketing of a host of consumer goods and services. Since that time there has been no end to (in fact, there continues to be a marked increase in) harsh criticisms about the role and function of television in American society. Some have scorned television's discourse presented in various forms of news programming which, they claim, provides little information about world proceedings, and even less context about vital events affecting the lives of the American public within and beyond the borders of the United States. Such criticisms have pointed out the way American news content is devoid of meaning—treating tragic human affairs (including death) with only tacit attention, while giving more credence to "human interest" stories that are simple and require no reflection or analysis—"light" viewing no more serious than the sitcom or game show that immediately precedes or follows.

Still more critiques of television include its myopic representation of various racial minorities, characterizations ranging from criminal to simple-minded and comic, to down-right inferior. This is echoed by claims of television's erroneous representations of a host of various marginal discourses from religion to anti-government causes. Other scholars have staked a claim bashing systemic issues regarding media ownership, claiming that the concentration of media restricts access and solidifies imperialistic power that can be wielded against the interests of average Americans, as well as downplay the importance of "educational" programming that has some "real" social benefit. Further, many critics have extended this allegation, casting a scornful eye at the hegemonic effect such concentration of media ownership, coupled with American military and cultural might, has had on other countries across the globe. For these critics, the ownership and importation of American television technology (satellites, cable, etc.) and programming serve as a global conveyor of American values threatening local, indigenous cultures across the world not yet tainted by Western, American ideals, morals, and ethics.[2]

Perhaps no one has been a more forceful and unrelenting social critic of television and its influence on American culture than Neil Postman. In his widely read book, *Amusing Ourselves to Death*, the "Great Satan" role of the former Soviet Union during the Cold War has been ascribed to television in our postwar age.   Communism does not hold a candle to television in its threat to American society.   In this book and other writings, Postman accords television almost sole blame for all American social ills.   Television, as he tells it, has single-handedly robbed us of American democracy—turning our politicians into publicity hounds, voters into victims of deceit and disinformation, and government bureacracies into building blocks of an invisible empire which serve as an inpenetrable wall between government power and populist political action.   For Postman, television, in one fell swoop, has destroyed our country's educational system, dumbing down both teachers and students alike, and is the underlying cause of rampant child and adult illiteracy.   It is the ultimate mind-numbing device responsible for stealing our individual and collective abilities to think and question.

Don't get me wrong.   As a former political operative and current educator, I am inclined to agree with much of Postman's assessment of television's influence on these two aspects of our culture.   I have witnessed first-hand the ignorance of many American voters on issues of national importance, the growing number of Americans unwilling to participate in the political process, and egotistical politicians who get over on the American public aided by their good looks, athletic abilities, or shallow (but motivational) rhetoric, without having the faintest idea about public policy or the business of government.   As well, as an educator I continue to be perturbed by the sight of heavy eyes and hearing the beleaguered moans of faintly attentive students after I have spoken for ten consecutive minutes without an audiovisual aid or dramatizing some aspect of a lecture.   Perhaps it is television's fault that many of the highschool students I teach on occasion label me, well—boring!

Be that as it may, my problem with Postman's wholesale critique against television is not his scope or content.   Rather, my objection is that he excludes the very possibility that television can have any constructive, positive role in our culture.   For Postman, entertainment and education— classroom, social, or political—are mutually exclusive.   If we agree with this assessment, as many such social and media critics do, then we have an even more significant problem when it comes to what I see as a considerable social deficit in our society: what young people (who will eventually become adults) know (or, more appropriately, don't know) about issues of death and dying. A brief look at the many arguments criticizing television violence helps us to understand our shortcomings regarding the impact television programming about death and dying can have on our culture, and its relationship to the general lack of death education that I argue enables us to mediate the mediated messages about death seen on the screen.

Death and Television Violence: The Missing Link

In our drive to relieve children of the staggering burdens of adulthood they were saddled with throughout much of the industrial age, it seems that our contemporary society has moved from one end of the extreme to the other. The accepted view these days is that children are not adults; they do not have the rational or emotional capacity that adults have to cope with the world, and therefore should not have to deal with adult problems. Children are a protected class of people—perhaps the most protected class. This desire to shield children from the rigors of the adult world is, perhaps, no more evident than in our attempt to control their exposure to media, especially violent media in television, film, video games, and the Internet. Over the past decade, scholarly and popular books on the subject of media violence, on television in particular, account for more than one-third of all of the books published on the general topic of media. Many nonprofit groups currently pursue a mission of monitoring violent television programming and lobby against its purported harmful effects. The federal government contributes hundreds of thousands of dollars each year to aid scholarly research that will determine the causes and effects of media violence on children.

While there are mixed results and conclusions of such endeavors, public scholarly and popular opinion seems to cling to the view that, as a whole, children, who are exposed to multiplied thousands of violent images by the age of eighteen are negatively affected. Critics of media violence argue that high levels of exposure to violent images on television contribute to increased anxiety and aggression in children, and mental and experiential dissociation between children's fantasies and the real world; these maladies are said to increase the likelihood of antisocial and violent behavior. This is, of course, a very generalized and simplified explanation of popular findings on the subject, but it is nevertheless clear that there is a distinct affinity for many to link exposure to violence with what we generally view as negative and unproductive behavior, thus making the case that decreasing such exposure will result in fewer instances of such conduct. W. James Potter's *The 11 Myths of Media Violence* characterizes the primary arguments of these critics more precisely: a) Children's exposure to media is high; b) children have difficulty distinguishing between reality and fantasy; c) children's ability to deal with the media is limited by developmental stages; d) children have a lack of experience; and e) children are especially vulnerable.[3]

Though I do not wholly disagree with, or object to, the findings of media violence critics, or the agenda of activists in this arena, I do believe they themselves do some harm by pursuing their agenda to significantly curtail or even eliminate children's exposure to violence in media; they unduly focus on the *act* of mediated violence as the underlying problem, when it is in actuality only a symptom. In the following few pages I argue that critics of media (primarily television) violence actually produce the same violence they seek to protect children from by making a case for a dual censorship of sorts that eliminates the opportunity for children's development of sensory, conceptual, and moral awareness of death (death being conceptually intertwined with violence).

Media Violence and Education: A Deconstruction

In order to effectively assess the theoretical nature and role of media violence, we must understand precisely what both violence and education is.

What Constitutes Violence? Critics of media violence, as a whole, commit what I refer to as the fallacy of conceptual myopia. This is to say, they advance a sociopolitical and educational agenda by proffering singular and limited conceptualizations of that which they are seeking to challenge; this stems from their imposition of myopic definitions and conceptualizations of what constitutes violence, as well as what counts as education, in advancing their claims. The commonly held definition of violence as it is depicted in media sees it such as: a) an act or observable behavior that b) inflicts willful, physical harm on a victim, the consequences of which are c) somatic injury and/or death, or that inhibits the victim from acting— examples of which we have no trouble visualizing. Such definitions bear much fidelity to standard lexical uses and interpretations of the original term that refers to the exercise of physical force, to cause damage to persons, or to forcibly interfere with another's agency. While violence critics see this conceptual and etymological fidelity as a vindication of how they view media violence, they generally do not take into account alternative and commonly used definitions of the term that I believe alter not only what we think of as being violent, but how such violence is to be mitigated.

Before proceeding, let me justify the relevance of this discussion to the overall thesis of this chapter and book as a whole by describing briefly why the subject of violence and that of death, as they relate to media, are inseparable. I make no distinction between acts of violence and death as they are depicted on television primarily because the two are both etymologically and empirically linked. First, death is the ultimate experience that inhibits individual agency and freedom; it is the cessation of life itself, that which is ultimately feared about violence. As early as the sixteenth century, the term was used almost interchangeably with the term violence, especially that which resulted in bloodshed or murder, as well as with various weapons or means of commiting violent acts. Second, television violence, more often than not, ends in death. While not scientific, surveys I randomly conducted over a two week period of shows that are considered fraught with violence showed that more than two-thirds of all the acts of violence catalogued resulted in death that was either immediately apparent or implied from the circumstances regarding the acts portrayed in the violent scenes. Thus, when people view violent acts on television, they also receive an either explicit or implicit image or understanding that someone has died as a result.

As early as the eighteenth century, a departure from the original conceptualization of violence did not view physicality as a necessary condition of violence. It also broadened the notion of constraint associated with the term. This new version of violence saw it as "undue constraint applied to some natural process, habit, etc., so as to prevent its free development or exercise," a definition used in contemporary times primarily in political contexts. Defining more precisely what constitutes "undue constraint" and what is a "natural process" as it relates to children's development of attitudes about death and dying, is key to how I see objections to violent programming as itself producing violence.[4] I argue that children undergo a natural and necessary process of developing attitudes, conceptualizations, and interpretations about death. This is to say, even without familial and cultural intervention into the life cycle, children naturally become intrinsically aware of and concern themselves with the idea of death and dying. This awareness is a process that begins not too long after birth and continues throughout the course of one's life. In Europe (whose culture of death avoidance and fear has been historically akin to our own) children often immersed themselves in their own private world fraught with contemplations about death and dying. Even though the experience of the public death had long faded from the scene, children absorbed the primary media of the day—media which had begun to assume primary reposnibility for representing the experience of death. As Ninian Smart once noted, "Literature, representing or interpreting daily experience, also incorporated death as part of that experience. The death of a child from illlness, disease or violence...was an integral part of literature and offered a dramatic and credible, yet important, turn to a plot."[5] Smart recognized, as did those of that society, that the immersion of children in a fictitious, yet real, world of violence and death was a fundamental part of a child's developing the ability to, as Smart puts it, "live in the light of death." This exposure was seen as a part of the normal and necessary development of an adult attitude toward death in which the fear of death would not rule one's thoughts and actions, or inhibit one from living life to the full. This attitude was to be cultivated from childhood.

But even less abstract and contemporary is the fact that health professionals generally agree that children naturally confront loss, violence, and death at an early age, though we have chosen still to shield them as much as possible from the experience. That is, our rhetoric of protection does not seem to match what are the commonly held empirical findings about child development and the experience of death and dying. We seem to, at least in theory, agree that optimally adults should possess some modicum of maturity when it comes to death and dying, yet we somehow think this occurs via some magical, instantaneous process when an individual suddenly turns twenty-five. Consider the following:

- Preschool children between the ages of two and six years old are cognizant of death, though they see it largely as a temporary experience;[6]

- By age six, more than half of all children understand death as a permanent event, and by age nine, most children do;[7]

- At age nine, children actively begin to express a curiosity about the details and mechanics of death and dying.[8]

While health professionals note that certain forms of intervention (or non-intervention) during this developmental process influence *how* a child comes to view death and dying, the process itself exists and continues irrespective of such intervention.

The Violence of Censorship. Making the case that intervention into or constraint of this process is "undue" is perhaps more difficult to substantiate since it is a value claim. Thus, I can only show that the case here is similar to others in which claims of undue constraint have been made and upheld to some degree. Let us begin by specifying some more concrete terms for "undue" that will aid in making the necessary comparisons and claims: viewing undue constraint as either unwarranted, excessive, unnecessary, or unjustifiable. Thus, we can pose three questions in order to decide whether intervention into a child's process of dealing with death is undue: Is there sufficient backing for why one would intervene? Is such intervention beyond what is reasonably expected in similar cases? and Will such intervention mitigate the negative effects said to justify this intrusion?

Media violence critics argue, as stated earlier, that it is necessary to intervene and protect children from how much they are exposed to and think about death (as a result of the violent act), because exposure to such instances of death at an early age, when they do not have the full reasoning or emotional capacity to distinguish fact from fiction, will result in increased agitation and aggression and ultimately will lead to the violent acting out of such aggression. Referring again to Potter and his conclusions about the research findings that undergird this proposition, we see that the premises of intervention render this argument as unwarranted. Potter's reading of the evidence leads to the following conclusions:

1. Children are not especially vulnerable to violent media images; in fact, older people are, as a class of people, more vulnerable;

2. That children require special protection from violence because they lack the ability to distinguish fantasy from reality is a faulty permise; we underestimate the ability of children to know the difference when research shows that they are capable, as adults are, to make sophisticated judgments that consider multiple factors; we also overestimate the ability of adults to make such distinctions;

3. Children are no more unable to cognitively process the meaning of violent images than adults; some children are equally

developed and able to do so;

4. That children have no "real-world" experience to ground their interpretations of media violence is a logical fallacy because age and experience cannot be equated; thus, age cannot either increase or decrease the level of risk associated with exposure to violent images; and

5. In general, research does not demonstrate a high degree of likelihood that children are any more susceptible to the negative effects of violent television viewing than any other class of people.[9]

These conclusions demonstrate, at least to my satisfaction, that the premises for shielding children, as a special class, from images of violence in the media, are largely unwarranted. There is little justification for why such intervention is necessary for children who, in many ways have the same cognitive and emotional capabilities as adults, and whom we do not single out for protection. Violence critics' response to the question "why intervene?" does not meet the logical burden of establishing that media violence is especially problematic for this group. This failure, I believe, is enough to qualify their pursuits as "undue" intervention. However, let us turn from whether such actions are warranted to whether or not they can be considered excessive.

I do not believe it is useful to address the issue of excessiveness in this regard, by trying to quantify what is an appropriate amount of intervention and whether such intervention is measurably more than is necessary. However, if we consider the form of intervention that is generally sought to combat the "problem of violence"—censorship—we can compare cases in which such actions are imposed and determine whether censorship in the area of media violence meets the criteria for such intervention in other cases. Whether media producers should limit the amount and substance of violent television programming, or whether parents should control what their children watch, media critics believe, in part, that mandating violent programming as unacceptable for children and imposing limits to their viewing will mitigate much of the problems said to be associated with exposure to violence. There are many other situations in which censorship of both speech and exposure is imposed. The important question for our purposes here is, when we compare these other examples to that of censorship of media violence, is this form of prescription comparatively excessive in this instance? Another way to phrase the question is, is the problem of media violence as significant as other problems that have merited censorship? Let us look at two such examples that have been the source of state-sponsored censorship: racially offensive speech and pornography.

What is seen as racist speech is said to result, in many cases, in individual and group expressions of violence, and to impede on one's constitutional right of equality and equal protection; the result of pornography as a form of visual speech is also said to violate the rights of women in much the same manner. Though I do not agree with certain forms of censorship as a way to deal with such problems, we have as a culture, primarily through the arm of the state, expressed that these forms of articulation have result in the violation of rights that we hold ideal—inclusion and protection of every citizen without regard to racial, gender, or other such differences.

The next question we must ask to complete this argument is, are the probable consequences of violent media exposure on par with what has been generally accepted by the courts as the outcomes from "racist" language and the depiction of pornography? The answer to this question is no. Our corporate values as expressed by agents of the state demonstrate that we view the circulation of obscenity and the articulation of violent speech as significantly greater concerns, threatening what we see as more cherished values. If we look at each of these arenas as forms of speech, and accept the claim that Matsuda, Richard Delgado, and others argue, the courts have been much more apt to argue that racist speech and pornography lead to violence[10] than do violent images on television.

This disjuncture seems a bit unusual. The courts and other proponents of curtailing racist speech and obscenity through censorship must make the case that certain forms of language actually constitute violence—the foundation for the claim that such actions violate the civil rights of others. In the case of media violence, we have a form of articulation that is undeniably violent by any reasonable person's definition. It seems more likely that this would be a better candidate for censorship than others, given this circumstance. The disparity of judgment between the cases is based on how we collectively evaluate the extent of the said effect in each case. That is, the effects of media violence in children—heightened aggression—have generally been judged as not extending beyond the individual. As such, aggression is viewed as an individual problem warranting individual solutions—medication, restraint of some kind, and the like. We assume in this case that an individual, or an agent acting on his or her behalf, has control over the individual in terms of mitigating such effects.

In the case of racist speech and pornography, the consequences are said to extend beyond the individual to the broader society; such consequences render the victims of such violence in this case as impotent, necessitating state intervention in the form of censorship. Simply put, these instances are seen as threatening both individual and collective civil liberties in a way which is so extensive as to render the victims of such speech powerless; the former case threatens the singular individual thought to bear sole responsibility for his or her own emotional and psychological well-being and of having the power to do so.

The final test of whether censoring television violence from children counts as undue intervention—whether the remedy will indeed mitigate the problem said to exist—can only be inferred, rather than conclusively proven. That is, if we accept the conclusions given earlier by Potter, then we must necessarily conclude that shielding children from violent images will accomplish little in the way of alleviating heightened aggression and actual violent behavior. If intervention is unwarranted because of the non-differential effect violence has on children as opposed to other groups of people, then it can be reasonably concluded that the effects of little or no exposure to violence would be minimal in this regard. We can draw this conclusion as well, given the fact that a plethora of variables work together to determine aggressive or violent behavior and the aforementioned fact that there is a relatively weak causal link between exposure and heightened aggressive feelings and/or behavior.

If we conclude, then, that intervention into the violent viewing habits of children as a special class is undue, and inhibits a natural developmental and maturation process in regard to death and dying, then it can be said that it therefore constitutes violence under the aforementioned definition. A final question is in order then: What is lost if such censorship were imposed? Are there critical elements of developing a reasoned and emotionally mature conception and relationship to the experience of death and dying that are lost when we are shielded from the concomitant depictions of death and violence in a mediated format such as television? I believe there are—at least in theory. By shielding children from violent television images, we deny them the very impetus for critically evaluating the forms of violence and death that do exist in reality. By imposing parental or industry censorship, we create an extremely disingenuous, if not patently false, contrast between the mediated experience and the reality of violence, death, and dying. Such an extreme contrast also conforms to a definition of violence that, though used more often in other contexts, is applicable here. What if children were exposed to violence-free, death-free television viewing? Television violence critics argue that because of their limited abilities, children are likely to internalize a fantastical, skewed notion of the world from viewing violent images. What view of the world would they likely receive, then, if there were little or no violence to be exposed to?

If the perfect world of zero television violence were suddenly to become a reality, children, and perhaps others, would view the world as one where no one ever solved their problems through violent means—a world where husbands do not kill their wives out of anger or chemically induced psychosis, where criminals talk their way out of their bank robberies, giving up their own lives and freedoms instead of acting out of self-preservation and killing those who would thwart their efforts; a world where frustrated members of minority communities would dialogue rather than riot when they, yet again, are faced with being systematically violated by those sworn to uphold their interests, or when crooked cops cheer a misguided bullet that happens to kill just another piece of scum; a world where a doctor's malpractice does not end in prematurely causing one's death, fathers do not protect their families by killing intruders, starving children do not die of malnutrition because others do not provide to feed them, and mediation, rather than war is the primary solution for international conflict. As unreal as the world would be in which a superhero kills hundreds of men all by himself to protect the innocent, so too would be a world—whether actual or mediated—where no violence exists.

What more precisely constitutes violence, given such extreme censorship, is that without the realization of all such evil that manifests itself in violence and death, we have no impetus to question the very act of violence and death itself. It sounds almost cliché, but there is no pleasure without pain; no understanding of what it means to live and live well, without an understanding of violence and death. Thus, if we are to look to television and other forms of media as a way of helping us engage the realities of the world, our exposure to death and violence is a necessary component of being able to be so engaged.

Before drawing this point to a close, let us turn briefly to another bias of media violence critics that rounds out my overall argument regarding how media can be helpful for children and others to critically evaluate, question, and learn from the images of violence and death they see on television.

Rethinking the Meaning of Education. An explicit bias held by many media violence critics, as previously stated, is that entertainment (that which includes some form of death and/or violence) and education are mutually exclusive. To demonstrate media producers' seeming unconcern for targeting children with violent images and their willingness to make great leaps to justify the "educational" value of violent programming, James Hamilton cited industry executives when making the claim that in response to the FCC's requirement for stations to provide educational programming, they largely justified existing violent programs by

> ...claiming that noneducational programs were actually educational. These efforts reached such extremes as stations claiming that GI Joe was educational programming since it dealt with "issues of social consciousness and responsibility" and that Geraldo and Beverly Hills 90210 were educational since they dealt with issues of sexuality.[11]

Though such a characterization sprung no doubt from a desperate attempt at public relations, and in order to side-step the cost of developing new programming, I do not view it with the same absurdity that Hamilton attributes to it. Critics of media violence focus all too often on particular acts of violence while seemingly ignoring that such acts occur within some larger social context or within some larger story plot (though there are, of course, many examples where this might be a stretch). But the reason that Hamilton and others cannot accept that violent images that are connected to or grounded in some other valid social context or around some social issue can be educational is that they assume a very limited view of what constitutes education. They infer from their explanations an acceptance of a purely transmission or banking model of education in which educational content is directly relayed from a source who "knows" to a receiver who needs to know. Such transmission, in the context of educational television, must be expressed explicitly in the images and verbal language of a particular program, and must require little cognitive or emotional effort to decipher its overall message.

This limited view of education applied to the context of television programming not only is premised on the erroneous notion that children are incapable of making complex cognitive judgments and distinctions, but ignores what I believe more adequately constitutes education. Education is less about transmission than it is about an active engagement that necessitates individual interaction, the confrontation and contestation of difference and critical thought premised on the primacy of questioning.

This is why censorship of violent and death-related images from children and others constitutes violence—it removes them, at least virtually, from the world. It substitutes the simplicity and comfort of ready-made answers and dogmatic, authoritative instruction for the messiness, illogic, and oft unexplainable that constitute the everyday existence of most of us who are not above being human—adults as well as children. If education is supposed to, in at least some respect, prepare the young for adult life, then we do violence by not giving the opportunity and tools—imbuing to children themselves the necessary agency to make sense of the world in which they will one day live in and have to deal with largely on their own. When we shift our conception of education from one of simple transmission to that of creating occasions and opportunties to critically engage the mediated and real world (which are effectively the same; that is, a mediated experience is nonetheless an experience constituted in a world that is very much "real"), we see that censoring violence and death makes less sense than it might otherwise.

I conclude this section with an anecdote and question regarding an example of what media violence experts have been citing frequently over the past couple of years as a case supporting their arguments—children's reactions to the (real) violent images that circulated on and following September 11, 2001. Hundreds of experts commented that children were confused by many of the images and questioned: "Why did that plane keep hitting the building over and over? Why are there people screaming and crying and running in chaos? Why would someone do this? Why does this seem serious, since no one has really died—like the Arnold Schwarzenegger movie I just saw? Do we really think that children would have been better off not seeing such images, thus refraining from posing such questions? In terms of the actual images they saw, what was the difference between their reaction to this and watching *Collateral Damage,* for instance? That is, if a child were to indeed interpret the latter as an actual, real event, could it not generate the same questions as the former? If so, I ask again—would they be better off not having been exposed?

Given the conclusions of this section, why are we as a society so focused on protecting children from the so-called harmful effects of television programs rife with images of violence and death? Some media violence critics and I agree that television or entertainment programming can be educational, yet programming featuring violent content is exempt from what they see as an acceptable form of educational programming. Why is this so? I believe that it is, in part, because we do not want to deal with the fact that we are largely ill-equipped to deal with the multitude and variety of questions likely to be generated by children—helping to bridge the gap between what they can grasp enough from the content of such programming to formulate a question or articulate how they understand it and what they may lack in terms of fully making sense of the depiction of violence and death they see. I conclude the chapter by demonstrating our unpreparedness—our (adults') inability, inexperience, and unwillingness to help children deal with violence and death in media and real life—choosing rather, as media critics do, to simply ignore such a responsibility by imposing censorship and/or the production of programming void of complex, socially relevant content.

Silence as Protection: The Role of Death Education

In the United States, 8 million people suffered through the death of someone in their immediate family in 2002; 800,000 new widows and widowers were the results of such deaths—among them, 400,000 people under twenty-five.[12] Gerald Koocher, Chief of Psychology at Boston's Children's Hospital, notes that "Kids are encountering death more often and at a younger age." "It's just inevitable," he says.[13] As recently as 1999, the U.S. Social Security Administration reported that 1.9 million youngsters under age eighteen (more than 2 percent of American children) had lost one or both parents.[14] More than 55,000 people age one to eighteen died in the year 2000.[15] Regardless of such facts, the old adage, "an ounce of prevention is worth a pound of cure" seems to be applicable to every major social problem in America, except these negative aspects associated with death (when considering the individual and social aftermath of death).

What do children know about death, both prior to and following such an experience? Answering this question leads us to question two primary groups of people who spend the most time with, and have relatively the most influence on, young people—teachers and parents. It is no surprise that we have so many adults who fear, ignore, and avoid death, and suffer from the complex social and psychological problems associated with it, when our system of education is so ill-eqipped to deal with such issues. This is compounded when government agencies and professional organizations, in the service of education, help maintain the reality that issues of death remain at the periphery of education. When teaching a recent class attended by several students who were currently educators, I casually asked the question, should death be a topic dealt with substantially in the K-12 classroom? The answer—not only a resounding "no," but "hell no." While only one was bold enough to attach the expletive to his response, I am quite sure that the others would have said the same thing if they had had the nerve. Nevertheless, I was not at all surprised by their response. Why would any teacher want to subject their students on a regular basis to the anguishing and depressing realities of death? Don't their young, malleable minds have much more productive things to think about without being distracted by something that likely will not happen to them for a long time? And besides, even if it did turn up in the school-sanctioned curriculum, what teachers are prepared to talk to their students about the myriad of issues surrounding death and dying?

Let us begin with the latter question first. To ask such a question about teacher preparation in discussing issues of death is to make a very important observation about what teachers are not prepared for in the classroom. And, when we talk about teacher preparedness, our first place to look is at the college classroom where teachers receive their foundational training and certification, which, for many today, includes graduate education. I was interested to see what, if any, preparation was given to prospective teachers for discussing issues of death and dying. After surveying the available courses offered at some of the top-ranked teacher education programs in the United States, I found that of the top eight programs,[16] including those at Columbia, Stanford, William & Mary, and Cornell, among others, no program offered its students a course in which issues of death and dying were the central topic—either at the undergraduate or graduate level.

Giving these programs the benefit of the doubt, I decided to look beyond just the three-year survey of regular course offerings for each department and assume that students might go beyond the limits of their own programs to explore such topics in other areas. I looked for these in departments where the topic of death is more likely to be offered—sociology, psychology, religion, and social work. If we use this as a gauge, it is clear that students preparing to be professional educators have startlingly few opportunities to gain some education about issues of death and dying.

Of the top teacher education programs, the University of Texas (in religion and psychology) and the University of California at Los Angeles (in sociology and social work) had the most out-of-department course offerings dealing primarily with death and dying—each school with two courses each. Two other universities, the University of California at Berkeley and Boston University, had one such course, and Cornell, Indiana, William & Mary, and Stanford each had none. Taking the average number of courses offered in this area, with the average number of out-of-department courses available in these departments, the odds that a teacher-in-learning would take such a class is approximately 1 in about 120—eight-tenths of 1 percent chance. Even factoring in that students, on average, have the ability to choose five such elective courses, the odds increase to only a tenth of 1 percent. Given this, we see that it is likely that most teachers complete (and have the opportunity to complete) their education with little knowledge about death issues to pass on to their future students. This translates into having little guidance in dealing with future students they will surely encounter, who are likely to experience the death of someone close to them while under the teacher's tutelage.

Government agencies and professional organizations designed to support education and educators in their endeavors also offer little help in mitigating the shortcomings discussed above. If anything, they exacerbate them by encouraging educators to shy away from gaining knowledge of, and preparing for, discussions of death-related issues with their students. From the U.S. Department of Education and Department of Health and Human Services, to national teacher organizations such as the National Education Association and the American Federation of Teachers, the advice to teachers is strikingly similar: Death is bad and grief is hard; talk to your kids about it because they *will* want to talk to you; here are a few tips of what you might talk about but, since you are not really equipped to do so, your best bet is to send them to a school counselor, who can then send them somewhere in the community where they can receive "expert" help. Not only are teachers urged to pawn off such problems on others (whom kids will likely have little connection with or trust in), but the advice coming from these sources is primarily aimed at children *following* a crisis, and offers little about how they might discuss such issues with students prior to, and in preparation for, such experiences. This flies in the face of widespread findings that demonstrate that discussing death-related issues prior to the experience of death has a positive effect on young people's attitudes and emotional well-being as they transition into adulthood. Why, then, are such predeath discussions via the medium of interpersonal, face-to-face contexts largely avoided?

The topic of death, insofar as it is a part of standard educational curricula, or as a component of various aspects of it, is at the stage that many other social issues have been in vis-à-vis its location within educational settings. In the not-so-distant past, issues such as sex, drugs, and race, among others, were met with similar questions and criticisms when considered whether they should be discussed in school alongside the three Rs." Discussing such topics with kids is a responsibility of parents, it was argued. Children are not at an appropriate age to talk about such things. Teachers are ill-equipped to teach about them, and to require them to do so will distract them from teaching what kids really need. Furthermore, it would be too disturbing for kids to have to deal with such material, and it could be psychologically harmful to require them to do so. These were all common concerns voiced about the above issues—each of which today is standard fare in the process of primary and secondary education. Teachers receive much education on issues of health, human anatomy and reproduction, and sexually transmitted diseases; multiculturalism and racial identity; and problems, preventions, and solutions to adolescent drug use, and each of these is a regular part of the curriculum in most American schools in one form or another.

The concerns expressed about these topics have reared their ugly heads again in today's debate about the role of teachers in dealing with issues of death in the classroom, and are, like the others, easily addressed. First, it *is* a responsibility of parents to teach and discuss such issues with their children. But how many parents do you know who actually successfully fulfill their responsibilities in any area of parenting, especially given the fact that close to half of American children are likely to live with only one parent? Furthermore, when parents are themselves largely ill-prepared and ambivalent to broach the subject of death with their children, what can we really expect? Second, children are equipped, at varying levels, to deal with issues of death. Most experts acknowledge that children can develop a "healthy" understanding of death by age seven.[17] Others point out that infants as early as eighteen months express identifiable reactions to the death of someone close to them. Most grief experts encourage children of all ages to be allowed to attend funerals, downplaying the risk of "trauma" at what many consider to be an inappropriate event for children.[18] And yes, teachers are ill-equipped as I have previously discussed, yet such is not necessary, and the problem could be easily addressed.

Conclusion

The stimulus struggle that Desmond Morris[19] argues takes place late in adulthood begins in childhood, manifest as playful curiosity. Children, whose development stems from the natural urge to investigate, explore and discover their environment, express the need and desire to change and grow, and to create and re-create the world around them. Losing the stimulus struggle at age sixty has the same consequences for children who are not allowed to do what comes naturally at age nine or ten—to get to know themselves, and their world—and themselves vis-à-vis the world. That is, they essentially die; not in a physical sense, but in the sense that they lose the ability and desire to engage in the necessary conditions for maturation. They lose the ability and will to be engaged, to challenge, to question, answer, and question again every facet of their daily lives; the creative, dynamic living of the child soon goes the way of the insipid life of the one who has checked out at age seventy and is merely waiting for death to save him from living.

One cannot—or at least should not—privilege out of hand the experience of seeing someone killed and carted off to a grave by grieving loved ones or the experience of attending their own grandmother's funeral. They are very different experiences, no doubt. Yet, they both are necessary and important in terms of our continual wrestling with the inevitability of our own deaths, and that of others.

NOTES

[1] This transformation of television use from public good to commercialization is a typical pattern of use of the medium from its original introduction in both American society and other societies around the world which have instituted its use in later times following its use in the United States. The topic is a centerpiece of media studies and theories regarding the diffusion of innovation of media technology.

[2] See Ben Bagdikian, *The Media Monopoly* (Boston: Beacon Press, 1992); and Armand Mattelart, *Mapping World Communication: War Progress and Culture* (Minneapolis: University of Minnesota Press, 1994).

[3] W. James Potter, *The 11 Myths of Media Violence* (Thousand Oaks, CA: Sage, 2003).

4   Judith Butler makes a similar argument, claiming that the court's censorship of racially offensive language, as well as pornography, constitutes violence because it inhibits the necessarily interpellative nature of linguistic discourse and discussion. She argues that the court's usurping of the power to define what is or is not offensive robs individual citizens of their own agency which enables them to decide for themselves what is offensive and act to counter such offensive speech. See Judith Butler, *Excitable Speech: A Politics of the Performative* (New York: Routledge, 1997).

5   Ninian Smart, "Death and Dying," in *Man's Concern with Death* ed. Arnold Toynbee (St. Louis, MO: McGraw-Hill, 1969), 25–35.

6   Dan Schaefer and Christine Lyons, *How Do We Tell the Children?* (New York: Newmarket Press, 1993).

7   Frances Sheldon, "ABC of Palliative Care: Bereavement," *British Medical Journal* 316(7129) (1998): 456–458.

8   Muleady Seager and S. C. Spencer, "Meeting the Bereavement Needs of Kids in Patient/Families," *The Hospice Journal* 11(4) (1996): 41–66.

9   Potter, chapter 4.

10   Butler, chapter 3.

11   James Hamilton, *Channeling Violence* (Princeton, NJ: Princeton University Press, 1998), p. 78.

12   See the National Mental Health Association, located online at: www.nmha.org.

13   Jonathan Kaufman, "Grief Enters the Classroom Curriculum," *Pittsburgh Post-Gazette* 21 February 1999, sec. A, p. 13.

14   Grant Pick, "Too Young to Grieve," *Chicago Tribune*, 18 July 1999, sec. Magazine, p. 10.

15   U.S. Department of Health and Human Services. Vital Statistics Branch. National Vital Statistics Report, *Deaths: Preliminary Data for 2000*. Volume 49, Number 12.

16   Rankings were taken from the 2002 issue of *U.S. News & World Report* rankings of universities and special programs.

17   "Coping with Death in the Workplace," *Protective Service Training Institute of Texas* http://www.utexas.edu/ssw/psti/newsletter/pdf/v84.pdf.

18   Dr. Cendra Lynn, death education professional and founder of "GriefNet," one of the most popular grief and death education organizations. See its website at http://www.GriefNet.org.

[19]   Desmond Morris, *The Human Zoo* (1969; reprint, New York: Kodansha International, 1996), chapters 6–7.

CHAPTER TWO

Death, Home from
Its Holiday?

In *Death Takes a Holiday, Sort Of,* Vicki Goldberg suggests, and I believe rightly so, a correlation between the declining visibility of death in actual experience and the increase in mediated depictions of death and dying. As she describes, death in eighteenth-century Europe was a prominent and public affair. Whether it was the death of a monarch, commoner, or criminal being executed, the events that surrounded the deaths were paraded before all the community, providing spectators with an occasion for personal religious reflection and communal affiliation (and in the case of public executions, a deterrent to crime). The bodies of the dead were visible and, in some cases, handled by members of the community. Religious ceremonies such as receiving the Eucharist were an indulgence open to all who wished to participate.

By the twentieth century, the concrete experience of death was rendered largely invisible by several interrelated factors: new technologies that affected decreasing mortality rates; the decline of public executions; the heightened sense that we should protect children from certain experiences of the "adult" world; and the emergence of a professional class of funeral directors who assumed the responsibility of caring for the dead. When death declined as a public spectacle, new forms of media—from print to electronic—began to assume the role of meeting the needs once fulfilled by the genuine, embodied experience of death and dying. Such representations, though removed to some degree from actual experience, still "offer more or less realistic or exaggerated versions of how we die," in Goldberg's view. She, however, leaves several important questions unaddressed. First, if mediated representations of death and dying are characterized in terms of their realistic or exaggerated depictions of actual experience, what are the criteria for making such distinctions? That is, what are the marks of fidelity by which to judge the fitness of such representations? Second, as we became more temporally removed from the time when death was a central aspect of public life and discourse, how have media depictions navigated between these two poles of realism? Have we tended toward one end of the spectrum more than the other over time? Third, are or can such representations be an adequate substitute for the experience itself? The first two questions are addressed in the content analysis of television programs that is the focus of this chapter. The third question is left open until the end of the book after having had an opportunity to explore it beyond the confines of the analysis here.

Before I begin this analysis, let us return again briefly to Goldberg's use of the term "holiday," which is an errant characterization in at least two respects. Insofar as "holiday" signifies a dormancy in death's visibility in both actual public experience and in media—an escape from normalcy, a vacation—the meaning only holds for the time period preceding her writing; it is not necessarily an adequate representation of the case across an extended period of time from then to the present. Additionally, a "holiday" not only refers to a momentary escape from the reality of daily life, it also most generally entails a celebration. In this regard, Goldberg's analogy does not hold and is even contradictory in some respects. This is to say, the period that Goldberg refers to is partially characterized by invisibility, but the invisibility belies the related aspect of celebration more or less inherent in the colloquial usage of the term "holiday." I make this point not to create an argument with Goldberg where there is not one, but to demonstrate the dynamic aspect of time as it relates to representing death in media and the way in which it problematizes any general characterization about its appearance outside of "real" experience. The invisibility and celebratory nature of death and dying in mediated representations oscillates its presence and intensity not only over long periods of time, but between different media and different genres of programming. Depictions of death and dying in news programming has maintained a fairly predictable form, for instance.[1]

However, when we look at how death has been represented in television, outside of news programming, a discernible pattern emerges over the past thirty-plus years. Throughout several genres of television programming, particularly soap operas and hospital/medical dramas, there has been a noticeable increase over the years in the frequency that death is depicted, the depth and breadth in which the subject of death is discussed (the qualitative contexts), and the explicitness of its presentations. Along with this general pattern, however, divergent trends exist between each of these program types. As I look at a variety of examples from these program formats throughout the 1970s, 1980s, and 1990s, I address what I believe are the most critical questions for our understanding of this phenomenon: How do we characterize the unfolding pattern of death's depiction from its isolation and avoidance in the 1970s, to the trend of general openness and explicitness in the 1990s and up to the present? What is the relationship between television's treatment of death and dying and some aspects of the larger culture at work at the time? Finally, what is the significance of the shifts that have and are occurring on television and in the broader cultural context in terms of the future of mediated depictions of death and our society's understanding of and attitudes toward issues of death and dying?

Death throughout the Decades

A comprehensive study of death's depiction on television is as unfeasible as it is nonsensical, to certain degree. As previously mentioned, death is a primary and pervasive subject of fictional drama. To study it in this way would likely lead us only to the general conclusions discussed in the previous chapter, that is, citing the scale of violence and killing that fill the television screen across all television genres. Because such a focus highlights only one end of the spectrum—the hyper-exaggeration of such representations of death—it affords us little in terms of understanding the relationship and continuum between realism and exaggeration, or the way it has played out over a long period of time. It makes more sense, at least to me, to begin such an analysis by bracketing certain genres of television programming inherently biased toward a single—exaggerated—portrayal of death and dying, focusing more on those in which the experience of death is depicted as more or less a "natural occurrence."[2] And so it is in the analysis that follows.

Making such distinctions in order to conduct a fruitful analysis of death representations also allows us to formulate some reasonable criteria for judging the relative realism or exaggeration expressed in such depictions. Unlike many other forms of experience that become the subject of television content, the empirical fact and experience of death is systematically codified in demographic statistics. While such data gives only a limited understanding of death, to be sure, it does provide the basis for one set of interpretive guidelines: comparatively evaluating the general frequency of death's occurrence, and its causes within television and among the general population. Our shared collective experience of death and dying serves as a reasonable basis for a second set of criteria. Certainly, we all experience death in different ways, both individually and culturally. However, we share the same realization that the experience of death both enacts and requires certain actions and reactions and invokes a set of new relationships. In short, the experience of death, we all know, is linked to a broader context beyond the individual who dies. Thus, a second criterion we can use to ascertain an understanding about the nature of death representations is the degree to which television programs invoke these related contexts. These two criteria are the basis of the following analysis of death representations over the last three decades and focus on two television program formats in particular: daytime soap operas and prime-time medical dramas.

Death in the Afternoon: The World of Daytime Soaps

The daytime soap opera as a television genre has its roots in radio and arose to prominence on television in the seventies. At this time the "big three" television networks adopted the one-hour serial format to cultivate and deliver to advertisers the female demographic, who at that time were composed largely of homemakers. Often referred to as "stories," these programs centered on the everyday lives of seemingly ordinary individuals. The family was the primary nexus of the majority of its content, along with the dynamic relationships that extended the family into its own personal world of friends, extended relatives, coworkers, and other members of the larger community. While no soap family or related characters resembled any family or characters most of us have ever witnessed or experienced in "real" life, the daytime soap characters can be viewed, in large part, as Jungian projections of our shadow selves. They express a caricatured understanding of them and extend elements of routine daily life to the limits of the absurd. In doing so, it makes visible our cultural anathemas for those living in restricted moral environments such as the United States. It explores and expresses those things seen as inappropriate for social life and public consumption—sexual deviance and promiscuity, rampant jealousy, and unbridled hatred inspiring all kinds of violence, murder, and mayhem.

By the end of the seventies, daytime soaps accounted for a vast majority of television advertising revenue, sustained by millions who regularly tuned in to share in the lives of their favorite characters. Many viewers watched multiple shows, which were staggered throughout the afternoon television schedule. Soaps continue to be, a powerful genre of television programming, in large part because their stories are unending (and without beginning for that matter);[3] main characters persist for long periods of time, giving audiences ample opportunity to emotionally invest in a particular character or unfolding drama. Though the original soap opera demographic has changed significantly since the seventies, many viewers continue to engross themselves in the fictive, but in some sense real, television world, enhanced to a significant degree by the diffusion of video recording technology in the early eighties, and the rise of the Internet in the nineties. These mechanisms allowed many to remain plugged in to their "stories" despite the requirements and increased rigor of contemporary work and family life.

Soap operas provide an excellent forum for studying representations of death and dying for at least two reasons. Their serial format and focus on "typical" family life implicitly provide a context for death and dying to occur as a more-or-less natural aspect of everyday family life over an extended period of time. That is, observing family life for one or two years, much less ten or twenty, one would necessarily expect death to occur as an inevitable reality of screen life, as in actual. Second, these daytime dramas have been cited in the past in terms of the amount of death and violent content that fills their stories. Some medical professionals have even speculated about the "health risks" of such programs.[4] The earliest, and perhaps only, study of death in daytime soaps was conducted as a part of ongoing studies in the late seventies by researchers at the State University of New York at Buffalo. As early as this time, scholars recognized that death and experiences potentially leading to it were prominent features of this television form and could thus have some bearing on our individual and collective perspective about the meaning of (or, in this case, the meaninglessness of) death.

The following analysis focuses on three daytime television dramas from their origins in the early 1970s through the end of the last decade and include: *All My Children* (beginning in 1970), *General Hospital* (1963), and *One Life to Live* (1968), all of which continue to air to this day.[5]

Health, Trauma, and Drama in Prime Time

The medical drama format has been popular since the mid-to-late 1960s, and each new decade has brought with it a new variety of such shows. They each share a common theme, but often focus differently on various kinds of medical experiences. This program format necessarily deals with the possibility of death as a primary theme, focusing on experiences that can and may lead to it and, as will be seen, on death and the dying themselves. While the soap opera presents a view of family life that draws its audience in large part from the audience's emotional investment in, and identification with, the character and story of the show, an arguably more complex scenario contextualizes the prime-time medical drama. The institution of medicine is one of the most prominent in the United States. It is the place where people go when they are sick, and doctors and other medical personnel control, to a large degree, whether their patients live or die. Like any institution, the medical community has always dealt with issues of public legitimacy in terms of their methods and approaches to treating disease, the patients who carry them, and what kinds of medical treatment are afforded to the general public. Their institutional image is largely related to that of the hospital as the primary setting for the practice of medicine. This issue became a central area of concern over the past thirty years, due to a host of new medical technologies that helped to solidify the institution of medicine as a giver and sustainer of life, rather than as a place to simply anticipate one's death.

This struggle over institutional image was thus a prominent feature of television dramas focused on such medical settings. The proportion of people who lived, compared to those who died, was a constant source of contention, negotiated between television executives and medical professionals alike. In his book, *Playing Doctor,* Joseph Turow provides a telling example of such a scenario during the production of *Trapper John, M.D.* The first episode of the seventh season featured the story of Trapper, a cardiovascular surgeon, performing an artificial heart transplant. The original script ended the story with the patient's death, due to complications in surgery. But, as Turow tells it,

> At least that's how Whelpley (the head writer for the show) and the producers had intended it to end. *Trapper John's* permanent M.D. advisor, Walter Dishell, had not voiced any objections to the patient's fate. Indeed, blood clots, strokes and death were unfortunate norms among actual artificial heart patients of the day. But when the producers sent the script to Dr. Robert Jarvik they received a startling surprise. He suggested firmly that the patient ought not die. In fact, he expressed strong reservations about the patient even getting a blood clot.[6]

Then, as it continues to be now, it was in the medical community's best interest to express faith in this new medical technology, to present an image of improved medical knowledge and expertise that would increasingly keep death at bay.

While this example illustrates the symbiotic nature of the relationship between the television industry and the professional community in the production process of shows such as these, a range of such issues typify and help to distinguish programs in the medical drama genre over the past three decades. The first of these is, logically, the issue of life versus death, that is, whether patients tend to live or die. The second is one of focus—whether shows centered more or less on doctors and other medical personnel, or their patients. The way these issues have played out in this context has shifted significantly over the past thirty years. The death-conquering doctors of the seventies and early eighties gave way to the more nuanced focus on individual patients and the increasing probabilities of death over that time period. This is seen in the medical programs analyzed here: *Medical Center* and *Marcus Welby, M.D.* (1969–1976), *Trapper John* and *St. Elsewhere* (1969–1976; 1982–1988), and *Chicago Hope* and *ER* (1994–2000; 1994–the time of this writing).

The purpose of the following analysis is not to focus on, or add to, the descriptive knowledge of soap operas or medical dramas as a genre per se, but rather to use them as an avenue for understanding the prevalence and divergent methods of representing death in general on television. Several issues are important to understanding the nature and degree to which such representations have appeared over the last three decades: the frequency of death's occurrence; the nature and causes of death; who is chosen to die; and the contextual complexity surrounding depictions of death (including expression of grief and the occurrence of funerals and other such memorials).

General Trends in Frequency of Death

Deaths have increasingly become commonplace in both the world of soaps and medical contexts (Figure 2.1). The total number of television deaths more than doubled between the 1970s and 1980s and increased more than 10 percent between the 1980s and 1990s. The rate of increase holds when taking into account the broadcasting time difference between soaps (which air for one hour, five days per week) and prime-time medical dramas (which appear for only one hour per week and are absent for several weeks between seasons). The dramatic rate of increase over the thirty-year period is even more significant when considering that in the 1990s, despite the above time differences, the portrayal of death and dying in

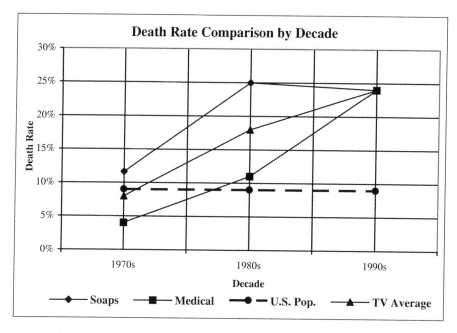

Figure 2.1. U.S. population death rate calculated from U.S. Census Bureau.

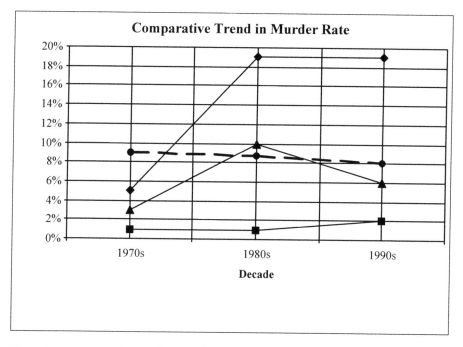

Figure 2.2 U.S. population murder rate calculated from U.S. Census Bureau.

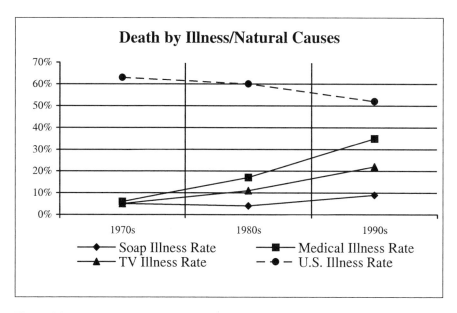

Figure 2.3. Percentage of deaths by illness/natural causes, by decade, genre and U.S Population. Population mortality statistics compiled from U.S. Census Bureau Data for each decade.

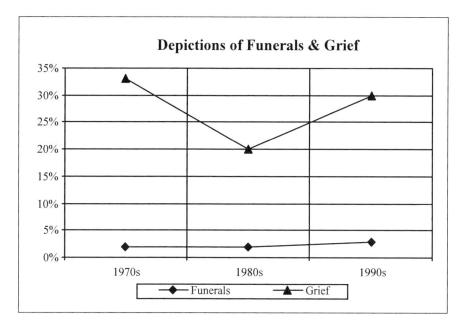

Figure 2.4. Total percent by decade of number of depictions of funerals and grief in all television shows included.

medical dramas were virtually equal to those in the daytime dramas.

Viewers of both soaps and medical dramas were likely to see more death in their respective favorite programs, yet soap opera viewers likely became more accustomed to such depictions. Though there was a significant increase in soap opera characters' deaths between the 1970s and 1980s (during which time they doubled), the frequency of death in the 1970s far outweighed those of the medical programs. Rather than continuing an upward spiral following the dramatic increase between the first two decades, however, occurrences of death in the daytime leveled off, remaining virtually the same between the 1980s and 1990s. The upward trend has been, however, more steady and pronounced in medical dramas. Their numbers doubled between the first two decades, though they were still, at the end of the 1980s, significantly fewer than their soap counterparts. Then, in the 1990s, there seems to have been an explosion of sorts, the number of deaths catapulting to the level of frequency found in soaps. Though the increase between decades for the medical dramas was only about 13 percent, when taking into account the aforementioned time differences between the program formats, this increase in the last decade is quite significant. That is, in the 1990s, the number of deaths that occurred over a five-hour period per week on network soaps was equaled by shows taking up only one hour per week in comparison.

Another way to understand the overall frequency of death on television in general, and in particular program genres, is to compare television death rates to that of the actual U.S. population over the same period of time. On average, death in television only came close to mirroring that of the actual population (which has remained virtually the same over the past thirty years) in the 1970s[7]. In the following two decades, television deaths doubled that of the general population in the 1980s and tripled it in the 1990s. A somewhat different picture develops when we differentiate between soaps and medical dramas, comparing the death rates with the population average rate. In the 1970s, the medical drama death rate was about 4 percent less than the population, while soaps were about 3 percent above. When medical show death rates climbed to only 2 percent above the population in the 1980s, soaps soared more than 15 percent above. As mentioned earlier, the death rate for both shows was about equal in the 1990s, both more than double that of the U.S. population.

Explanations for the unexpected decline in deaths within daytime soaps in the 1990s, the virtual nonexistence of death and dying in medical dramas in the 1970s, and their dramatic increase in later decades cannot be clearly

made without considering the remaining aspects of such depictions—the
types of deaths most often depicted, those shown killed, dead or dying, and
the circumstances surrounding them.

Causes of Death

In the world outside of television, causes of death are extremely varied. In
these television programs, however, certain forms of death are depicted
more than others, in a much more narrower fashion than in the general
population. Here, too, a discernible pattern is apparent over the three-decade
period in general, and between the two program formats in particular. Deaths
on television generally take the following forms: accidents, suicides, murders, short-term or long-term illnesses, or miscarriages. While various forms
of illnesses—from cancer to Acquired Immune Deficiency Syndrome
(AIDS) to Sudden Infant Death Syndrome (SIDS) and the like—occurred the
most, murders and accidents followed close behind, each representing 33
percent, 28 percent, and 24 percent of the total numbers of deaths, respectively.

Though the time between the 1970s and 1980s showed the greatest rate
of increase in numbers of murders (9 percent) (see Figure 2.2), accidents (6
percent), and illnesses (4 percent) (see Figure 2.3), the only form of death
that increased significantly between the 1980s and 1990s was illnesses,
which doubled between the two decades and accounted for the greatest percentage of death types in the 1990s. Suicides were depicted the least, com-
prising a mere 3 percent of the total numbers of deaths (though their numbers
did rise marginally in each decade). Portrayals of miscarriages were also
relatively infrequent (4 percent of the total), and their numbers declined from
the seventies to the nineties.[8] As might be expected, murders dominated the
daytime soaps, while illnesses dominated the medical dramas. Additionally,
the percentage gap differences between each type of show and their depictions of death by illness or murder were substantial, a 25 percent difference
in the number of murders (soaps dominating), and a 16 percent difference for
illnesses (dominated by medical dramas).

How do these trends in the cause of death relate to those in the general
population? The overall murder rate on television was significantly below
that of the general population in the 1970s. In the following two decades, the
number has been about the same, rising only 1 percent above it in the 1980s

and falling 2 percent below in the 1990s. Again, however, there are significant differences between program types. The fidelity between TV murder rates and that of the general population is obfuscated in large part due to the skyrocketing of murders in soap operas, which were more than double that of the population in both the 1980s and 1990s. The murder rate on medical shows are virtually nonexistent throughout, remaining between 1 to 2 percent over the three decades, and significantly below the rate of the general population.

Illnesses, which comprise the vast majority of causes of death in the general population, are seen significantly less often on television in general. However, the rate of increase in deaths of this type has risen significantly in general over the decades, as well as in each show format. While the rate dipped slightly in the 1980s for soap operas, it more than doubled in the 1990s. The rate of increase in medical dramas steadily inclined, doubling its numbers between each decade. The numbers of accidental deaths followed a similar upward trend, with rates of death in general on television mirroring the general population much more closely.

Who Dies?

If "only the good die young," then television is full of good people. The degree of change in the numbers of the different groups of people who appear dead and dying here distinguishes to some degree our expectations of who should die most often and those with whom we are most comfortable dying. Medical dramas, significantly more than soaps, depict a wider range of classes of people who die. While adults (largely young to middle-aged) die most frequently in both types of programs, the elderly, young children, and teenagers die more in medical dramas than in soaps, which hide from view the dying images of the very young and old. The only exception to this is the frequency of infants and newborns who die in soap operas, accounting for about 6 percent of deaths in that format. Though a relatively low percentage, infant deaths here are more often than not connected to the number of miscarriages or births of children whose severe medical complications were known prior and whose life expectancy was extremely short. This is about the most that can be said here about who dies on television.

It would be quite inaccurate to make the same comparisons here to deaths in the general population because the details of each person's age who dies on television is not given. Therefore, the larger categories of the very old, very young, and those in the middle are the only ones that make much sense.

Funerals and Expressions of Grief

One of the primary elements distinguishing mediated and actual realities of death and dying is the degree to which such deaths are contextualized. Typical expressions of death and dying on television overall are largely devoid of such contexts. On television, people just die; they do not grieve, and if so, only for a fleeting moment. They do not plan and carry out funerals and burials or experience the process of probate; there are no death certifications or autopsies. If television is progressing toward more "real" depictions of death and dying, we would expect to see more contextualizations of death and dying in these and other terms. In this analysis, I accounted for two of the above experiences—that of individual and public grieving and the depiction of funeral or memorial services.

While grieving and funeral depictions have steadily increased over the decades (see Figure 2.4), they each continue to appear relatively infrequently when someone dies on television. Funerals, shown the least often (in only 3 percent of the total numbers of deaths occurring), doubled between each decade. Individual and collective grief was virtually nonexistent in the 1970s, marginally increased in the 1980s, and saw the greatest rate of increase between the 1980s and 1990s, when the number doubled. Funerals appeared about equally in both soaps and medical dramas. However, when looking further, these depictions were greater in length in the medical dramas and more focused on the actual grieving and memorial behaviors indicative of them. When funerals appeared in soaps, they were generally short, and they focused more attention on the continued plotting and scheming of the living characters rather than on the circumstances dealing with the deceased. In addition, when compared with one another, soaps were more often bereft of any kind of grieving when dealing with one who has died. Such expressions of grief occur two-thirds more of the time in medical dramas than in soaps.

Here, too, it makes little sense to try to make any kind of quantitative comparison of "realism." While it seems that grief has become more commonplace among those who die on television, many of the experiences following someone's death that we typically engage in have only begun to creep into the contextual scenarios provided. Funerals, memorials, interactions with funeral directors or probate lawyers, etc. still only appear anecdotally in terms of the frequency in which they appear. The statistical data here paints one picture of how representations of death and dying have changed over time. General details about what was going on in the broader cultural context during these times add to our perspective of such developments and changes.

The Changing Reality of TV Death

In 2001, Home Box Office launched what would turn out to be a hit series, *Six Feet Under*. In 2003, the Showtime Network responded with its own brand of "death TV" in the series *Dead Like Me*. And this year, in 2004, the A & E Network introduced the first-ever reality television death series, *Family Plots*. Each of these shows, in very different ways, moved the experience of, and circumstances surrounding, death and dying from the margins of television programming squarely to the center. Just prior to the appearance of these programs, a host of new "autopsy" documentary series sprang up on several cable networks, captivating audiences with the disgustingly fascinating images of death's physical realities. Several new reality shows set in various hospital emergency rooms infused a new sense of "reality" into a context we were used to seeing, in some more or less exaggerated way, on network television. They exposed the frightening anticipation of death's probability, as real doctors operated on real patients whose outcome was indeed an all-too-real matter of life and death. The ever-taboo mediums and twenty-first century soothsayers of the type we have all seen on late night television commercials—panhandling their psychic abilities—soon found their way into "mainstream" households in the Sci-Fi Channel's *Crossing Over*. And even the major television networks continued to forge new—if only slightly—ground in terms of the role that death played in much of its programming, from sitcoms to cop shows. Many such recent programs, though they are mixed two-parts drama and two-parts comedy, were one hundred percent about death and dying and the circumstances surrounding it.

When we juxtapose the trends discussed in the preceding analysis with our present media environment in which death, as a natural occurrence, seems to abound more and more, we may be tempted to look for cause. What caused the shift from what seemed to be a blatant shielding of our eyes from real-life death on the screen at the beginning of one era to now? But I believe a more prudent and implied question is expressed in my explanation of such occurrences: What we see now was not caused by a singular or even complex set of circumstances in the mediascape or otherwise in our lived experiences; rather, what preceded in the programming and social contexts of now bygone years paved the way for what we see now. The prior representations of death and dying, as they began to shift and change over several decades, made our "new" era of death-related programming possible and plausible—for both television audiences, media executives, and other commercial entities they accommodate.

In a way, the prior programs from the seventies and beyond were market-testing the idea of death's reality as a conceivable source of entertainment in a society that became increasingly more acquainted with death's realities in the everyday lives of their own families and those vicariously experienced by others in this country and beyond. It is clear and understandable that in the seventies, Americans wanted to see anything but death in their living rooms. The country, reeling with the brutal images of thousands of its brothers, fathers, and sons returning home in uniform body bags that laid bare their bloody bodies mangled in a Vietnam jungle, was all too eager to forego more of the same for what many saw as a well-deserved escape into a serene world of not-so-socially relevant television.

Women of the seventies found solace and sought sexual fantasy in the world of daytime soaps, providing a much needed temporary escape from the twenty-four-hour-a-day rigors of raising their children and taking care of their husbands and homes. Men on the television screen, much unlike their husbands, provided a mediated life where the family dramas that ruled their own lives were writ as large as possible on their twelve-inch sets. Even though much drama did ensue, only on occasion were viewers made to vicariously experience a death in their television families. And when they did, they could be assured that it would be brief, and somewhat unemotional. Additionally, more often than not, those who did "die" were returned to them—their deaths having only been faked in order to breathe an air of dramatic continuity. The hospitals where many of these family dramas were played out were filled with people finding miraculous cures, new loves, and renewing old relationships with distant family or newly discovered mothers, fathers, and children. Death in the afternoon was fleeting, highly dramatic, largely accidental, and most of the time criminal—inflicted on the innocent by evil characters motivated by jealousy, pride, contempt, and hatred. The television viewer rarely had to attend a funeral and was given little time to grieve with the individuals and families who suffered mortal loss. Deaths were meaningful only insofar as they paved the way for happier circumstances or provided just consequence for another's evil deeds.

When the men folk returned from their world of work and other extracurricular activities, their wives had new stories to tell, not only about their own work day, but about the screen events they had witnessed unfold between their favorite characters on their stories. When a husband and/or father wanted to relax after a long day of work, he, together with his wife and children, was also assured that he and his family could find entertaining pleasures in the hospital and medical dramas scattered about the three-or-four channel television dial. Parents did not have to worry about their children witnessing the adult realities of death and dying. Men could trade in their troubled identities for that of the television doctor, whose prevailing macho persona and god-complex personality commanded medical students, nurses, and other hospital personnel, all in the name of "doing what they have to do" to cure sickness and disease. Wives could find in these characters a man with the caring sensitivity of their fathers; benevolent physicians whose bedside manner rivaled that of the parish priest comforting the sick with the assurance of renewed health. The doctor's office or hospital hallways were filled with people for whom, though they may have had physical ailments that stimulate thoughts of death, a mere shot and a healthy dose of good cheer were enough to send them back on their way to their own lives that we experienced little of.

The reality of television death in the seventies was, in many ways, no different in the abstract than the lives being lived by those who watched. The number of people who died on the screen virtually mirrored those in the general population. The kinds of people who died on television were largely the same as those viewers witnessed on the six o'clock news—murderers and those they murdered, and accident victims. And on the television serial, as in the news they watched, such images were fleeting and shied away from the messy details that surely engulfed those who really lived them. The TV world of the seventies was in most every respect one where we could largely escape and revel in our ever-deepening fear and denial of death. The circumstances of work, an ever-expanding desire for middle-class and upper-class wealth and the pleasures it afforded, and a not-too-distant past that we all wanted to forget became our collective ethos.

The world of the sixties and early seventies—mired in bloodshed, ideo-logical critique brought on by the deaths of those to whom we were inti-mately connected, and the all-too-often experience of attending wakes, funerals, and national memorial ceremonies—drastically changed. Those who once raised their middle finger in disgust to God, government, and the "silent majority" who seemingly sanctioned or acquiesced to the deaths these critics held them responsible for began to become enmeshed in a hedonistic world that allowed them to forsake the death scenes of previous days for a variety of newfound toys and material pleasures. And with this shift in focus, the dead disappeared, only to be dealt with in the private lives of individuals and families unencumbered by meddlesome neighbors or bureaucrats—and definitely not a national television audience.

If the seventies laid the foundation for an ethos of detachment, denial, and fear of death in American life (supplemented and sustained by the form and content of television production), the eighties seemed to respond to this expression of collective national sentiment with a modicum of paradoxical nostalgia. The previous decade of denial seemed to arouse a sense of longing for what was absent both in actual public discourse and in the multitude of television narratives. The death and destruction ever-present in the sixties and early seventies that precipitated the posture of personal and collective denial in the real world and on the screen were increasingly visible in the following decade. AIDS, which reared its head as a national plague, inspired fear in doctors and lay-citizens alike; we did not know from whence it came, nor did we know what would be left in its wake. What was first seen as a gay and/or drug user's disease soon affected a sense of collective vulnerability from which the Marcus Welbys of the world could offer no protection, no cure. The disease was as nationally pervasive as it was intensely personal, as a new generation of men and women—old, young, and the unborn alike—suffered without impugnity by death's forceful hand.

The violence the disease wrought on the body made fragile shells of those who were once in such immaculate physical condition, turning the strongest among us into the most weak and frail. And the families and loved ones—of whom no circle seemed to be untouched—were forced to care for those who could no longer retain control of their bodily functions. They were disgusted but retained a sense of extreme personal responsibility. Others took the easier rode traveled—abandoning friends, family, and other loved ones, ashamed of what they had become and the lifestyles that so transfigured them. To those who opted for this reaction, the reality of death that we had become so accustomed to being disinterested and disengaged in stared at them through the sunken and squinted eyes of those whose condition simply reminded us that whether we were poor or wealthy, gay or straight, religious or atheist—none of us was exempt. And this made many of us keenly aware and afraid. But rather than refuse to relive these realities through our sources of entertainment, as we had done in the past, this time we dealt with it individually or collectively, personally or vicariously. We watched the horrors of death in our own lives unfold in many of the same respects on the television screen. The unscrupulous, power-hungry, and ever-conflicted and conflicting characters of daytime soaps and a new breed of television doctors flashed these harsh realities on the television screen—and we watched anyway, despite the pain and sense of extreme mortality they inspired.

The world of the eighties began to make a little less sense to us than the decade before. We began the new decade captivated by televised images of innocent American citizens being held hostage—imprisoned, tortured, starved—by an enemy that caught most of us unawares. On a fall afternoon many of the pre–Generation Xers felt what our mothers and fathers felt more than a decade before, when we heard the news that our president had been shot. We watched with our parents the images of Reagan and Brady as they took a bullet from a would-be assassin, fell to the ground, and were wheeled away to the hospital in a chaotic circus of insecurity and uncertainty.

In a country with increasing technological prowess, we collectively watched one of our own—an unassuming public school teacher no less—disintegrate in a cloud of fire and smoke in a tragic space shuttle crash. We expected astronauts to face the possibility of such destruction as a part of their profession. But when Christa McCauliffe joined their ranks in this terrible tragedy, it instilled in a new generation of Americans an anxiousness about the world and our own mortality that we had before then never experienced. This was compounded by the weekly attack drills many of us practiced as schoolchildren during the height of the cold war. Reagan's Wild West persona insisted that "some men just need killing," and it seemed, at least in our minds, that it would soon play out in the doomsday scenarios we were forced to simulate. And just when we thought the threat had subsided, George Bush Sr. helped to ensure that we would have a host of new enemies, inspiring and ensuring that the next generation would have some anxieties of impending death of its own.

Wars and rumors of war, a destructive pestilence that attacked us personally like the plagues of Egypt, and a general sense of collective apprehension

clouded the national landscape and informed our public debates; the competing images of reality and contradicting notions about moral values and public
policy began to take hold of our television fantasy worlds as they had not
before. The everyday world of our sensory experience and our mediated fictional worlds began to collide, compete, and control, to some degree, our
national debates about a host of new issues, including those related to death
and dying.

Television doctors increasingly found their patients' circumstances on a
same plane of prominence as their own characters were in the previous decade. The conditions that brought patients to hospitals became much more
serious, much more traumatic. Increasingly, rather than leaving with a clean
bill of health, the patients escaped the corridors of the hospital wards only
through death's door, as audiences intensely looked on. The horrors of the
AIDS affliction and many others inspired more than their share of television
content in both soap operas and medical dramas. The individual and collective tragedies multiplied in the lives of countless families, played out on the
screen in a more or less similar manner that many had really experienced it.
The death rate in the general population was simultaneously exaggerated and
understated in television dramas; a juxtaposition of death's realities seemed
to offer viewers not only a choice of television programming, but a critical
space from which to interrogate the nature of life, death, and its place in our
own lives and in the dominant discourses of the day.

Soap operas and medical dramas seemed to give us something we did not
have prior: an increasing contextualization of the experience of death,
whether expressed in the exaggeration of murder victims in one, or as the
tragic end of illness and disease in the other. Individual and collective grieving began to supplement more and more of the television death experience,
encouraging us, to some degree, to share in the underside of death, rather
than quickly jump from death right back into life again—never having to
really fully experience and understand the fictional deaths of the television
characters, and therefore our own. In many circumstances we moved away
from the "shotgun death" where our eyes are taken from one death scene to
the next, and on and on without any sense of understanding the experience of
what happened in between. The dead of previous decades began to be rescued from their relative invisibility and were given form. This time they had
names. Families cried when they died, attended their funerals, laughed and
grieved, fought and made peace. Doctors found themselves more and more
having to discuss with family members in grave detail how and why their

loved ones would soon die. Still maintaining an image of the omnipotent healer, they nevertheless were portrayed as having to deal with the conflicting realities of their own power and powerlessness in the face of death, as well as the emotional pain and anguish of the dying and their loved ones who now surrounded them at their hospital bedsides.

To be sure, the 1980s television junkie did not look for death when she turned on the tube; yet, when increasingly faced with such realities, she did not turn away to other things. She did not change channels in search of some "light" viewing. She did not, as her counterparts in the seventies may have been apt to do, refuse to continue to look on. She did not refuse to be emotionally taken in by the death scenes plastered across the screen. Something about her and the world in which she lived allowed her to resign herself to, realize, and confront the literal meaning of the soap introduction: "like sand in the hourglass, so are the days of our lives." On the other end of the television screen, producers, too, found themselves weaving narratives of death and dying more often, and in a much more complex manner. However, the scenes did remain somewhat covered with a thin veil of expected etiquette, still limited to some degree by what audiences would and would not tolerate. Attempts to mirror death's reality too closely were met with a sense of some remaining reticence, making it possible for a show such as *St. Elsewhere*, for example, to be cancelled—in large part because it was seen as being too "dark."

But like the seventies did for the eighties, the 1980s world of television drama paved the way for what proved to be a dramatically new and daring decade of programming in the 1990s. Shows revered as "too edgy" in the eighties, and their death narratives tempered with just the right amount of personal dissociation, became the basis for pushing the envelope in many respects, including how much and in what manner death would continue to be represented. Rather than the drastic change that occurred between the 1970s and 1980s, the way of representing death on television in the 1990s can be described by one word—more. More death, more illness, more suffering, and more pain. More kinds of death. More kinds of people dying in more places, more people mourning the dying and dead, and more memory of the dead by the living. The context that death began to be increasingly enshrouded in was expanded and exaggerated; while it was regarded by some as poignant social critique, it was reviled by others as still an unwanted invasion into the heart and soul of our emotional core. Some welcomed the new no-holds-barred way of fictionalizing death and dying for the television screen, while others lamented the injection of this old taboo into a new context of public discourse.

The pushing of the envelope in terms of how television dealt with death in the 1980s, and its expansion in the 1990s, differed in respect to motivation. At least this seems to be a plausible speculation. This is to say, the death-related programming of the eighties sought to provide viewers what they rejected in the 1970s, which largely eschewed using entertainment media as a forum for social criticism. Its seeming hyper-expansion in the nineties, on the other hand, seemed to try to explode our sensibilities and taboos with extreme vigor—imposing its own relevance on the discussion of death-related issues—much as it had done with concomitant issues of sex and sexuality. The same prevailing predilection to allow previously profane words such as "ass," "asshole," "shit," and others to flow from the lips of network television bad boys and girls found itself in the same expression that made it plausible and acceptable for dead and decayed bodies, guts spilling out in full view on a coroner's table, to become a new television staple.

Representations of death and dying changed significantly between the 1970s and 1980s, while the 1990s extended the nature and style of such representations even further. It seems that programs that have sprung up in the past two or three years may arguably be the beginning of another significant shift in this regard. After having discussed here the long-term trends, I turn our attention now to the possibilities that particular shows in this new "genre" of death TV may offer us in terms of expanding the public nature of death-related discourse and influencing our larger cultural attitudes about death and dying.

NOTES

[1]   Susan D. Moeller, *Compassion Fatigue: How the Media Sell Disease, Famine, War and Death* (New York: Routledge, 1999).

[2]   Philipe Aries uses this qualifying phrase to describe the normal, natural occurrence and process of death, to be distinguished from such things as killing (or being killed), etc. I use it here to signify that the deaths that occur within these shows are part of the normal course of the lives of the actors in the fictional narrative. That is, dying or death is not *the* focal point of the drama itself, though it may be an aspect of it. This distinguishes it from programs such as those in the cop drama where violent crimes and/or death are the central aspect of the show.

[3]   George Comstock, *The Evolution of American Television* (Newbury Park, CA: Sage, 1989).

4 Tim Crayford, Richard Hooper, and Sarah Evans, "Death Rates of Characters in Soap Operas on British Television: Is a Government Health Warning Required?" *British Medical Journal* 315(7123): 1997, 1649–1652.

5 Each of these programs are all featured on the ABC network. They were selected primarily because they were the only shows with comprehensive episode guides that are available from throughout the entirety of their existence. They each also began as thirty-minute shows and expanded to the one-hour format by the mid-seventies.

6 Joseph Turow, *Playing Doctor: Television, Storytelling and Medical Power* (New York: Oxford University Press, 1999), xi–xii.

7 This number excludes instances of murders and routine, violent deaths.

8 A substantial number, about 8 percent of the deaths that occurred, were of unknown cause, that is, they were not able to be ascertained using the episode summaries provided.

CHAPTER THREE

Death Becomes Them

Reading Six Feet Under

In the spring of 2001, when the trailers introducing HBO's new series *Six Feet Under* first began, I had just finished a year of doing interviews with funeral directors throughout parts of the South, Southwest, and Midwest. Without fail, most were initially reticent to speak to me. I had expected this given that usually when you heard about funeral directors, it was because of some scandal. However, when I would meet them face-to-face and explained that I wanted to understand their industry and their work, their hesitation gave way to a keen, childlike sense of enthusiasm. They answered my questions in great detail and elaborated them with myriad stories ranging from the sublime to the comical. Many of them spoke long after I had stopped my tape recorder, and some, I think, would have gone on for hours had I not suggested over and over that I had all that I needed.

Funeral directors work in the shadows; dark ones at that. Few of us are interested in what they do, and many are quite disgusted at the thought. I could see through my interactions with them that few people talk to them; some talk about them, in order to publicize the latest instance of consumer price-gouging, but few talk to or with them. So, a sizable cohort of morticians sat on the edge of their seats anticipating what HBO would offer the world when they dared to discuss a business that no one really cared to talk about. Their anticipation was much like their interactions with me—reticent, but then hopeful, ready for disappointment, but eagerly hoping for the best— that someone would actually show them and their world to a world that new little about them, and to do so in a way that did not show the same old distorted picture of a group of demented, expressionless necrophiliacs who would just as soon carry on a conversation with a corpse as interact in a normal way with those of us among the living.

Many more Americans anticipated the show's debut for a different reason; they simply had not seen, much less heard of, a show such as this on television ever before. The idea of a show focused on a family of undertakers seemed repugnant, yet strangely inviting, for many. With this attitude, along with the reputation of HBO and the show's famed architect of dramedy, Alan Ball, American audiences were primed for the first undeniably different program to hit the small screen in our collective memory. Three years and a host of accolades and awards later, the show has proven to be even greater than its predebut hype. It has spawned at least two new shows that mimic in some way the substance of the show—Showtime's *Dead Like Me,* and A&E's *Family Plots.* It proved to the television world that death and entertainment were not oxymoronic; that we could handle such grave subject matter displayed and discussed without all the typical trappings characteristic of traditional television death.

But *Six Feet Under*'s success is due to more than just its novelty as a mode of entertainment. When its newness wore off, people found it, as it was from its beginning, socially relevant, sophisticated, and powerfully poignant in its message and influence. It was as much a form of social commentary and critique as it was simply great television. This and the following two chapters focus on this aspect of the show's success; its ability to influence traditional attitudes about death, dying, and the relatively unknown and little-considered business of dealing with the end of life. In this chapter I begin by laying the groundwork for how *Six Feet Under* manages to simultaneously entertain and make socially relevant arguments about a range of issues regarding death and dying. I focus on the most important elements in this regard: the substance and style of its introduction, and the characteristics of its primary characters—the Fisher Family. Both elements are constructed in such a way that they are allowed to serve a plurality of functions.

An Introduction to Death

They say familiarity breeds contempt. If so, then one might likely believe that the introductory scene to *Six Feet Under* has nothing new to offer. The familiar motifs associated with death, recognized so widely that they are almost cliché, are all there. The passing, even rushing, of time is seen in the movement of the clouds, the dramatic budding and wilting of flowers, and the inevitable transition from noontime to dusk. Men in black—not the figures who conceal government secrets, but funeral directors—are characteristically adorned, as are the sleek, jet-black hearses that deliver bodies to the cemetery. We well recognize the cold, sterile, and impersonal environment whose atmosphere is evident, signified by the long stretches of white tile and the abundance of metal objects associated with the dim corridors of basement-level hospital morgues. The bright light at the end of the tunnel beckons the souls of the dead with the promise of amazement and wonder, while the omnipresent raven, hovering and in flight throughout the scene, reminds us that it (death) will soon, too, come for us. From the white sheet that conceals the corpse, to mourners draped in black veils; from the serenity of the modern cemetery park to the very phrase "six feet under"—the readily recognizable collage of symbolism seems to signal that the show is about to take us on a journey of the familiar, a ride we have all been on before in our television viewing experience.

But the familiar patchwork of death imagery should not be read as simply a statement, a mere succinct explanation of the content that will fill the viewer's visual field for the remaining fifty-five minutes or so. Nor should it be interpreted only in terms of its typicality of form as a cinematic introduction that foreshadows what is to come. The symbolic unity of interwoven death imagery is both at once statement and question. Its foundation of familiarity is a necessary component by which to interrogate the familiar itself. Beyond setting the stage for an ongoing narrative, the introduction alerts us to the fact that the primary focus of the remaining episode and episodes looks to question that very familiarity with which we have come to think about death and dying.

But the introduction here does not solely consist of visual stimuli; music anchors and accentuates the ethos its visual substance communicates. Though our viewing experience and interpretive realities privilege what our eyes see on the screen, the simultaneity of hearing creates the possibility for a dissonant synthesis; music—this single stylistic element—accomplishes this, telling us not only what to see, but *how* to look at it. While all that our eyes see in this brief span of time is unquestionably familiar, the style of music that accompanies it is unfamiliar, questionable. Ours is a culture whose etiquette largely requires refraining from emotional expression generally, and views anything other than somber reverence as a sign of disrespect when in the company of the dead. An atmosphere of solemnity is cultivated at wakes, funerals, memorials, or any other such events, and music is as much part of that atmosphere as any. Our acceptable range of tolerance for this air of reverence and respect generally requires the absence of music or that which is slow and of low pitch—nothing that would arouse the emotions of those who are present. Despite this, certain subcultures and death traditions in the United States incorporate a wider array of music in such ceremonial observances, theirs being conducted in a much more celebratory style and tone. But the music playing throughout the *Six feet Under* introduction is reminiscent of neither. We are surrounded visually by death, yet with the accompanying music it is hard to decide whether we should be standing calmly at attention or skipping around the countryside like Ken and Barbie. The music—the music is the question mark. It is that which asks "what is this" about all that we are seeing—the imposition of a question where what we see does not beg for one.

And so it is in this liminal space—in between the figurative forms of the familiar and unfamiliar, the literary genres of comedy, drama, and tragedy, the experiential world of agency and inaction, uncertainty and inevitability, life and death—that we enter the world of the Fisher family as a surrogate space in which to question death's realities.

The First Funeral Family

The family is generally regarded as a unit in and of itself; it is a dynamic system whose definition and characteristics cannot be reduced to its individual members. In keeping with this understanding, *Six Feet Under* as a literary text, does not offer us a traditional protagonist in the sense that there is a single character who propels the action of the drama throughout, or from one episode to the next. I should say that there is no *visible* or embodied protagonist. In this case, death—personified in a variety of anthropomorphisms—drives the narrative. Death is the primary association by which the family and each of its members are defined. The Fishers' most distinguishing characteristic is the family business, a family-owned/family-operated mortuary located in the Southern California suburbs. The identities of each of the family members are constructed, to one degree or another, by their relationship to the business of death and all of its concomitant experiences. And as with most other aspects of the show, the characters serve a dual function, one that fits them to a particular story and one that communicates a more substantive message. The following details of each character in the remaining pages, along with descriptive examples of their disposition, demonstrate how this dual function works throughout the pilot episode and the remainder of the series.

Nathaniel Fisher: The Shadow of Death

Nathaniel Fisher, the family patriarch, is a fifty-something-year-old man who has always been in the funeral business. His life has, since its inception, been the life of the family. He possesses the required ability to dissociate death from his own personal feelings and emotions, yet on a number of occasions it is evident that, while he masks them well, he nevertheless is emotionally invested in his work. So, while he would not hesitate to flick his ashes into an ashtray sitting atop the chest of the man he is in the process of embalming, he sees his work as a way of helping people in his community at a time when they most need it. It is his sincere belief, not a pretense for self-gain.

It is tempting to see Nathaniel as the protagonist of the show. It is his death in the opening minutes of the first episode that serves as a primary catalyzing agent for the remaining actions of the family. After his death, Nathaniel also reappears to various members of the family, and to others who have died or are dying. He posthumously maintains a prominent role in the family—inciting new reflections and advice that lead them to embark upon particular courses of action; however, his character changes dramatically. He is no longer Nathaniel Fisher; his reappearances transfigure his character from that of the family patriarch and head of the family business. He is the embodiment—the representative, if you will—of death itself. I return to his role as such later in the chapter.

Ruth: The Order amid the Chaos

If Nathaniel Fisher is both father figure and the symbolic incarnation of death, then the characters of the remaining family members are also dually constructed vis-à-vis this figurehead, their relationship or perspective regarding death itself; how they see Nathaniel in his posthumous recurring presence is, in large part, how they see death and themselves in relation to it. Ruth, the family matriarch, has lived the traditional life of an American wife and mother. Her identity is intimately intertwined with her husband's, and it is not until later in the show that she begins to make a distinction between the two—to "have a life of my own" as she often puts it. Having fulfilled this wife/mother/consummate support role for most of her adult life, she is inclined to look after the needs of her offspring before herself. Her interests, of which she is generally unaware, are marginal, while those of her children take center stage. Her character reveals a particular stance toward death and dying—the need to maintain order and control. When she loses her controlling grip, she is prone to increased anxiety and emotional instability. She is hypersensitive to the needs, as well as the actions, of others in the family, allowing her to supplement and complement her rigidity in the face of the chaos often going on around her.

"I'll be home for Christmas" plays in the background as Nathaniel drives casually around the suburban L.A. streets, smoking a cigarette and singing along to the music billowing from the sleek, new black hearse he is just purchased for the business. He is on his way to the airport to pick up his elder son who is flying in from Seattle back home for the holidays. His daughter, the youngest of three children, drives to a party at the same moment in her eyesore of a vehicle—a hideous pea-green hearse. Ruth is preparing dinner in the company of her youngest son, who is seated resolutely with perfect posture at the table, reading the newspaper in his funeral director "uniform." Nathaniel, relaxing during his leisurely drive, answers the car phone; Ruth is on the other end of the line and immediately inundates Nathaniel with questions. "Did you take your blood pressure medication?" "Can you pick up some milk at the store?" "Are you smoking?" Nathaniel says "no" to her last question, but Ruth knows he is lying. "Forget you'll give yourself cancer and die a slow and horrible death," she chides, "you should not be stinking up that new hearse." "People want things to be nice when there's a funeral. They don't want their loved ones riding around in something that smells like an ashtray," she continues. Nathaniel grudgingly extinguishes his cigarette to appease her, then hangs up the phone. He immediately begins to light up another one. Turning his eyes away from the road to grab the hearse's cigarette lighter, he is suddenly hit by an oncoming bus and killed; he dies not having seen what was coming.

In the next scene, Ruth, not yet knowing what has taken place, turns to her younger son: "I think your father's having some sort of midlife crisis," all the while ignoring the fact that she has just cut her finger. "I'd much rather him buy himself a fancy new hearse than leave me for another woman." This comment is met with a strange stare by her son, as if to say, "Where the hell did that come from?" Ruth insists that she is fine, despite her now bleeding finger, and quickly reminds her son that he has a funeral that he should start getting ready for.

As her son consoles mourners at the funeral downstairs, Ruth begins removing her pot roast from the oven as she continues to prepare for dinner. The phone rings and she answers, a bit perturbed that someone has interrupted. "Hello? This is Ruth Fisher," she says to the caller on the other line.

"Yes, I'm his wife," she continues. Annoyed at the caller's questions that seem to veil the real reason for the call, she asks, "What is this about?" Then there is a period of uncomfortable silence. "What!" she screams, hurling the phone across the kitchen floor. Her oven mitt still on, she subsequently backhands the pot roast off the stove and across the floor. In an uncontrollable fit she then begins doing the same with everything she can get her hands on—dishes and other kitchen utensils—screaming in short, high-pitched screams, "Ah! Ah! Ah!…"

The funeralgoers downstairs hear the screams and stare inquisitively at the ceiling. Ruth's son excuses himself and walks up to the kitchen to find his mother sitting, curled up on the floor in front of the stove. When he suddenly notices the chaotic scene, he asks what the hell is going on. Then he notices his mother as she continues staring straight at the floor. "There's been an accident" (pause). The new hearse is totaled (pause). Your father is dead (pause). Your father is dead, and my pot roast is ruined," she says in a calm voice, her face bereft of expression.

A few scenes later, Ruth's controlling character and need for order is demonstrated when she, her eldest son who has just arrived from the airport, and her daughter are at the hospital morgue. Her oldest son has just returned from identifying his father's body. Ruth inquires, "How did he look?" "Dead!" her son sarcastically replies. Her outward displays of anger having quickly subsided, she begins to think about business as usual. "Will there need to be a lot of reconstruction?" she asks in a soft, quiet tone. "[Your brother] is not that skilled at the really hard stuff. [His assistant] usually does that. He's quite gifted. You don't think we'll have to have a closed casket, do you? I would hate to send that message." "What message?" her son frustratingly asks, expressing some of his ignorance of the funeral business. "That we're not equipped to handle a major restoration, or that we're not proud of our work," Ruth answers.

Despite her momentary loss of control when she first learns of her husband's death, Ruth must maintain a calm grip on reality and does so by reacting rationally and cerebrally to events that might stir emotion and propel her into a spiral of chaos.

Nate: Baby Learns to Run

Nate, the eldest son, is a runner—both literally and figuratively. From the time he was a child, he eschewed his father's work; frightened to observe it and resolute on never engaging in its practice. When he became an adult, he dashed his father's dream of his two sons joining him in the family busi-

ness—Fisher and Sons Funeral Home—and moved far away from home to
Seattle, Washington. There he lived a life close to nature, worked as a man-
ager at an organic food co-op, and formed relationships with other hippie
throwbacks who had also escaped all the drudgeries of normal, urban life. He
does not so much fear death as he simply does not understand it. His agnostic
posture leads him at times to flagrant emotional outbursts and intense self-
reflection—both hedonism and restraint—not quite sure which is most useful
or appropriate in trying to resolve life's dilemmas. He displays intense emotional sensitivity toward others, but at times can be callous and brazen in his
reaction to others who enter his relational network, not giving a damn about
his actions and reactions. He believes in fate, though this orientation toward
both death and life is clearly never quite satisfying.

While Ruth is sharing the news with his younger brother there at the
Fisher home, Nate is in an airport closet consummating an illicit sexual encounter with a total stranger he met on his flight in from Seattle. In the midst
of engaging in their postcoital kisses, they both let each other know that they
"never do this," debating whether or not to exchange names. Nate's cell
phone rings. He assumes it is his dad and answers, only to find out that his
father is dead. "What?" he asks of his brother on the other end of the line.

The woman that Nate has spent the evening with, Brenda, graciously offers to give him a ride to the hospital; they converse about themselves and
their families en route. Brenda is in no hurry to get home to her family,
whom she describes as people who "get off on tormenting each other." "Actually, we're pretty normal," Nate replies to Brenda's question about his family. "My mom's a control freak," he says. "My brother, well, he's a control
freak too. And, my sister…well, I left home right before she was born, so I
never really knew her that well. She's kind of wild like I was."

Nate, suddenly turning his thoughts toward his dad, comments that he
"rode his ass" all the time. Obviously angry, he starts to yell in an irritated
and annoyed tone, "How could a man who's so fucking scared of everything—who never had an accident or never even a speeding ticket in his entire fucking life—how could he have a car wreck?" Brenda's reply to his
rhetorical question repels him all the more, but her statement reveals the nature of Nate's fear and ambivalence regarding death. Looking toward him as
if she were going to dispense some priceless pearls of wisdom, she says in a
soft, inquisitive voice, "Are you mad at him or the fact that we're all going to
die?" Nate, put off by her question, not wanting to be reminded of this real-

ity, asks in a demeaning tone, "Are you a shrink?" "No, God, no," Brenda replies. "Both my parents are." They both laugh as they speed on to the hospital.

The scene that perhaps most solidifies Nate's character takes place at the hospital morgue, when he finally goes in to identify his father's body, at the behest of his mother who said she could not do it because it is work and she did not want to see her husband this way. The coroner opens the steel drawer and uncovers his father's lifeless body from under the white sheet; his face still bears the horrible wounds caused by the accident. Nate stands there staring into his father's face as the coroner awaits confirmation. "Well?" the coroner asks, as if in a hurry to get the moment over with. Seamlessly, the camera angles toward a close-up of Nate so that we see only a partial view of the coroner's back and the sleeves of his white lab coat.

"Well, well," a voice says; Nate suddenly realizes that it is his father speaking, not the coroner. Nathaniel is standing right there, alive and well, where the coroner was standing. Dumbfounded, Nate stares at him in disbelief as his father, with a tinge of sarcasm, but serious in tone, says to him, "Well, well. The prodigal returns. This is what you've been running away from your whole life, buddy boy. Scared the crap out of ya when you were growing up, didn't it?" As the camera reveals Nate's growing anxiety and fear set in his face, it quickly goes back to Nathaniel who continues smiling, lovingly mocking Nate's attempt to escape not only the family business, but death itself. "And ya thought you'd escape. Well, guess what?" Nathaniel asks. After a brief silence he continues, a frightening seriousness countenancing his face as if to say, "this is something that you should never forget." "Oh nobody escapes," Nathaniel says to Nate, looking directly into his eyes and shaking his head. The camera returns to Nate, who is still standing, staring in disbelief. The suspended moment in time fades, and the figure of Nathaniel is replaced once again by that of the coroner—who picks up where he left off. "Well?" he asks again. "Yeah, that's him," Nate responds, still troubled by this confrontation with his dead father.

Not only does Nate's mind oscillate between fear and resignation when it comes to death, his emotions are constantly a visible sign of that struggle. In several scenes it is as though his emotional struggles were used to stimulate his thinking about the nature of death and what his orientation to it is, or should be. The first of such examples takes place as he is sitting on a bench with his sister during his father's viewing. At first they are just chitchatting, catching up on each other's lives, if you will; Nate has just admitted that he is "barely holding it together." After revealing to his sister the many disappointments of his life, he introspectively, but audibly, makes what he thinks is the summary comment about his life to this point. "I'm gonna be one of those losers who ends up on his deathbed saying 'where'd my life go?'" he says with a nihilistic tone in his voice and corresponding look on his face. Their conversation is interrupted by a woman who seems to be a professional funeral goer, one who hardly knows the people whose funeral she is attending, but nevertheless receives some form of pleasure or fulfillment out of attending anyway. She walks up to the two of them, glasses pulled down halfway on the bridge of her nose, looks at Nate, and offers the typical condolence, "I'm sorry about your father, but he's in a much better place now." Nate, irritated, frustrated and unsure about the truth of her comments, quickly snaps back, "You're so right about that!" "Who the hell is that?" he yells at his sister.

After Nate and his sister have continued with their conversation, the next interruption that stimulates one of these emotionally speculative moments is when Ruth begins to break down after just having viewed her husband's body lying out in the slumber room. Before she is able to let out much of a cry, her younger son quickly rushes her out of the room through a curtain where she can continue her outbursts in private. Angered at his brother's actions, Nate turns to his sister; the following conversation ensues:

Nate: What, she's sad, so he has to get her out of sight?

Sister: They always do that the second someone starts to lose it. They take them off into that room. It makes all the other people uncomfortable, I guess.

Nate: (loudly) This is not about the other people.

Sister: (quietly admonishing Nate) Volume!

Nate: (as Nate makes his following speech, we see on the screen a flashback to the scene which he is describing) When I went backpacking through Europe after I quit school, I went to this island off the coast of Sicily. This volcanic island. And on the boat over, there was this pine box. Somebody from the island who was being returned to be buried there, and there were all these old Sicilians dressed up all in black, waiting, just lined up on the beach. And when they got that coffin to the beach, these old Sicilian women just went ape-shit, screaming, throwing themselves on it, beating their chests, tearing at their hair, making animal noises. It was just so—so real. I mean, I'd been around funerals my entire life, but I had never seen such—grief. And at the time, it gave me the creeps, but now I think it's probably so much more healthy than—this.

In a similar scene where he must again confront death head on, Nate is standing over his father's grave, his casket having just been lowered into the ground. The family is cued by the presiding clergyman, who takes a salt shaker filled with earth and sprinkles it over the casket. "Looks like he's salting popcorn," Nate disgustingly quips. The clergyman beckons the family to follow his lead in saying their final good-byes. Nate's younger brother goes first, followed by his sister, then their mother. When it is his turn, Nate grabs the salt shaker and hesitates, walking off to the side of the grave, unsure of how he wants to proceed. He settles by the grave and kneels down, taking the time to peer inside and contemplate what is taking place. He grabs a handful of the dirt that is to cover his father's body; he looks at it as it runs through his fingers and back onto the pile. His younger brother quickly goes over to him and begins a heated conversation, in earshot of all those gathered, who are standing there calmly taking in the scene.

Brother: (whispers) Nate.

Nate: No! I refuse to sanitize this anymore.

Brother: This is how it's done.

Nate: Yeah? Well, it's whacked. What is this stupid saltshaker? Huh? What is this hermetically sealed box? This phony Astroturf around the grave? Jesus, David, it's like surgery. Clean, antiseptic, business. He was our father!

Brother: Please don't do this.

Nate: You can pump him full of chemicals. You can put makeup on him, and you can prop him up for a nap in the slumber room, but the fact remains, David, that the only father we're ever going to have is gone. Forever. And that sucks, but it's a goddamned part of life, and you can't really accept it without getting your hands dirty. Well, I do accept it, and I intend to honor the old bastard by letting the whole world see just how fucked up and shitty I feel that he's dead! (He throws the fistful of earth onto the coffin.) God damn it!

Priest: Um...Amen.

Ruth: Wait.

(Ruth lifts up a handful of dirt and throws it on the coffin. Then another, and another, and another. She begins sobbing and crying, as her hat falls off, and she continues to throw the dirt. Nate's brother tries to stop her.)

Nate: Let her.

(Nate holds his brother back, while Ruth weeps and hugs Nate. His brother just stands by and watches.)

In these and other such similar scenes, Nate's attunement to his own emotions and to the circumstances of those around him provides him the opportunity to deal with his demons. There is never an end in sight for him; there never comes a point in which he is settled with regard to the realities of death and dying. Like a shadow, it follows him all the days of his life. This aspect of his character is significant given how the show continues after this pilot episode. As time moves on, and the circumstances of the Fisher family's life branch out in new and far-reaching directions, other elements of the plotlines—Ruth's search for a new partner, the younger brother's relationship trials, or the sister's exploration of her professional pursuits—often take center stage, sometimes leaving the topic of death at the margins. But it is with Nate's character that the event and possibilities of death are ever-present as a source of conflict and contemplation. From this time forward he must struggle with assuming his new responsibility as a partner in the family business; his girlfriend's (Brenda) father dies; a subsequent girlfriend herself dies; and Nate's own life is at one point in jeopardy when he finds out he has a growing brain tumor. Death is always looking over his shoulder, like the ever—present raven shown in the show's introduction; he must constantly wrestle with what to think about it and how to act in light of its omnipresent possibility.

David: Master of the Mask

David, the middle child and Nate's younger brother, is in many respects the complete opposite of Nate. Unlike him, after graduating from high school he fulfilled the wishes of his father by attending mortuary school, ignoring his real desire to practice law. Clearly bitter about his decision, he rarely lets on that it is anything but what he wants. He acts out of familial responsibility, now increased by the fact of his father's death. He masks his emotions to such a degree that one questions whether he is even capable of expressing such. It is clear that he feels deeply, which is most evident in his relationship to his longtime friend and partner, Keith.

David reacts to the horrors associated with death with a posture of stone-cold dissociation and often comes across as disinterested; he feigns concern with a mask of statuesque resoluteness that always veils his countenance. Like his mother, he is a control freak who requires a well-ordered environment. He is generally nonconfrontational until the emotions he has so deeply internalized cannot help but come out in a burst of straightforward scolding toward family members and others he comes into contact with. He is in every sense his father's son but blames his father often for his own shortcomings. He is stable yet confused, his real identity and his mask at constant odds with each other.

A glassy, stunned look is pasted on David's face when his mom revealed the news to him of his father's death. Having assumed the responsibility of notifying the other siblings, he first calls Nate. With a grim look on his face—halfway between crying and screaming, but keeping his emotions under firm control—he makes the call. "I'm so sorry, Nate," he says to Nate on the other end of the phone. "I hate to have to be the one to tell you." He speaks in a solemn voice like that of a doctor relaying bad news to a patient about to die. Hunched over the kitchen counter, staring at the wall, David continues to ask Nate if he can meet his mom and sister at the morgue to identify their father's body. A moment later he calls their sister; in the same calm voice he says, "I've got bad news."

Meanwhile, David returns to the wake he was overseeing. With perfect, upright posture, he stands amid all the people politely and reverently greeting each other, offering condolences and conversing; he shows that he is the rock in the midst of the shaking figures who surround him devastated by their loss. With his hands folded in front of him and a look of calm control on his face, he all of a sudden lets out a horrific scream. You laugh in anticipation of the reaction he will get from the rest of the crowd gathered, but you soon realize that it did not actually happen. It was merely a projection—a dream of what he really wanted to do at the moment. But he hides the mix of emotions churning inside of him, because this is what he does—this is what he is obligated to do. David's character is always at odds with Nate, both literally and figuratively. Having followed in his father's footsteps, he has learned to deal with death in the manner dictated by his professional position—to maintain a posture of order and control lest the mourners with whom he works day to day lose control in the face of their grief. He sacrifices his need and prerogative to emote, thinking that this is the proper way to comfort the grieving.

Claire: A Caricature of Fear

Claire, the youngest of the family, is fitted with all of the trappings of a typical teenager, which also signify her posture toward death and dying. Unbridled fear and uncertainty have overtaken her psyche, and it spills over into every experience she lives. She is constantly concerned with how others see her, often escaping her tormented world by isolating herself from others and from the circumstances or opportunities that present themselves. Like the typical adolescent, she is prone to mood swings, oscillating between intense depression and fits of mania, often within a short period of time. She fears death like she fears adulthood, both of which constantly fuel her anxiety and lack of self-assurance. Claire represents the polar oppositions mentioned in my introductory chapter; her stance toward death is simultaneously one of fear and curiosity. She deals with her fear by displaying some modicum of detachment and disinterest. She has no problems, for instance, cutting off the foot of a dead man lying in their basement mortuary and sticking it in the school locker of her lover to punish him for telling all of her classmates that she sucked his toes during a make-out session in the back of the pea-green hearse she uses for transportation.

At the time of her father's death, Claire sits on a couch next to her boyfriend at a friend's house. In a smoke-filled room crowded with teenagers who look like they are in the middle of a backstage party at a grunge rock concert, her boyfriend offers her some crystal meth. "This is just speed, right?" Claire asks before she agrees to indulge. "Promise me this isn't crack. 'Cause tonight I've gotta spend Christmas Eve eating dinner with my demented family; it's going to be weird enough without being high on crack." Her boyfriend, Gabe, takes a hit himself, then passes her the glass pipe, assuring her. "No, it's just crystal meth," he says. "It just makes everything burn a little bit brighter."

She has just taken her first hit when her cell phone rings. "David, hi," she says as she gets up off the couch to move to a part of the room where she can hear and escape the advances of her boyfriend. "So, is Nate there yet? She hears the news and there is a moment of silence. "Yeah, sure, I'm on my way," she replies to David's assumed question of whether she can make it to the hospital. Stunned, she brushes her long, red hair out of her eyes and walks back into the room where her friends are talking and still getting high. "I...I have to go," she says as she starts to tear out of the room. "No fucking way," her boyfriend responds. "Wait, wait, wait, wait," he says quickly. "Come back, okay?" "I don't think so," Claire responds, on the verge of crying, her agitation heightened by the hit of meth she has just inhaled. Facing the crowd of drug groupies gathered in the room, she explains, "My dad just got hit by… a bus…and it broke his neck…and he's dead." As she simultaneously explains to them what has happened and reasons with herself to get a handle on just what is going on, she continues. "I gotta go pick up my mom and bring her to the morgue so she can identify his body." Her friends laugh at what they think is a story induced by her meth-related paranoia. She blurts out a slight chuckle as well, but quickly returns to her anger and anxiousness. "No, I'm not kidding! she yells defiantly. "This is actually happening." Throwing her hands in the air, she continues, now staring directly at her boyfriend. "And I'm high on crack!" "Crystal," Gabe corrects. "Whatever!" Claire yells back. "I guess… this… whole.. hellish… experience I'm about to go through is just going to burn a little bit brighter now, right?" she says. "Great! Thankyou! Fuck!" she screams at him, walking quickly out the door.

After picking up her mother, Claire reluctantly chitchats on their way to the morgue. Ruth is doing most of the talking, free-associating about the hearse, about Nathaniel, while all Claire can muster is the occasional "yeah" or "uh-huh." Her agitation, heightened no doubt by the drugs she has just inhaled, finally comes out when she says, "You're kind of freaking me out right now." "Claire," her mom begins. "Are you having sex? Are you doing drugs?" When Claire asks what has stimulated this inquiry, Ruth responds, "Your father's dead. I can't even remember the last time we talked about anything important. I just need to know you're okay." Hoping it will end the conversation, Claire assures her mom that she is indeed alright.

Claire, Nate, and Ruth are the first of the family to meet at the morgue. After Nate greets and hugs his mother, she admits to him that she cannot do the identification. Claire then quickly pulls Nate aside to tell him that she is high on meth, not sure if her "meltdown" is being caused by the drugs or the fact that her father is dead. Nate chidingly responds, "You cannot do this to me right now! Look, I have to go identify our dead father's body. Now I'm sorry you're having a bad drug experience, but deal with it," as he walks away from her. She is, as she will frequently continue to feel—alone, an outsider in fear of engaging with her family, avoiding human interaction and life itself.

Federico: Laughing at Death

While not a member of the family by blood, Federico was adopted, in some respects, into the family by Nathaniel Fisher. A somewhat troubled

Hispanic youth, he was spotted by the elder Fisher, who found him curious about his work as an undertaker. Nathaniel nurtured his interest and paid for him to learn the trade of embalming, which he subsequently put to use working for the Fisher family business. Federico is, in many ways, the symbol of detachment. He often refers to himself as a "restorative artist" who prides himself on being able to reconstruct the most hideously disfigured dead bodies in a way that is palatable for viewing by the deceased's relatives and friends. He is often chided by David for being disrespectful of the dead, frequently using foul language while in their company or eating lunch next to or even on top of the bodies that are the canvas of his art. It is clear that Federico has accepted the fact that death is a part of life; he is cognizant of the fact that like those around him who die, this, too, is his destiny. His acceptance of the reality is seen in his ability to joke in death's presence.

Two scenes in the first episode typify this aspect of his character. In the first, he has begun the embalming process on Nathaniel, late on Christmas Eve. When Nate enters the embalming room, Federico takes a Polaroid of Nathaniel's face. As he does, he looks up from the embalming table to see Nate, excited to see him after so long. "Nate!" he yells. "Whassup?" he asks, throwing his hands in the air. As he goes to shake Nate's hand, he momentarily remembers that some sadness and condolences are in order. "Ooh... Uh... I'm really sorry about your dad, man." Nate just looks down at the ground. "But, you know, when your time is up, it's up, right?" Federico exclaims. Nate hesitantly nods his head in agreement, though it is obvious he has not quite accepted that reality as Federico has. After Nate and Federico shake hands, David enters the room and asks Federico about his progress on his father's body. David unexpectedly gets a call on his cell phone and leaves the room. In his absence, Federico takes a break from his work and brings Nate over to the wall to show him pictures of some of his "work."

Federico:	Okay, here it goes. This is the one I'm most proud of. (He shows Nate a picture of a dead husband and wife, with serious bullet wounds in their faces.) The husband, okay, got fired, flipped out, shot his wife point blank in the head, right? And then turned it around and shot himself in the mouth. Some seriously closed-casket shit, right? Now look at this. (He shows Nate a picture of the same couple, after he has worked on them. They look perfect, as if they are sleeping.) Huh? Hah! Hah! Like the bride and groom on top of a cake! And then we cremated them. What a fricking waste. (He shows Nate a picture of his young son.) Actually, this right here is my best work.
Nate:	Wait a minute. This kid was just born like last month.

Federico:	Be four fucking years old in April. Can you believe it? Shit! Oh...Vanessa's pregnant again!
Nate:	Hey, you stud! (laughs)
Federico:	(laughs) Hey, it wasn't planned. But, you know what, neither was this one, and he's the best thing that ever happened to me. (Kisses the picture.)

Later at Nathaniel's viewing, the woman who accosted Nate earlier with condolences captures Federico's attention. Federico is reluctant to engage her in conversation until the woman mentions the name of someone familiar to him.

Chatty mourner:	My aunt Shirley was laid out here.
Federico:	Aunt Shirley, huh?
Chatty mourner:	Mm-hmm.
Federico:	Hmm.
Chatty mourner:	Shirley Hamilton. Terrible accident. Lost her ear.
Federico:	(smiling, delighting in his recollections) Oh, yeah! Yeah! I know Shirley! I remember Shirley!
Chatty mourner:	Really?!?
Federico:	Yes, yes. I was the person who sewed her ear back on. That was me.
Chatty mourner:	Really?
Federico:	That's my work!

The members of the Fisher family exhibit the typical reactions to death and dying outlined by Kubler-Ross's theory of the stages of grief that an individual goes through throughout the grief process—denial, anger, bargaining, depression, and acceptance. In this first episode, we see that each of the family members runs the gamut of these stages, to one degree or another, in response to Nathaniel's death. And as in actual life, it seems as though the family members express the symptoms of several of the stages simultaneously, while others seem not to express them at all. Like many aspects of this show, however, the family members' expression of these personal various mourning rituals is only one aspect of their dual function.

Because this is the first episode of a serial program, the writers must begin to establish the identities and character of each personality involved. Given this purpose, the expressions of grief by members of the Fisher family take on an added quality. They not only exhibit particular emotional expressions of grief, but their fundamental nature of their individual characters also reflects a quasi-permanent orientation toward death, constituted, in part, by the given reactions of a particular stage or set of stages of the grief process. It is these orientations toward death and dying in general, extrapolated from the elements of particular circumstances of mourning, that extend with each character throughout the life of the series: Nate's bipolar reaction to death; Ruth and David's need to maintain control; Claire's consummate fear and anger; and Federico's acceptance. As such, death itself is the central figure that drives the actions and circumstances of each of the players here; plots constantly churn as the relational matrix between the family and its individual members intertwine with the main player—death.

As I previously mentioned, the construction of these characters in this manner allows the show to accomplish more than formulation of the theatrical elements of the show, laying the groundwork for conflict and resolution, etc. The precise way that the characters are constructed vis-à-vis their orientation toward death and dying provides the basis for raising substantive arguments and stimulating social criticism about various issues of death and dying in the world beyond the television screen. In the following chapter, I demonstrate more precisely how such arguments are made given these characters and other signifying elements of the show.

CHAPTER FOUR

Rhetorical Invention
Structure and Argument in Six Feet Under

Aristotle lamented the fact that logical appeals based on human reasoning were not enough to accomplish most persuasive goals, thus acknowledging the appropriate use of pathos and ethos as acceptable tools of argument.[1] If emotional appeals were needed to supplement logical appeals to the thinking mind in Aristotle's day, the emergence and domination of new communication media—particularly visual media—almost require that they play an even greater role in television programs' ability to produce persuasive arguments about relevant social issues. This is to say, arguments derived from the pathetic and ethical environment surrounding a given issue not only provide important argumentative statements; they, more importantly, give such arguments the required force necessary to captivate audiences, stimulate inquiry, and facilitate attitudinal and behavioral change.

The matter is not that emotion and aspects of individual credibility are utilized at the expense of rational, well-articulated arguments. Rather, in visual, electronic media, they are foregrounded. Nevertheless, they are intimately entangled with the arguments themselves that are based on accepted conventions of logical reasoning. That is, in cases where emotional and ethical appeals appear alone, they are most effective when they link themselves to logically articulated arguments made elsewhere in other contexts.[2]

Perhaps more importantly, appeals to emotion and source credibility are a necessary component of one of the most fundamental purposes or means of argument itself—dialogue. In summary, the foregrounding of pathos and ethos as a source of argument in electronic media is (or I should say, can be) sophisticated, in the truest sense of the term vis-à-vis the classical Greek origins of rhetoric and argument.

If *Six Feet Under* does indeed serve to communicate a rhetorically persuasive message, then several questions are in order that frame the remaining discussion. First, what are the primary arguments made, and how do we extrapolate them from the variety of visual, verbal, and auditory signs presented? Second, from where does the show draw the content and evidence for its arguments? In what existing social context or arena of discussion are the arguments presented situated? would be a different way of asking this question. Third, how are the arguments made? That is, what stylistic elements of production are used to both ground the arguments and frame the dialogue it seeks to stimulate? And finally, to what ends are the arguments made? This question is necessarily addressed on two fronts, the least important of these is, what rhetorical message do the writers/producers intend to communicate? The more appropriate question is, what is left unanswered and/or ambiguously argued, such that viewers themselves adopt the framework given in order to substantiate the arguments given or produce new ones? In short, how do the arguments presented by the show contribute to the establishing of dialogue regarding the social and political aspects of death and dying in American culture?

The primary arguments (established in the pilot episode) are twofold: that the commodification of the death ritual process leads American citizens to make decisions about the disposition of loved ones without considering the ironies, contradictions, and inconsistencies evident in our decisions; and that by allowing death to play a prominent role in moderating daily life, we can renew and strengthen a sense of connection with others within a particular family or community. These two principal messages are established, in large part, by the decisions made about the context in which to frame the show itself: within the boundaries of a family and business.

Grounding the various narratives of *Six Feet Under* in these two settings accomplishes several important tasks insofar as they allow them to communicate the previously stated arguments. First, both groups (families and commercial enterprises) are essentially ecological in nature. No business enterprise, no family can be understood apart from the dynamic relationship each of them has with individuals and entities within and beyond themselves. For instance, we do not get a clear picture of David's character without knowing and understanding his relationship to his significant other, the church group he is actively a member of, and his other nonbusiness related interests. Similarly, we cannot understand him without considering the relationships necessary to the operation of the business, including those who purchase the funeral home's services, the larger elements and figures within the funeral industry, professional organizations to which he and the others belong, etc. The dynamic and interrelated nature of the family and business as the stage setting for the unfolding drama here allows the show both to accomplish both its primary commercial purposes as well as to create and communicate a message that is important and relevant to the society as a whole. That is, these environments in which the show is framed are familiar to all, though they may be more specifically well-known to others. They are natural settings rather than otherworldly or outside the American cultural range of understanding. Such circumstances as these provide the backdrop for the remaining reading of how *Six Feet Under* accomplishes its rhetorical and dialogical task.

Commercial Satire: Critiquing Commercialism

The rampant commercialism that has overtaken the American death ritual process is what is usually cited as the most prominent aspect of our culture's dissociation between life and death, the living and the dead. And, it is plainly evident that much of *Six Feet Under*'s programming is designed to highlight the degree to which market values have shifted our focus away from the dead to the material niceties in which they are enshrouded. The most forceful arguments regarding this disconnect are made in the first episode's use of what I refer to as "pseudo-advertisements." In terms of its dramatic production, these commercials serve the structural purpose of introducing the thematic content appearing in each of the four acts that comprise the episode.

But the commercials have a secondary, and in my view primary, purpose indicated by the fact that the "commercials" do not serve the intrinsic purpose of its own form. This is to say, they are packaged as actual advertisements—they attempt to promote a product and/or brand name—yet there is no actual or intended audience to receive its commercial message. That is, the producers of the pseudo-ads do not intend for the *Six Feet Under* viewer to actually purchase them. Additionally, these ads promote products that are rarely—if at all—the subjects of broad, commercial advertising appeals, primarily because the market is too miniscule to warrant mass appeal. There is no need to market embalming fluid, for instance, to the masses.[3]

So, assuming that these are not actual ads that promote actual products to actual consumers, they must serve some alternative role. Alternatively, we can discount them as having a singular descriptive purpose as well (beyond the degree to which any act of description is always already perspectival), the production of a particular reading at the expense of other perspectives. In actuality, the advertising form here is a metaphor which serves to rhetorically articulate a point of view. Presenting the message in the structural form of an advertisement equates the purpose of advertising in general—selling and the cultivation of need and desire—with what the producers argue we have essentially succumbed to in terms of how we deal with death and dying.

Just as millions of people are persuaded everyday by commercial advertisements to believe they want or need this product or that one (or that buying is an end in itself), so, too, have our beliefs about how we dispose of our dead been shaped by salespeople who help to create, sustain, and capitalize on our consumer impulses, the *Six Feet Under* ads argue. While the form in which the message is packaged makes this metaphorical link, the content of the ads themselves and the tone in which they are presented satirize rather than sell, mock rather than market, and invoke critical reflection rather than evoking desire. When we look at each of the four pseudo-ads, then, we see their dual purpose as both a dramatic tool and as argument and critique; each of the purposes are integrated in articulating the singular message of the ads, separately and collectively.

The first ad that introduces the first act of the episode follows:[4]

Image:	(Soft, light instrumental music plays in the background throughout.) A tall, white female dressed in a long, black evening gown and wearing long, white gloves on each arm, next to a new hearse. She faces the front while her left hand is outstretched, showcasing the vehicle.
Voice:	Sleek, sophisticated, seductive…
Image:	The woman walks the length of the vehicle as she eyes and strokes it with her left hand.
Voice:	The new Millennium Edition Crown Royal Funeral Coach…
Image:	The woman again faces front, now at the back of the vehicle, her right hand outstretched toward the vehicle, head cocked to the right with a seductive smile on her face.
Voice:	Because your loved one deserves the very best in style and comfort.

The correlation of the primary images in the ad is clear: The hearse represents the new vehicle Nathaniel is driving to pick up Nate from the airport;

the saleswoman, Ruth, who insists that he keep it in immaculate condition, suitable for the dead and those accompanying him or her. The visual presentation of the two images are consistent; they are both, "sleek, sophisticated, and seductive." But the satire here is presented in the comparison of extremes—between the realities of our commercial environment and the details of death. The reality of our media environment is that sex sells everything, disregarding any need to present any fidelity between signifiers and that which is signified.

That a mechanistic vehicle signifies our dominant sexual desires and standards of beauty and attraction demonstrates the degree of dissociation commonly relied upon in our culture generally. The same form of dissociation expressed in the advertising message is at work in the link between sex, beauty, eroticism, and—death. Society as a whole has generally come to grips with the merging of sexuality and commodification. But the satirical exposure of our foolishness here is that the same semantic and experiential development of the link between sex and material products is threatening to become our cultural reality of death and dying. That is, the more we allow our commercial impulses to serve as a primary motivation in dealing with death, the easier it will be to accept that a dead man actually gives a damn about the condition of the vehicle that drags his lifeless body to the cemetery, where he will be laid in the ground to decay and putrefy. In actuality, the ad argues that we have already reached this point; the folly in continuing this reality is its eventual acceptance as normal—our refusal or reluctance to challenge it.

Act 2 opens with a commercial promoting embalming fluid, foreshadowing the upcoming scenes that focus on the embalming and restoration work of Nathaniel's body, performed in part by both Federico and David.

Image:	(Rhythmic, seductive music plays in the background throughout.) A pair of feet of a white male, descending at 45 degree angle from left to right.
Voice:	(Male) For a body that's firm, yet flexible...
Image:	Partial view of man's stomach, with left hand resting on top, descending at a 45 degree angle from right to left.
Voice:	For skin that begs to be touched...
Image:	Close-up image of the man's face and upper torso, at a 45 degree angle from left to right; his eyes are shut, with no facial expression.

Voice:	For the velvety appearance of actual living tissue, top morticians rely on Living Splendor Embalming Fluid.
Image:	Full image of man in the background, draped in a long chair with his right arm hanging off the chair. In the foreground, a tall plastic bottle with a label that reads, "Living Splendor."
Voice:	Living Splendor: Only real life is better.

The ad bears some similarities to the first. The background music, as well as the tone and pace of the announcer's articulation, suggest an air of sexuality and eroticism. But two slight, yet significant differences alter our interpretation of the ad from the first. The first difference is the gender of the referent; in the first ad a female, the second a male. Second, in the first ad the two figures, the product and its representative, simultaneously occupy the visual space of the ad; in the second, the male figure precedes both the presence and our knowledge of the advertised product itself.

The difference in its interpretation is that where sex (represented by the female image) sells in the first ad, the appeal of the second ad is one of vanity. Sex, whether in actual experience or in its representation as a selling point, is constituted within a relationship including more than one person; it takes two to tango. Vanity, on the other hand, is embodied within an individual and appeals singularly to other individuals. That is, the woman in the first ad beckons the viewer to *have me,* to *possess me* (by having this product), while the man in the second summons us to *be* him—the perfect physical specimen. Its later connection with the actual product in this case suggests not the ability to attain something through the acquisition of a possession, but the reverse: Through this possession you can attain this ideal of bodily improvement.

The extreme, even comic nature of the figures is that it purports that in death we can be something that we could never be in life (or that we would want it at all). In light of the differences in interpretation between the two ads, however, the irony is much the same: How foolish to desire, expect, or require this ideal when one is dead, or seek it on behalf of someone who is. When most of us fall so short of this physical perfection in life, why take great pains to achieve such on a body that, in death, has no value in terms of what the "perfect body" might be used for (to be an object of another's desire or one's own self-indulgence)? The ad here ridicules notions proffered by members of the funeral industry that the dead should be "presentable" for viewing, for the benefit of the living.

The commercial introduction to act 3 is closely related to the second, both in terms of what is seen, but also regarding the content of the scenes the acts introduce. The third ad continues and extends the narrative scope of dealing with the body; in this instance it is the cosmetic aspects of preparing the body for viewing that is the subject of focus.

Image:	(Airy flute music plays in the background throughout). A woman seated in a chair with the back of her head facing the screen. Another woman faces the screen, looking directly at the other. four bulbs of a cosmetic mirror sit on the right.
Voice:	(Female) She looked her best every day of her life…
Image:	The woman facing swings the chair around so that the other woman now faces. The woman has a new coat of makeup and is dressed in a night-gown, expressionless. The other woman leans over looking at the other's face as she smiles.
Voice:	Don't let one horribly disfiguring accident change that.
Image:	A black circular table on which several cans are stacked, one rotating at the top. The label on the front of them reads, "Wound Filler."
Voice:	Use new Wound Filler cosmetic molding putty; now faster-setting and self-sealing…
Image:	Same as second.
Voice:	To help make masking unsightly wounds a breeze!

In the third ad, the appeal to vanity is much more explicit, providing additional signifiers such as the vanity mirror and lights which guard against making the slightest of mistakes in constructing another's appearance. Another difference here is the presence of an additional human figure, whose significance and characterization are tied to their relationship to the other (the deceased). The male figure of the second ad is presented alone, existing in his natural, self-attained state; he is unaffectedly, and through his own efforts, physically beautiful. In the third ad, this beauty is attained only with the aid of another. Thus, the ultimate difference between the messages of the second and third ads is one of focus: the absurdity of desire on the part of the individual in the first, and in the second, that of the mortician who deludes himself or herself into thinking that the perfection they can bestow is of any real consequence. The corpse, in essence, functions as a self-polishing mirror legitimizing and validating the mortician's worth and reason for professional existence.

The introduction to the fourth and final act turns our attention away from the specific subjects of death targeted in the preceding three; it shifts from our relationship with different aspects of the funeral business to the family and other mourners. The images, and the underlying tone of their use, suggest that the extreme nature of the delusion presented here is even more preposterous than those presented in the first three.

Image:	(The song "Shake Your Booty" plays in the background). Six young men and woman clothed in shorts, summer dresses, and khakis dance in a synchronized routine, each with their arms out stretched holding an indiscernible object in their hands.
Voice:	(Male) Ashes to ashes and dust to dust...
Image:	Two of the characters, one male, one female, face the screen, their heads cocked to the right, smiling brightly and holding what looks to be salt shakers in their hands.
Voice:	...is easy as pie with Franklin's new leak-proof earth dispenser.
Image:	All six characters appear; three in the front are kneeling, three in back are standing, all of them shaking the dispenser from side to side.
Voice:	Say good-bye to soiled fingers forever!...
Image:	A solitary woman, with a partial view of two of the male figures, continues dancing, now waving the dispenser. The name "Franklin Funeral Supplies" appears in the bottom left of the screen.
Voice:	Only from Franklin Funeral Supplies...
Image:	Same as previous, with four of the characters in view. a red line streaks under the letters "fun" in the name on the screen.
Voice:	We put the fun back in funeral.

The music utilized in the first two ads was slow and relatively monotone, concocting the erotic atmosphere and feelings they were intended to evoke in the viewer. The background music in the final ad is a rendition of "Shake Your Booty," a popular, upbeat, and entertaining piece that evokes the performance of the Gap-like characters in the ad itself. Also different here is that the product being advertised needs some explanation: Its existence and utility are not readily apparent to the viewer. The ad pushes the boundaries of extreme absurdity in this case by inventing a product, rather than featuring one that actually exists and has use-value. One does not realize what the object of sarcasm is until the scene that follows, when the family and friends of Nathaniel are gathered at the cemetery for his burial.

The harshest comment yet, the ad argues that the carefree and entertaining posture presented in the ad reflects a culture that has become so emotionally withdrawn that it cannot even allow itself to publicly break down in the face of what is arguably the most dire of life's circumstances. The show's articulation of how devastating a consequence this demonstrates is revealed in the ad's primary interpretation: In light of such extreme denial and emotional restraint, our internalized sorrow is equal to the playfulness expressed in the ad. The jocular style and manner of the characters' comportment corresponds to the way in which we feign acceptance of death, denying it by capitulating to conventions and convictions of emotional restraint.

I stated earlier that emotional appeals, when presented in isolation, draw their rhetorical significance from logically-stated arguments presented in other contexts. In the case of the individual and collective ads here, Jessica Mitford's *The American Way of Death*[5] is the source of rhetorical invention, grounding the ads' arguments. Alan Ball, the creator of *Six Feet Under*, consciously draws on Mitford's work, which, in part, also incited the show's development. The credibility of the arguments present in the ads is linked to that of Mitford herself, who gained notoriety for her groundbreaking "exposure" of dubious funeral industry practices, and continues to be the standard polemic on American death industry practices.

It is no exaggeration to say that Mitford believed the funeral industry (and its national professional organization, the National Funeral Directors' Association of America) embodied and produced everything wrong about how we as a culture deal with death and dying. In her view, the professional industry sought to dupe the American public into paying to the hilt for unnecessary goods and services. She argued that from its inception, the industry confronted both a marketing and image problem; its remedy was to persuade the public that morticians themselves were not the macabre and morbid creatures perhaps more frightening than the Grim Reaper himself and to conjure a method to capitalize on a service traditionally accomplished simply and sincerely by family members or others closely connected to the family of the deceased. Mitford contended that,

> A new mythology, essential to the Twentieth-Century American funeral rite, had grown up—or rather has been built up step-by-step—to justify the peculiar customs surrounding the disposal of our dead. And just as the doctor must be convinced of his own infallibility in order to maintain a hold over his clientele, so the funeral industry has had to "sell itself" on its articles of faith in the course of passing them along to the public.[6]

To some degree, then, the arguments made in the ads stem from previously articulated arguments. But significant differences exist, both in the manner in which they are articulated and the potential effects of the message. The first difference lies in the medium in which the two messages are expressed, Mitford's in print media and *Six Feet Under*'s in an electronic, visual medium. Mitford's writings provide the appropriate ground of argument that allows *Six Feet Under* to utilize the stylistic elements of its medium to supplement them. This difference in the medium in which arguments are made has a significant effect on the tone and force of the message. Print media that rely on grammar, syntax, and linear structure to express their message, are generally literal, explicit, and direct; the language of images is, however, figurative, implicit, and indirect. Mitford's arguments leave nothing to the imagination. Her disdain for the funeral industry is clear, her arguments against them rationally and logically explained with little need for interpretation.

The rhetorical possibilities are much broader, however, for the arguments presented in *Six Feet Under*. The arguments here that rely on imagery and other electronic forms (notably music and audible articulation) shroud the argument in some degree of mystery, rendering its persuasive message indirectly and possibly as even secondary in importance. It is the difference between a child being told by a parent "you shouldn't do that" and the child experiencing what is denied and concluding, "I shouldn't do that." The message of *Six Feet Under*, like that of the child's experience-prior-to-understanding, requires an intervening struggle prior to understanding. The message is not obviously discernible, and perhaps it may never be so. But I think most parents would agree that the lesson learned from the child's experience is far deeper and more meaningful than the simple admonition absent the struggle of "finding out for oneself."

This leads us to another notable difference between how Mitford and *Six Feet Under* articulate their arguments: the potential effect on the reader or viewer. Mitford's writings are a closed text. This is to say, though one may certainly read and reread, accept or refute, the primary argument made remains the same. In *Six Feet Under*, however, the text does not simply and primarily offer a particular point of view or argument as much as it establishes the grounds of dialogue with the viewer—above and beyond the degree to which any experience of textual engagement is, by definition, dialogical. Dialogue, if we adhere to its definitions by scholars such as Plato, Gadamer, and others, is fundamentally predicated on the question. Questioning, in this regard, both precedes, constitutes, and is the ultimate purpose of dialogue; the question is both the beginning and the end of the message. For *Six Feet Under*, unlike Mitford, the question—inciting dialogue—is the desired end, not the dogmatic acceptance of the argument itself. Its purpose is to establish the primacy of the question, that which initiates and stimulates open debate (among viewers in this case).

So, while the arguments of Mitford and *Six Feet Under* parallel each other to some degree, the former ends with a concrete and dogmatic answer, the latter with the question. In *Six Feet Under*, the viewer is invited to question the veracity of the claims made. Mitford argues that the way in which our culture deals with death is fundamentally flawed by commercialism, and most thanatologists have tended to proceed in their own investigations with the categorical and carte blanche acceptance of this notion. The veracity of the claims made in *Six Feet Under* is similar to Mitford's, but the author(s) characterize their arguments as questionable, inviting the audience to dialogue with the text—to free associate and question the text vis-à-vis their own experience and knowledge, and via their identification and connection with the characters and other aspects of the text. *Six Feet Under begins* a dialogue; it makes the rhetorical case for an appropriate beginning and proceeds with openness, with the "answers" always lingering from episode to episode, season to season, and beyond. This aspect of the show is what sparks the critical reflection with individual viewers, but also that which sparks dialogue beyond the text—between multiple viewers. I take up this aspect of the show's influence in the following chapter.

The Persistence of Memory or How Death Mediates Life

While *Six Feet Under*'s critique of materialism may be its most explicit message, I believe it articulates a more general, and more significant, argument about our relationship to death and dying.

On the one hand, it renders transparent the reality that death is a part of life. But beyond this, it argues that we should accept, rather than deny, this reality, claiming that doing so will allow us not only to become more aware of our own actions, but also to be more deeply connected to, and aware of, the lives of others with whom we interact throughout the course of our lives. In short, it argues that living in the light of death will compel some modicum of ethics—promoting a sense of duty and responsibility insofar as our relationship to others is concerned. This message is presented most fervently in the posthumous role the father plays, depicted through his continual reappearances to each of the family members. As the "shadow of death," if you will, Nathaniel's new character role serves as the impetus for individual reflection and future actions of the living. Individual family members' minds and actions are influenced or altered vis-à-vis their relationship with their father, and hence, with the reality of death itself.

Self-Reflective Conversation

The scenes in which Nathaniel reappears to the living come about as a self-reflective conversation between them. They also serve to solidify the nature of a particular individual's character and relationship to death and dying. For example, he appears to David at one point when he is working on reconstructing Nathaniel's facial damage. The father asks David to let Federico do the work since he is better skilled at the job. He does not want David to "mess up his face," though David quips that it is too late for that. In response to his father's criticism, he reveals that he has denied himself the pursuit of his own dreams in order to learn this business his father is criticizing his application of. The scene underscores David's character of denial and emotional masking for the sake of order and responsibility. Other scenes, however, articulate the father's primary role in his deceased state.

The Passed-on Passes Judgment

While in her room getting dressed for her husband's viewing, Ruth adorns herself with jewelry and double-checks the style of her hair as she silently stands in front of the mirror. She looks down at the chest of drawers to pick up one of the cuff links to complete her outfit. In quiet contemplation, she looks up into the mirror and suddenly sees her husband sitting on the bed behind her. In a revealing tone, but one of acceptance and forgiveness, Nathaniel simply says, "I know, Ruth. I know everything." He does not say what exactly it is he knows. But Ruth later fills in this gap, acknowledging to

Nate and David that she had long been having an affair. Nathaniel's revelation is not an instant of a child getting caught with his or her hands in the proverbial cookie jar, however. She does not realize she is caught and then abandons her wrongdoing. The scene demonstrates that the reality of death can and should impress upon us to reevaluate life's actions, to consider their impacts on our individual selves and others, and proceed having carefully made such considerations. In fact, in this instance, though Ruth initially harshly chastises herself (telling David and Nate that she is a whore because she was unfaithful to their father), in the following episodes she continues her relationship with the man she was having the affair with. Nathaniel's revelation of knowledge allows her to come to terms with and reassess the nature of her affair, but also allows her to continue a course of action that will permit her to consummate more meaningful relationships, something she was denied throughout her marriage.

Father Death Knows Best

Another significant scene of Nathaniel's reappearance is with Claire during the end of the father's burial ceremony at the cemetery. While standing, nonchalantly listening to Father Jack's words around the graveside, Claire looks up and over into the cemetery parking lot when her father mockingly yells, "Amen! Amen!" following Father Jack's closing prayer. She sees her father sitting on the hood of one of the limousines in the cemetery parking lot, dressed in shorts, hat, and a flowery Hawaiian shirt, carelessly sipping on a fruity, red drink with one of those paper umbrellas stuck in it. His attire belies the nature of the "real" atmosphere—the chilly, winter Southern California climate. Once the service concludes, Claire quickly walks over and sits down by her father (who is now sitting in a lounge chair), happy to see him. They begin to converse as each of them smokes a   cigarette.

Claire:	You're really lucky, you know that?
Nathaniel:	You kidding? It was over in a second. I didn't have to be afraid of it. I didn't even have to think about it.
Claire:	No more bullshit.
Nathaniel:	No more responsibility.
Claire:	No more having to care.
Nathaniel:	No more boredom.

Claire: No more waiting to die.

(Nathaniel laughs at her last comment.)

Claire's conversation with her father here is driven by her own fear of death and the anxiety that constantly envelops her, keeping her from being able to make life decisions or articulate any clear plan for her future. Her father, as she sees it, has been spared these drudgeries as a result of his death. She sees her father's death as an escape from the pains of life, and it seems as though Nathaniel supports her views by presenting his posthumous state as one of carefree revelry in this ultimate freedom. But the most significant aspect of this conversation is not Claire's dreams of what death entails or Nathaniel's appearance of happy-go-lucky entertainment.

The most noteworthy aspect of the exchange is Nathaniel's laughter at the end of the conversation. To this point, each of their comments parallels in agreement throughout the short exchange. But Nathaniel turns the tables on her with his laughter. Seeing death as the answer to a life ever dogged by death's possibilities, Claire wishes to join her father. But his laugh is not one of agreement; it is a veiled statement of fact. The laughter itself signals agreement, but its tone contradicts it—saying, to Claire, in essence, "You don't really know. You may want to consider this a little further." Apparently, this point eventually comes across to Claire later in the series. At this moment in the series, and throughout many of the remaining episodes, one wonders whether Claire's constant depression will lead ultimately to suicide. But she has, till this time, decided that perhaps death is not all it is cracked up to be.

Running

The most noteworthy reappearances by Nathaniel throughout the episode are to Nate. Nate is the one person of them all who is searching; he is the only one open enough to continually contemplate the realities of death vis-à-vis his regular life routines. After the scene mentioned earlier, the next appearance to Nate by his father is at the beginning of act 2, as we begin to enter the embalming room. Nate has transformed into himself as a child. He walks into the embalming room where his father stands, cigarette gripped between his lips, an ashtray resting on top of a dead man's body. He enters with caution; a look of extreme reservation covers his face, expecting to be repulsed by what is there to see. "Heya, buddy boy," Nathaniel says. Sensing

Nate's hesitance, Nathaniel motions to him and says, "Come on in. It's okay." Nate takes a few steps toward the embalming table, his eyes transfixed on the body his father is working on. Removing the cigarette from his mouth, Nathaniel senses a good opportunity to introduce him to his work. "Say hello to Mr. Bloomberg," he says, smiling. "There isn't anything to be afraid of, Nate. Mr. Bloomberg is dead. I'm getting him ready so his family can see him for the last time and say good-bye to him." Nate remains silent, his reserved look intensifying. Despite no reply from Nate, Nathaniel further explains, "It'll make them feel better. That's what Daddy does."

At that moment, Nate's little brother, David, walks into the room, "Bang! Bang! Bang!" he yells, pointing the legs of a doll toward his dad, who indulges him for a moment. Suddenly, Nate demonstrates some curiosity about what he is doing and walks even closer toward his father at the embalming table. Nathaniel leans over the table, cigarette back in his mouth, holding a pair of rubber gloves. "You can touch 'em if you wear one of these," Nathaniel says, lunging toward Nate. "He won't care." Nathaniel smiles, still holding out the gloves toward Nate, as David looks on. Nate then turns around and runs out of the room. And he has been running ever since— from the business of death, and death itself. The remaining scenes where Nate confronts his father's apparition fittingly take place while he is running.[7]

Poker

The next of these scenes begins in the Fisher's kitchen the following morning. Claire is sitting at the table about to eat breakfast, when Nate enters the room. He grabs some coffee and then sits at the table next to Claire as he begins scanning the newspaper. Ruth is standing near the stove cleaning when Claire asks her if she remembers a stuffed dog she had as a kid. Ruth does not answer. Claire, taking it as an invitation to continue explaining, goes on to tell her that after she lost it, Ruth made her another one out of old dish towels. She hated the new dog and threw it on the roof. "I hated that dog," she says about her recollection. "No! I don't remember," Ruth replies harshly. Disregarding her response, Claire continues to describe that when she began to feel sorry for throwing the stuffed dog on the roof, she asked her dad to go up and get it. Nathaniel refused, however, saying she should not have thrown it up there in the first place. Ruth then criticizes Claire for that being the only memory of her father she could think of at the moment. "God, I was just remembering," Claire responds. Frustrated, Ruth turns around and throws her dish towel to the ground. "He was a good man!" she yells as she bolts out of the room. Both Nate and Claire turn their heads toward her in shock. "I'm going running," Nate immediately responds as he quickly leaves the table.

In the ensuing scene, Nate runs through the neighborhood; part of his course takes him through the cemetery where his father is buried. It is unclear whether or not he does so intentionally, but it is nevertheless significant as it prefigures what takes place in the remainder of the scene. Shortly after leaving the cemetery, he comes to a stop at a street corner, leans over to catch his breath, and while still bent over, turns his head in the direction of oncoming traffic. His eyes lock in on a bus quickly headed his way. As if he has decided to face his fear—the experience of his father's death—he slowly stands upright again, stepping boldly into the street, almost daring the bus to hit him. It does. The screen fades momentarily to black. The bus driver rushes out of his vehicle and stands above Nate's body lying there. He does nothing but simply observes, Nate's blood now gushing and pooling from the gash to his head. But Nate's eyes are open. He is fully awake and is suddenly propelled through some kind of wormhole, traveling briskly toward a glaring bright light—presumably that path we all take after death.

As with other such scenes where outrageous and unexpected occurrences take place, this event is not real. Nate never actually steps foot away from the corner where he first stopped. The scene provides an opportunity to again use a visual metaphor as a way of communicating a message to Nate by death's agent—his father. When Nate hits the end of the tunnel, he is inside a hospital morgue, looking at his father who sits with three other people, each of whom are dead. Black and white, male and female, old and young—they are all represented at the makeshift table, which is actually the drawer of the morgue's corpse storage unit. Each of the individuals seated at the table are naked and, most importantly, playing poker.

While we do not usually associate poker with death, it is, in many respects, the perfect metaphor. The players' nudity signifies our vulnerability in the face of death, the poker chips the fact that life is always already at risk. The game itself is one of chance, each player's hazard mitigated not by their own volition, but by the rules of the game itself. In poker, the rules rule. The proverbial chips fall where they may, and one either folds or puts in. In either case, each of the players enters the game with an equal chance of winning or losing. Odds may fluctuate, but in the end all share the same amount of possible gain or loss.

In death, the reality of the gambler's fallacy is ultimately confronted; playing more does not increase your odds of winning, and the fact that you are alive one day does not mean you have cheated death. The metaphorical linkage only breaks down because of one crucial element: choice. When faced with the possibility of losing in poker, one can always quit the game and cut his or her losses. But in the circumstances of life and death, everyone is "in the game."[8] This is the point that death—a.k.a. Nathaniel Fisher—and the chorus of the dead gathered there try to get across to Nate. When their game is interrupted by Nate's presence, each of them turns around and stares at him with the customary signal that one has intruded. Each of them holds their cards in their respective hands as Nathaniel, cigarette again dangling from his lips, says to Nate, "We'll deal you in next hand."

Each of the scenes I have described here may be viewed as the expressions of one's own conscience. Nevertheless, they also are figurative representations of each character's orientation toward death and dying and constantly moderate their attitudes and behaviors in this regard throughout the series.[9]

The complexity of *Six Feet Under* and the manner in which it accomplishes its dual task of dealing with the realities of death and dying in a way that is also entertaining, is exhibited in such scenes as these that occur throughout the series. Flashbacks or dream sequences are commonly used in dramatic texts. Their use here is fitting given that such occurrences are prevalent among individuals dealing with the death of a family member or friend. Memory is a way of holding on to the person lost and all that he or she had to offer. But using these dramatic strategies here allows for the diversity of function to be realized. We are not only seeing how members of the Fisher family remember their father; their memories are a way of driving the underlying message of the show itself.

My Father's Eyes

This is perhaps most exemplified in the final scene of the pilot episode—a scene where we see Nate, again, running. And it is in this concluding moment that the primary and most important message of the show shines through, though it, like all other such messages, is veiled in various forms of visual and verbal speech. Throughout this episode the identity of the characters has been developed, new symbolic linkages have been created, and the familiar iconography of death and dying has been recycled. This final scene on the final day of the pilot episode of the series begins with David falling vulnerably into the embrace of his partner Keith, exhausted from maintaining his composure throughout the entire ordeal. Meanwhile, Nate recalls happy memories of the family in days gone by, as he slowly awakens from his sleep. Later, Ruth welcomes him home from his time away and begs him to stay in town just a little while longer. Then there is Nate's run. In this final scene that features no speaking by any of the cast, the new and the familiar, along with lyrical and musical articulations, swirl together to provide both closure to the episode and its pervading message, and provide a map of the terrain yet to be explored in subsequent episodes. Only two of the characters that we now know will appear—Nathaniel Sr. and his son Nate—the dead and the living—death's shadow and the one upon whom it is most often cast.

The corner bus stop—that place where one waits for death with reverent contemplation—is the first stop on today's course. Nate's father is seated there this time, while Nate stands idly on the sidewalk across the street. Their eyes meet, but no words are spoken between them. They stand there separated by the great divide of the busy city street—their distance and separation no longer able to be bridged by the telephone by which Nate is standing. Then the bus—that vehicle that transports us through death's journey into the great unknown, comes for the father. The father and son's connection is continued as their eyes never turn from one another.

Nathaniel begins his trip, while Nate still stands on the corner—alone; it is not yet his time. But death's shadow, seated on the chariot that will deliver him to the next station stop, will not let Nate alone. As their eyes force them to part company, death directs the living's eyes to those of another, plastered on the side of the bus just below where he is seated. These eyes are closed in death. But the eyes—those of the stranger, the oft ignored, the young and old, the black, white, and all others along the spectrum—are what carry us through to the end of this final moment. The living see each other. Though just for a moment, they see. Sometimes they look back a second time; sometimes they countenance a smile. These eyes—they are the ones among whom the living must live. The eyes beg to be seen, and we cannot help but hearken to their request—for in them is the essence of life—that which remains after death has done its bidding. Life and death are intimately connected. We find "our" dead among the living, and death's imperative is toward life itself.

The HBO motto—"It's not TV, it's HBO"—lauds the difference with which they approach television production. "Everything we do is about doing things differently than somewhere else," says Eric Kessler, who devised the AOL Time Warner marketing slogan above. Yet in their succinct promotional appeals, they rarely explain why their network programming is "undeniably different." Industry critics generally cite the eighteen Golden Globe awards *Six Feet Under* has won, which focus on the unique qualities of their production of this and other shows. But *Six Feet Under*'s success should not only be assumed to exist simply because of the manner in which they create and produce programs differently than other networks.

As will be shown later, I suspect that the show's commercial appeal stems from more than this. *Six Feet Under* not only provides excellent entertainment, fulfilling the media needs of a diverse group of viewers; it traverses the gulf between mediated realities and our own embodied "real" lives primarily because it deals with an experience that unifies and pervades its demographic. By not framing the show according to the dual oppositions of absolute reality on the one hand (as we might have if it were presented as a "reality TV" show) or absolute fantasy on the other (the manner in which much of television's depictions of death have been portrayed), the show manages to carve out a creative space that is socially relevant, not only in terms of the primary focus of the show, but its engagement with the broader discourse on death and dying that has privately permeated American cultural life. Evidence of this fact, seen in the experience of viewers of *Six Feet Under,* is seen next.

NOTES

[1]   Aristotle, *The Rhetoric* (*The Complete Works of Aristotle: The Revised Oxford Translation*, trans. Jonathan Barnes, Princeton, NJ: Princeton University Press, 1984).

[2]   Andrew Light, *Reel Arguments: Film, Philosophy & Social Criticism* (Boulder, CO: Westview Press, 2003).

[3]   As an aside, this is one of the main reasons that funeral-related products are never advertised in mass, untargeted media such as television or newspaper advertising (though there are a few exceptions to this as of late). Generally, products are sold in face-to-face interaction between consumers and providers at the time one needs such products and services. Over the past few years, some of these products have been marketed over the Internet, though most of the time the sales pitch that accompanies them is fairly muted.

[4]   Unfortunately, storyboard scripts without their accompanying images can only be used here because of HBO's refusal to grant copyright privileges to reproduce them here for the purpose of academic study and analysis.

[5]   Jessica Mitford, *The American Way of Death* (New York: Simon & Schuster, 1963).

[6]   Ibid.

7 This particular scene showing Nate being offered the gloves by his father and his subsequent running away reappears three additional times in the first and second episodes.

8 The title of one of the subsequent episodes.

9 These reappearances by Nathaniel have continued throughout show, up to the current season (season 4).

CHAPTER FIVE

Affiliation, Critique, and Community
Viewers Respond to Six Feet Under

Questioning whether *Six Feet Under* viewers have particular "uses" for the show, and whether these needs are "gratified" by their viewing experience, is largely irrelevant. It is virtually impossible to quantify either the needs themselves or the degree to which they are gratified. Additionally, to assert that the need for gratification incites television viewing belies the manner in which most people approach their choice of television programming; this is particularly so for many who regularly watch *Six Feet Under*, where simple curiosity surrounding its novelty provides much of the driving impetus for viewing. It makes more sense to ask and know what draws viewers to the show and how they "read" or otherwise interpret what they see on the screen—qualitative aspects we can only ascertain by observing what individual viewers talk about regarding their viewing experience, to themselves and with others in naturally occurring conversation.

The responses of viewers tell us much about why the show is significant for them, with or without any motivating intention underlying one's viewing. Their explanation and interpretations of what is seen, how they feel in response, and how their future actions (of viewing and otherwise) are influenced allow us to gain access to and understand various, and perhaps disparate, perspectives of interpretation. It also allows us to generalize from such observations about its possible influences on American death attitudes and practices.

Six Feet Under demonstrates death's universal appeal; its viewers run the gamut of American demographics. The responses dealt with in this chapter cover two important demographics—youth and adults—and are drawn from two very different forums—one mediated and one through face-to-face interaction. These distinctions, I believe, provide a substantive basis for analysis of variety of factors including how others interpret the show (especially vis-à-vis my earlier readings of it), their motivations for engaging with it, the nature of their conversations with others regarding the show, and what may be the possible individual and collective outcomes of viewing.

(T)eens, (N)ecrophobia, and (T)elevision

Weaving together the "innocence" of children, the pariah of entertainment television, and the taboo of death in American culture is likely to be viewed by some as an explosive, unhealthy combination. I am sure many of my generation remember well the "educational" components of Saturday morning television programs (mainly cartoons) of the seventies and the eighties. To this day we can still recite a good portion of "I'm Just a Bill" from *School House Rock,* and can picture vividly the image of "Yuk Mouth," who taught us all the importance of healthy dental hygiene. Looking back, however, it is obvious that such programs were only peripheral to regular programming (they were around sixty-second commercial spots, basically). While they were entertaining, and minimally educational, we really just wanted to get back to watching *Scooby-Doo, Superfriends,* or whatever else captivated our attention at the time.

Given the fact that education stands at the margins of television programming—rightfully so or not—this chapter and book are largely about whether television, given its primary function as a medium of entertainment, can have some broader social value and relevance. That is, can television successfully entertain, educate, and elicit social critique and debate simultaneously? Can children and youth, who collectively watch hundreds of thousands of hours of television a year, see past the comedies, dramas, and tragedies that draw them to the television screen and take from them some useful lessons, questions, and reflections about life, death, and the combination of the two?

I did not intend to write this chapter in the original formulation of this book. It was not until a teaching experience in the summer of 2002, working with a group of exceptional highschool students interested in government, politics, and communication, that I decided that some of their stories regarding life, death, and television would be an important contribution here. One evening, in an assembly of two-hundred-plus students gathered on the Princeton University campus, I introduced my course in political communication at the opening of the summer program. As was customary (this was my fifth year with the program), I tried to say something that would stand out, something a little entertaining to help break the ice with these students who had not quite yet come to grips with the rigorous expectations they would endure over the next month. After mentioning my academic credentials, I informed the thirty-five students in my specific class that I study death—meaning that, like the drudgeries of dealing with death and dying, they would have a long an arduous month of class. The oohs and ahhs echoed in the auditorium, along with, of course, much laughter. Their fascination with the subject of death was quite apparent. Many students not in my class approached me following the gathering, asking why I study death. Others asked me where they could buy my first book. And my own students amusingly nicknamed me "Dr. Death."

In one portion of the course I spoke at length about how to critique visual images in television, film, photography, and other media and discussed in particular how such images could construct sophisticated arguments and stimulate debate about social issues, public policy, and the like. Partly to provide them with some lighthearted entertainment (they do not watch any television during the program) and partly to piggy-back on what I had already been researching for this book, I decided to use *Six Feet Under* as an example. I wanted to show them how one might go about interpreting the variety of messages in the show and the way in which it critiques our cultural values and public policies regarding death and dying, and the process of burial, mourning, etc. (though I did not reveal this up front). I asked them to complete an assignment that hinged on three tasks. First, I asked them to write down what experiences they had had in the past regarding death and dying. Second, I asked them to write what their perception was of typical portrayals of death and dying in popular media. Then, after showing them the first *Six Feet Under* episode, I asked them to write down what their initial thoughts were regarding the meaning of the show, and any personal reflections, if any, they received from it. The following are a few brief excerpts from some of their stories.

Rosemary

Rosemary, a sixteen-year-old girl from Florida, said she has not had to deal with death in her lifetime. She lost an uncle when she was younger, but has no recollection of him. However, she has had several friends who have lost loved ones and remembers them as "very bad moments in their lives." She says she is not scared of death. "I respect it," she says, as she explains that she herself had come pretty close to dying on two occasions. Though she does not seem to fear death, it is clear that she, nevertheless, is very much affected by it emotionally. She remembers that the tragedy of September 11, 2001, made her "cry for days." After some thought, Rosemary makes some more qualifications, admitting that perhaps she is somewhat afraid of death. "To be frank, I'm scared of death, whether it happens to my family or friends, or simply other people," she explains. This fear surrounding the death of others extends to those who die on television, she says, explaining,

> All I know is that whenever something sad happens in a movie or on television where people die, I bust out in tears and I can't control myself. Lately, I have noticed that death, like romance, is a major part of film productions—or at least the possibility of death, as well as regular people escaping it. Death had been portrayed as glamorous, romantic, inevitable, unpredictable, honorable, and as simply the beginning of a whole different world.

Despite this view, Rosemary sees something different in *Six Feet Under,* which gels with her experiences of death in her own life thus far. "The purpose of *Six Feet Under,*" she says,

> is to present life as it truly is: ironic, unpredictable, funny, strange. You see presented the realities that every man seeks to escape—death, pain, grief, addiction, treason—through that which every man wants in his life, humor.... It involves all human emotions in the search for the true meaning of life, by juxtaposing it with death. Life is, thus…an intricate pattern of situations that lead to the ultimate meaning, symbolized by the bright light at the end of the tunnel and the clouds in the sky. Death is seen as a natural part of the sequence of life; not an end in itself, but rather as the beginning point of a mystery that has yet to be figured out.

Anastasia

Unlike Rosemary, Anastasia has experienced death quite a bit. Only fourteen, she says that she has attended six funerals in her lifetime, the majority of which have occurred in the past four years. She recalled two of them, one a Jewish funeral she attended when she was five years old and the other the funeral of her grandmother. Regarding the latter, she remembers that "It was a true Catholic funeral.... There was a mass, and it was a very sad occasion. I was very close to her and was very upset." Anastasia believes that "the media never properly displays death. They make it seem like a joke," she says. She takes a simple, familiar lesson from *Six Feet Under*— that "you need to treat each minute as if it is your last." She continued, "When you walk out the door, don't forget the ten seconds it takes to say goodbye or give your parents or spouse a kiss good-bye. Don't forget about the five seconds it takes to say 'I love you,' because you never know if you are going to walk out that door and never see any of them alive again, or if they will see you alive again for that matter."

Adlin

Adlin, another Floridian preparing to cross the threshold into adulthood, wrote in detail about the three funerals she attended over the past few years, one of which included her next-door neighbor:

> He was sixteen years old, and he got killed in a car accident on his way back to school from lunch hour. He died at around 1:30 and no one knew where he was. Then I got a call from a friend telling me that he had been in a car accident and I had to go tell his brother. I remember getting dropped off in school with him that morning and then not seeing him again. I never thought that life could be gone just like that, especially when you are so young. His viewing was a sad one. He looked bloated because of the internal bleeding that had caused him to die, and I didn't like seeing him that way.

Her experiences have demonstrated to her quite clearly that "humans generally fear death," something she sees illustrated again and again in *Six Feet Under*. "In our speech, our actions, our beliefs," she says, "we avoid and mince the idea, the word, and the act of dying. We look for fulfillment and purpose in our lives for fear that life may be stripped from us spontaneously."

Simone

Simone, who is sixteen and hails from Brooklyn, New York, says her experiences with death have been limited to attending funerals (primarily Jewish) of people she did not know that well, of seeing people in the final stages leading to death, and television shows that describe the possibility of the afterlife. She observes that "Deaths are often quite violent on television, in order to attract the audience's interest," citing movies such as *Goodfellas* and *Scarface* as examples. She says that death, in shows such as these, "[is] portray[ed] quite differently on television and in movies than it does [is] in real life." Yet, she notices that while a show such as *Six Feet Under* primarily has entertainment value, it can also stimulate reflection. She writes:

> *Six Feet Under*…is in essence for entertainment value, although it brings about a reflection of how society views death nowadays and what are acceptable ways of grieving and mourning. Since it provides a new understanding of death, as well as its responsibilities in our society, it shows the internal struggle of those who have to

deal with death every single day. I believe that each character brings about a situation where he or she is suffering some sort of death, whether emotional, physical or romantic... I think the purpose of this show is to question the moral judgments of current society and to probe into why current society treats death the way it does.

James

Two of James's friends have died, as well as his grandfather. Of Mexican heritage, he has celebrated the famed holiday *Dia de los Muertos*, the "Day of the Dead," and considers himself to have had as much experience with death as many adults. Like his peers, he has seen the deaths of characters in many a movie or television program, where he finds death portrayed as a "somber experience." About *Six Feet Under* he writes:

> A lesson we can learn from this is that we can never be ready for death; it can happen anytime. This also presents a new idea—death itself is ironic. One issue that becomes obvious...is how we feel that we need to suppress our feelings when someone dies....Another idea that can be drawn is that all these formalities and fronts people put on at funerals come from a deeper underlying fear we have of dying. The reason, perhaps, that we downplay the fact that someone died is that we don't want to realize that it could happen to us. We pretend like the person who died didn't really, almost. We even dress dead people up and try our best to make them look alive because it sort of comforts us.... The reason we are so paranoid of talking about death and dealing with this subject is that we don't want to admit someday we're going to die as well. It makes us angry to think about it, so we don't. [*Six Feet Under*] persuades us to come to terms with the fact that we're going to die, so that, finally, we might appreciate life.

Nick

Much of Nick's (a native-born Texan) significant death experiences have, as they often are for children, been associated with inanimate objects and the fictional characters of children's stories. His description of his experiences of death and dying are worthy of note because they involve the deaths of these childhood figures and close friends, providing an interesting take on another fictional program viewed, in this instance, in considerable hindsight. The death of his childhood best friend—the consequence of self-inflicted injuries—was particularly painful. "It was awful," he says, "like a moment that I was turned into a real person." Fueled by the resentment Nick felt over what he saw as a selfish and stupid act, he refused to attend the funeral, though he says now he wishes he had.

Reflecting back to years prior to his friend's death, Nick writes about another set of friends, whose loss seems to have had as much an emotional toll on him as the other. "When I was five, Jim Henson died," he remembers.

Nick describes his loss, saying,

> That hit me like a brick, because his puppets were my friends and he was like a third parent. Odds are that I can still name every *Sesame Street* character and most of the *Muppets*. I had a few friends, but his furry little animals were the only ones that I really enjoyed. I resented the world and my parents. I was in the stage when you think your parents are omnipotent, all-knowing, and I couldn't understand why they refused to stop this from happening.

No doubt these two experiences, and others like them that Nick held back from describing, circulated in his mind while watching this particular episode of *Six Feet Under*. His prosaic account of the experience reflects significant insights—those we would expect from someone who has obviously contemplated these issues of death and dying from a very early age.

> The show is over. The credits and theme music roll in tandem. Now is the time to think about what was just seen, but the only thing that you get out of it is a memory of your own life and the times that you might have been the subject of the show. All you get is a word: death. But then you realize that the word and its contemplation is the only thing that you were supposed to get out of the show. A deeper meaning than "Gee, death is a funny thing?" Not really, for all that the show persuades [is of] the *feeling* of death. The feeling is an odd one. Like a wave, a death crests through everyone that the departed affected with his life. Some tear, others bend.

Daniel

The final set of my students' reflections is from Daniel, a sixteen-year-old, quick-witted Oregonian with a penchant for sarcasm. Though he has lost several grandparents, he says that he did not know them well and, as a consequence, was not very influenced by their passing. Unlike most of his classmates, he has experienced death very little and seems to have thought little about it over the course of his life thus far. "I've known a lot of suicidal people, and I know Professor Mac," he writes jokingly, "but these people never killed themselves.... Oh, man. I have no experience with death. It is as remote from me as can be," he continues to reiterate, adding that unlike many kids, he has not even had a goldfish that has died. "My goldfish are like seven years old," he says. Despite, and perhaps because of, this lack of experience, Daniel's interpretation of *Six Feet Under* expressed some nuanced explanation of what he saw, but as well generated many questions for him. "The purpose of the episode," Daniel writes,

> was to stimulate without offending, to connect rather than alienate. Thirty-somethings struggle with midlife crisis and self-doubt, regrets of their youth, antici-

pation of aging and death, reintegration into domestic life, settling into routines, honoring traditions, finding meaning, rejecting commercialism, and probably a bunch of other things; I don't know, I'm not thirty-five yet.... Although death is the subject matter, the episode's discussion of death is only a segue into the more meaningful discussion that centers around "raw" emotions and the ways in which they're suppressed by commercialism, routine, and tradition.... Death is a situation in which the human instincts of living people who experience it clash head-on with social norms, tradition, and routines. The mortician family has handled death with a long-standing set of routines and norms, but when a family member dies, the immense grief, recrimination, and self-doubts of the wife and children overwhelm the system they've set up for dealing with tragedy...

The show's tone is sardonic. That means it artfully mocks its subject, which is the sterile, commercial nature of American domestic life. It is also sardonic in its treatment of death. The episode is full of irony, like Ruth telling her husband not to smoke right before he gets hit by the bus; like this tragedy happening on Christmas eve; like the radio in the hearse playing "I'll Be Home for Christmas," although the poor guy obviously won't. By treating the subject matter with flippancy rather than seriousness, it mitigates [our] natural aversion to the morbid subject matter. Of course, by morbid subject matter I don't mean only death—maturity, domestic life, commitment, etc. are also morbid subjects to many...

...I have to briefly answer the question, "Why does this all happen [around] Christmas?" ...Christmas reflects the ideals of this particular episode—forging interpersonal relationships rather than isolating oneself, goodwill towards men, of course, but moreover the theme of death and rebirth. I'm not a Christian, but from what I hear this Jesus guy was nailed to a cross until he died somehow, but then he came back to life and revealed to everyone how they were supposed to live in good faith and harmony and selflessness. This is fitting with the message of the episode, except of course the irony that Christianity also produced all these dumb sanitizing rituals around death like sprinkling salt [confused by Daniel with the earth sprinkled from a salt-shaker-like dispenser] over the casket and solemnly reciting prayers instead of bawling your eyes out. No offense or anything; I think I have less tact than the producers of *Six Feet Under* do.

Many of these young people, some of whose stories are not included here, immediately recognized something in *Six Feet Under* that I did not when I first began to watch it when the program originally began. When I first saw the show, I was in the midst of writing my first book on the topic of death rituals, and so I could not understand why Alan Ball, the show's creator, would say in countless interviews that *Six Feet Under* is not about death. Yet the students in my course, seeing only the first episode, interpreted it in just the same manner that Ball has often described it—that the show is about life and that death just so happens to be an assumed and necessary fact moderating how life is lived.

I think several other important points can be made about these young people's responses. I believe that most of them were sufficiently entertained.

There were frequent moments of laughter as we watched; they tapped their peers on the shoulder and whispered comments in their ears about something they picked up on they thought was humorous; they were attentive, the "adult" situations that filled the episode were not lost on their youth. But as much as they were entertained, I think it is clear that they saw something more than an interesting and funny drama. They liked particular characters more than others, yet they seemed to understand, to some degree, that the characters and other symbols in the episode had more than just a surface meaning. There were conflicting interpretations, none of which were more correct than another. It demonstrated that their individual differences in experience did, as expected, lead to different perspectives on what they saw played out on the screen.

I think it is also significant that almost all of them recognized a drastic distinction between how they see death portrayed in traditional television programming and other media, and how it was dealt with in *Six Feet Under*. Even those who had had no significant experience with death and dying prior to having watched the show seemed to intuitively sense a marked difference. Finally, it is evident that they were viewing, being entertained, and thinking simultaneously. Certainly, some of that is expected by the reality of the setting and circumstances surrounding their viewing. Nevertheless, I think that the students, who might have easily used this as a time of relaxation or an opportunity to completely zone out—especially knowing that this was merely an exercise they were not being graded on—found something powerful enough not only to hold their attention, but to stimulate thought, reflections, and induce questions about what they were viewing.

The viewers I focus on in the remaining section exemplify this in a much deeper way since they are fans. Their responses to the ongoing program tell us much about what potential *Six Feet Under* has not only to stimulate individual thinking, but also to lead in building a community of like-minded viewers, critique norms and values surrounding death and dying in America, and promote the possibility of collective action.

Challenging Traditional Discourse; Constructing a Community of Death

Television, despite all of the criticisms against it, has always been the champion of public discourse. That is, television, perhaps better than any other medium, has been able to effectively, and often instantly, move an issue from the private sphere to the public. Whether it was the brutal beatings civil rights marchers received on the streets of Mississippi, the system of apartheid in South Africa, the ethnic cleansing in the Balkans, or President Clinton's personal affairs—the televisual image makes a powerful statement that "here's something we *all* need to address, something we all must talk about. And perhaps more important than what the end result is, the fact that an issue makes it into the public sphere, that it is recognized as being significant for the general public, is of supreme importance.

While television has served this role over and over, the format in which it appears, more often than not, is in news programming. I have throughout this book made a distinction about the various functions of television. Here again I make the distinction between news programming (which admittedly often blurs the line) from pure entertainment. This is to say, to the degree that news programming has become entertaining, it nevertheless has at least maintained the façade of being a tool of civic interest through the proliferation of information and social commentary. I distinguish this from shows such as *Six Feet Under* that are "pure" entertainment, meaning that they are governed more acutely by the rules of television markets—the ability to create, gain, and sustain an audience. While they may contribute to civic interests, they are primarily aimed at generating profit. The remainder of this chapter focuses on how television in this later usage can and is helping us start on our way to bring issues of death more into the public arena, to the masses of people outside of those who have particular interests in another's death beside their own well-being and that of their families.

As with most popular forms of entertainment, be it music, film, or television, there are those whose viewing and interactions are more intense. They are fans, and their participation involves much more than just viewing. "Fandom," according to Henry Jenkins, is "an institution of theory and criticism, a semistructured space where competing interpretations and evaluations of common texts are proposed, debated, and negotiated and where readers speculate about the nature of the mass media and their own relationship to them."[1] For fans, mass media productions provide not only an opportunity for viewing, but an impetus for a range of forms of participation, be it criticism, or artistic innovation. The lay fan/critic/artist is herself a producer; she has an audience of other fans that consume her work, and through their interactions they perpetuate a cycle of creation, criticism, and community.

While Jenkins has been most interested in this aspect of fandom—cultural production—others, like myself, have been more interested in the communal aspect of fan behavior. Nancy Baym, for instance, has demonstrated how participants in soap opera fan communities—banal as such programs may be—form and negotiate relationships that are, in many instances, more important than the actual viewing of a particular show itself.[2] In such cases, viewing is both an end as well as a means to an end. That is, some satisfaction is gained from merely viewing the program, but above this it serves as one's entry pass into a new relational network—a sort of cultural "currency" as Jenkins puts it. The significance of the "online community" discussed by Baym is, in part, that it broadens the sphere of participation and therefore adds to the quality of what takes place within it, beyond that of the fan communities Jenkins has focused on who travel to conventions and such and rely predominantly on interpersonal interaction. The online community allows greater participation, while essentially offering the same products— the tangible forms of cultural creations, as well as the more ephemeral bonds of community.

Both of these aspects of fandom are characteristic and important in the *Six Feet Under* fan community I discuss briefly in this chapter. However, I suggest that in this particular content there is perhaps a more significant connection between the television show itself, the fans who participate in the online community, and the content they produce in their naturally occurring conversations. I would argue that the social relevance of the show itself, as discussed in earlier chapters, allows fans in this online community the potential to influence culture beyond their specific community boundaries, and beyond the confines of their interpretations and reproductions of aspects of the show itself. In short, the content and social valence of *Six Feet Under* make it possible for fan viewers to make meaning by forming new relationships and creating new cultural productions. They provide the basis for more generalized social critique about their common ground—death and dying— and suggest the need and possibility for individual and collective action to challenge and alter attitudes and practices in this regard. They provide a different kind of agency that fan communities surrounding other shows either do not have or, perhaps, even care about.

HBO's *Six Feet Under* Fan Community

The following analysis focuses on conversations taken from HBO's *Six Feet Under* online community. While I focus on only two sets of representative examples, more than fifty thousand separate postings have been made on the site during its first three seasons airing.[3] It is significant as well that among this number of postings, about half are centered on topics of death and dying (including topic sections on "death and loss," "funeral directors and aftercare," and "immortality"). These are the areas I paid most attention to, though the actual circumstances of dealing with death and dying are also taken up in conversations in other topic areas. When comparing the content of conversations in this fan community with other familiar serial programs—such as soap operas, for instance—it is clear that while fans at the *Six Feet Under* site do direct much of their attention to typical fan activities (discussing characters, plots, anticipating endings, etc.), the nature of the show has induced much conversation regarding what many see as the driving themes of the show. Their participation in this forum allows them to gravitate toward other fans who discuss their various relationships between death and dying in the show, and their own relevant experiences.

Online discourse is obviously presented differently than typical interpersonal conversations. Because of the absence of a common physical location among participants and the synchronous nature of interaction, online discourse is presented in what is commonly referred to as a "thread." In such exchanges, one member poses a specific topic of conversation to which subsequent members post responses. However, the pattern of discussion is not necessarily linear in that when one member opens a discussion, successive postings by other participants may shift to a different subject. Later in the thread, someone may respond to the original subject despite the fact that the topic of the thread has changed. What is significant about this particular structure of discourse is that, unlike face-to-face conversation, participants who respond to others in this forum do so not out of obligation, but a need or strong desire to communicate and identify with others. Two separate discussions from this forum illustrate the way audience members are using *Six Feet Under* for specific purposes.

Magic, Emotion, and Communal Discourse

The first selection of conversation reiterated below centers on the form of interaction between participants. What is significant is what members of the online community receive from their participation, the driving motivations evident in their involvement, and the significance it has for understanding the positive relationship between television programming about death and dying and human action. The text of the conversation is provided below in its entirety before I comment on specific elements of the conversation as a whole.

Jimmysgal   Hi, everyone....I have a question I'd like a serious response. to. My
              girlfriend can't afford cable and lives down south, and so I send her
              movies and TV shows, etc. (the *Sopranos*, for one). I have been tap-
              ing *Sex & the City* and *Six Feet Under* every week for her, but so far
              haven't sent it to her, because...she just told me her cancer is recur-
              ring and she is not doing too well with chemo this time around. My
              question...do you think it is ok for me to send all the episodes so far,
              or do you think it would be too morbid??? Your thoughts, please.

Jilly_Mac   Hi, jimmysgal. What a good friend you are. :-) Those are sad cir-
              cumstances, but I think—if your girlfriend has a good sense of humor
              and you think she'd appreciate the show—you should send her the
              tapes. If she doesn't like it, she doesn't have to watch; but I'd give
              her the option to decide. I would think that someone facing the situa-
              tion she's in would need to laugh about it. Just my opinion, of course.
              (I hope things work out well for her.)

Jimmysgal   Jilly Mac...she does have a good sense of humor....Maybe I'm the one
              who is too sensitive....Thanks for your opinion....JG.

Nightwolf   Jimmysgal, my mother (when she was a mother) sent the movie
              Ghost and another I didn't recall to my aunt,. which is her sister.
              Well, she sent them to her to help understand more about the passing
              of her father. It helped my aunt a great deal...God rest her soul. By all
              means send the tapes to your friend. It's not morbid at all.

Toetag13   I agree...not morbid whatsoever. It might help her face things with a
              sense of humor and a good outlook. If you think it'll put a smile on
              her face then send her the tapes :) hugs, Jimmysgal. I hope she gets
              better. Go be with her if you can :)

S_C   Jimmysgal—A suggestion—Ask your girlfriend what she wants you
              to do about sending the videos to her. This may be the time to con-
              centrate strictly on what she wants.

Jetta_N   Jimmysgal, I think it'll help her deal with it. Watching *Six Feet Un-
              der* is helping me deal with the fact that I'm probably going to lose
              my mom soon. Send the tapes. Hugs, Jetta.

Toetag13   I agree Jetta. *Six Feet Under*'s helped me make peace with the loss of
              family members. Especially my cat's death. I find that its dark
              irreverence combined with not-so-perfect, good-at-heart characters
              makes it easier for me. I feel happier and more refreshed.

Toetag13   Yep Jetta....that's why I'm so drawn to the show. It's irreverent to-
              wards death yet totally honest and up-front. It helps me cope. Though
              I'm beginning to think I've totally lost it because I laugh at scenes in
              the show that no one else does. LOL.

Several important items are evident in this selection. First, what is most significant is not what is being said, but the tone with which it is said, as well as the structure of the conversation taking place. Despite the use of language, the discourse here is essentially magical. That is, it is fundamentally a display of emotion both from the initiator and each of the others who respond to his initial query. This emotion is evocative of the search for personal identity, communication, and community. In the opening line *Jimmysgal* gives us insight into his emotional state that provides the drive for posting his question. "I'd like a serious response" says unequivocally that he is in such an emotional state and that he is motivated by a deep sense of concern and attachment to his partner. Subsequent remarks also signal the depth of this emotion. *Jimmysgal* admits to *Jilly_Mac* that he is experiencing a heightened sense of sensitivity, suggesting that his personal state is one of significant feeling and that this emotion provided the impetus for him to seek out the advice of others regarding a two-part problem: How can I help relieve some of my girlfriend's suffering, and will watching this program help?

Second, while *JimmysGal*'s request is emotionally ladened, it nevertheless is a request for rational advice. He has a problem that he is trying to solve. However, the responses to *Jimmysgal*'s original questioning illicit primarily emotional responses as well. *Jilly_Mac* indicates this with her use of the emoticon used to signify pleasure and happiness: ":)". "What a good friend you are" is not simply a statement of fact; it is a statement of affiliation. She is saying that she knows what having a good friend is like—that she understands through his inquiries and the care it shows that *Jimmysgal* is what a good friend is like and that such a friend would reasonably make such a request. *ToeTag13* presents similar evidence that the conversational interchange is driven primarily by emotion by using the same emoticon in her first reply, adding "hugs" as a preface to her concluding statements, suggesting that *Jimmysgal* go be with his girlfriend. Obviously, this is used to denote an emotional act that would have been engaged in by her were she and *Jimmysgal* in the same physical proximity, even though they and other participants are essentially strangers.

Third, what is most telling is the additional manner in which conversants respond to both *Jimmysgal* and the other participants. For instance, *Nightwolf* responds initially not with an answer, but with the story of his mom sending similar tapes to his Aunt who was in a similar situation as *Jimmysgal*'s girlfriend. He ends with "The tapes helped her...God rest her soul." *Nightwolf*'s response to a question was his explanations of a shared experience, his advice being implicitly stated within the message of the story. *Jimmysgal*'s posting elicited a specific memory for *Nightwolf*; evidently, emotions of both sorrow and relief were at work as he read and contemplated his response. Again, the participants are building affiliation here more than responding to a request for advice. It is significant to the whole of this analysis that emotion is at the center of this conversation. Emotion provided the impetus for *Jimmysgal* to initiate his query, and it was followed up by responses from other participants that were largely emotional, and at the same time addressed his question.

Following this, a fourth item is significant here. The conversation that begins with *Jimmysgal*'s request for advice is responded to not only with one-way responses of advice. The other participants use the initial request as an impetus for their own self-reflection. This can be seen most prominently in the final exchange between *Jetta_N* and *Toetag13*. We see here that no longer is *Jimmysgal*'s request the center of concern. *Jetta_N* who begins by giving her advice, concludes her response with how the original topic reflects on her own experience of her grandmother's impending death. Following this, *Toetag13* leaves *Jimmysgal* out altogether in her response, shifting the conversation to respond to *Jetta_N*'s experience by reflecting on her own circumstances. This is further evidenced in the very next posting by *Toetag13*, where she does not acknowledge the original request for advice, but communicates feelings she has regarding the show vis-à-vis her own life and experience of coping with loss. The fact that *Jimmysgal* is absent from the discourse after the first two exchanges further indicates the changing structure and motivation of the discourse taking place between participants from beginning to end. Thus, we have here a very discursive interchange taking place in which one person's search for advice results in that advice being given, but which in turn is used as a means for other participants to work out their own problems, feelings, and insights.

Two important generalizations can be made about this body of discourse. First, the fact that it takes place among a group of "strangers" forming a community based on emotional bonds, mutual affiliation, and shared experience allows for a different and broader experience of participating in such discourses about death and dying. That is, with our core group of friends or family members, we generally know from experience how they might respond to certain questions or statements. So, rather than recycling familiar conversations which have taken place in the past with family and friends, this interchange allows participants to expand their range of perspectives and insights regarding death by making new connections which, because they are largely anonymous, provide a safe place to do so without the fear of ridicule or the judgments we might receive from known others in face-to-face interaction. Second, we see that the structure and tone of the discourse is driven primarily by emotion rather than rationality. That is, while the discourse is presented in a rational manner through language and other symbolic behavior, the primary motivation is emotional, to the end that an emotional and communal bond would be formed—both momentarily as the discussion around the particular subject continued, and as a way of maintaining this virtual space as a place where *Jimmysgal* and those like him could indeed receive empathy as well as "serious" consideration for such problems. So, while the casual reader might interpret this selection of discourse as essentially a request for advice, I would argue that this is only a minor part of what is taking place. This selection, then, is essentially a search for identity and connection among and between participants. They seek someone who knows what it is they have been through, and those who respond provide the necessary connection, while also fulfilling their own need or desire to express.

Finally, the uniqueness of the setting in which this discourse takes place is significant. The temporal constraints of face-to-face conversation require that when faced with a question, we are generally forced to provide an immediate answer. In doing so, we tend to disregard the buildup of emotional affect in order to give a reason or answer to a question. The immediacy required of such interactions often inhibits emotional development. In on-line conversation, however, participants may read one person's statements and respond in his or her own time. While there is some temporal constraint in that one generally needs to respond while a certain topic is still at the center of discussion, one is given the room to contemplate another's statements, develop certain feelings if they do erupt, and then contemplate their response in a way that best expresses both their thoughts and sentiments. Thus, this form of interchange moves participants beyond a dissociated, clinical relationship where one seeks out the advice of those who have specialized knowledge. Rather, it provides a forum for connection and building of community.

Challenging Dominant Discourses of Death

In the next set of discourse, we see the relationship between discourse produced by the fans of this show and the dominant discourse of death constructed largely by the professional, specialized sector of the funeral industry and others. Again, the full thread is provided below in its entirety:

Toetag13	"I'm sorry" is about all you can say about someone's loss...right? I can't stand it when people say "They're in a better place"....bullsh*t. They're gone and it sucks! Why can't people just say sorry? And why does everything have to be so damn antiseptic. It pisses me off. I've had too many losses in my family to really be bothered by death. Why can't I be allowed to deal with it in my own way? Why do people have to say all sorts of weird sh*t? Yeah, death bothers me...sure, I'm hurt when a family member dies. But just because I don't bawl my frickin' eyes out and wail constantly doesn't mean I'm not hurting. I am. Death hurts...death sucks...but hell, we're all gonna end up there in the end, right? I'm scared of death...but it's part of life and I've learned to deal with it. Sometimes I just wish people would let me and everyone else grieve in their own frickin' way. Sorry...I just had to let that out. sighs I've been needing to let that out for about ten years now...
Nightwolf	My bad...misunderstood your last post. Everyone grieves in their own different way. Some even shed a tear for those they never even met while paying respects to the family.
Leilah	Toetag, with all due respect, I think that maybe you are being a little hard on people. After all, they probably have undergone some sort of loss, too, and they are just looking for a way to try to comfort you (although failing miserably, from the looks of it). I, too, have gone through MANY MANY losses, and I just try to remember that people just do the best they can... they are just trying to sort things out in their own minds. After all, nobody REALLY knows what happens after death, do they?
Toetag13	Yes, maybe I am being a little too hard on people Leilah. But I've heard so much crap from people that I forget how to grieve in my own way. It keeps me wondering if I'm grieving in the wrong way. Maybe I am...
Maren	There is no right way or wrong way to grieve, it is different foreverybody.
Nightwolf	Toetag, like I tell people...certain people grieve in their own way. Not all people grieve the way other friends, family, etc. grieve.
UglyBlonde	Toetag, I agree with you completely. that "better place" comment makes me want to go postal, too. There's nothing in the world that's better than being alive and well...I've been through that one five times and I feel exactly the same way. The biggest difference between pets and people is that your pets are always there for you. When my brother died in 1980 (he was 24), my cousin laughed rather

uncomfortably at the wake when someone told a story about him. My mother was offended. She was also peeved that I managed to maintain a stiff upper lip. It wasn't until recently that she brought this up again and I explained to her that my cousin was probably nervous as all hell and that I prefer to cry in private and keep a stiff upper lip in public whenever possible. Being half British and half German will usually express itself that way. I have a bad habit of cracking dark sarcastic jokes when someone dies. It's my way of coping. At the last funeral I went to I got snapped at because I cracked a joke about the fact that there was a mattress in the coffin and the inside of the coffin was silk-lined. lol. The person's dead...why would they care? I really got in trouble when I asked to ride in the hearse...lol. Bottom line: I hate funeral homes, I hate body viewings, I hate how damn clean and antiseptic death has been made to be. Death is scary, dark, creepy, and gross to think about...don't make it what it's not. I got yelled at for not going up and looking at my great-uncle's body...I don't want to see that made-up, live-looking shell that was his body. It creeps me out. Death makes a lasting impression. I may have only been three when my grandma died but I remember my mom carrying me up to look at her dead body. I remember touching her hand and I remember how damn cold it was. But my mom taught me a valuable lesson by taking me to see her body. I learned what death was...and I'll never forget. It's made me live my life better.

Leilah   Toetag, I'll tell you what really bugs me at a funeral. When somebody says, "Now, if Brother Taylor were here today, he'd want me to remind you of your immortal soul and if you haven't found Jesus, you had better do it right away." Now that will make ME go postal! Or some lame preacher pretending that he knew the deceased when in fact he doesn't have a CLUE what that person was about. Those aspects of funerals really turn me off, and there is an abundance of that b.s. in the South.

While the first selection of discourse demonstrated the structure and motivation of participants to be the most prominent theme, the second reveals its content as most important. The participants here voice their frustration with certain "rules" that they feel strangled by regarding how they are supposed to think, feel, and behave in the face of death. In the course of the exchange, several entities are pointed to as the source for such frustrations. First, the funeral industry is chided for its role in making death "antiseptic," and its perpetuation of the belief that viewing the dead is a positive endeavor. Second, religious leaders are maligned for propagating the notion that the dead are in a "better place," and using the deceased's death as an impetus for the need for religious conversion. Third, other family members are castigated for imposing certain rules of etiquette during public funeral ceremonies, usually indicating what "appropriate" emotional display is.

Further explanation of these statements helps us to understand their significance. First, the delineation of the source of participants' frustration is provided largely by me. That is, while some do mention a specific person or group as the antagonist in this regard, most of the interactants appeal to some anonymous "they," "people," "somebody," or "everyone else." The inability to point to specific persons or entities as the cause of their frustration indicates, to a certain degree, the pervasiveness with which the specified actions take place. When making an appeal to anonymous generalities, participants express a feeling that such things take place often, and are everywhere in their experience, such that there seems to be an inability to say directly, for example, that "The funeral director did this," or "Pastor Joe said..." So, participants are not only expressing here their own feelings and personal experiences, their discourse is an expression of the degree to which they are indicative of a larger structure of cultural behavior and belief about death and dying, which they express they have no real control over. Through such discourse they are going further and making a critique about American culture in general—that our society has imposed certain rules and standards of behavior when it comes to experiencing another's death and how we deal with that experience—critiques not largely voiced in typical public arenas.

Second, a further indication of the pervasiveness of such discourse in the society as a whole and the influence it has on our behavior is indicated in *Toetag13*'s apology at the end of her opening remarks. Her challenge to this dominant mode of discourse on death has taken ten years to come to fruition. Her inability to express such feelings for so long attests to the power of this discourse in her feeling like it was something that could not and should not be said to anyone else she has come into contact with. Such statements, it is evident, were not within her purview to make public. It indicates further that multiple participants and entities in the society at large are complicit (mindfully or not) in perpetuating such discourses that discourage any challenge to prescribed norms of dealing with death.

What I mean to say here is that there is a system of etiquette that governs how we behave and interact with others during the process of memorializing and grieving the dead. Such rules of interaction, as Goffman thoroughly explains,[4] are not insignificant. Not only do they dictate our behavior and conversational patterns, but our compliance or deviation from them influences the experience itself and how others view and judge us in such situations. The critiques lodged by participants in this forum, then, are much more than the collective whinings of people who have too much time on their hands. Their critique, their discussion of changing the rules of the grieving game, is an effort to change the nature of the very experience of dealing with death and dying itself.

Though these conversations are taking place here in a limited arena, they are a necessary first step to influencing the broader array of attitudes we have about death and dying in our society, especially to the degree to which they correspond with similar conversations in other societal forums. The conversations here add to, for instance, recent conversations about death and dying stimulated by the wars in Iraq and Afghanistan currently taking place, raising questions such as: Who deserves to be publicly remembered? Should the public be allowed to see media images of dead soldiers returning so that we all have an opportunity to grieve? What should be the tangible by-products of our individual and collective grief? What religious perspectives and denominational representatives should officiate public memorial ceremonies? and What ethics should govern the rhetoric of those who speak for the dead, and who should be allowed to speak for them in the first place? That the criticisms and discussions indicative of the participants in the *Six Feet Under* fan community discussed here are taking place is significant alone.

That these conversations parallel and sometimes intersect with similar conversations in the broader community[5] adds to the possibility that such discourse may reshape various attitudes regarding death and dying and ways of dealing with it both individually and collectively. That a television show such as *Six Feet Under* can serve as an impetus for such community, conversation, challenge, and change by creating a forum for mutual identification and freedom of expression demonstrates the value of sophisticated programming that can both entertain and produce social, public goods as well as influence individual perspectives and ways of dealing with death and dying.

NOTES

[1]   Henry Jenkins, *Textual Poachers: Television Fans and Participatory Culture* (New York: Routledge, 1992) 86.

[2]   Nancy Baym, *Tune In, Log On: Soaps, Fandom, and Online Community* (Newbury Park, CA: Sage, 2000) 14–24.

[3]   The selections here are taken from the site as it existed between the first and second season.

4   Erving Goffman, *Interaction Ritual: Essays on Face-to-Face Behavior* (Garden City, NY: Anchor Books, 1967).

5   For instance, the various issues surrounding the September 11, 2001, attacks, including those who died, our collective grieving, the media images that circulated, and the political maneuverings that followed were all prevalent conversations within the fan site immediately following and since.

CHAPTER SIX

Myths of Death in Science Fiction
The Case of The Twilight Zone

T he prophet Hosea's people were destroyed for lack of knowledge, says the Hebrew Bible. Yet we who are modern may condemn ourselves to a similar fate, not because we lack knowledge, but because we are bereft of myth. Where are our myths? In the modern world, mythic ruminations have been replaced by scientific explanations. The gods and monsters of bygone days have been revealed for what they *really* are—their mysteries banished into outer darkness after unmasking the man behind the curtain. The randomness of the world has been substituted for a world where every human and natural action can be precisely predicted if we can just provide the correct regression equation. The irrationality of the world we once reveled in has been sacrificed on the altar of logic, the deductive statement, the formula, algorithm, and natural law. Science killed God—and thank God for that!

But it seems that by rejecting God (in the sense of a permanent, omniscient and omnipresent deity) and myth we place ourselves in a rather precarious position; the vitality of myth is indispensable to the creation and sustenance of communal bonds. Myths instruct us as to what it means to be one of a community.[1] Myths help us understand how we should both live and die, and nothing begs for mythic explanation more than our common experience of death. The reconciliation attained through mythic guidance expresses itself not in trying to overcome death or to remove its sting, but to foster a sense of acceptance—a resolute acquiescence, if you will. Such a perspective is possible in truly mythic stories of death where the world is connected through a vital energy or spirit allowed to permeate it. Death becomes not an end to be feared, but an experience to be acknowledged as merely a change in form, where death is but a return to life of simply a different kind.

So, to where should we look to find such myths in a modern world that largely rejects their validity, and in a society where escapist entertainments provide a covering shield from our fear of the unknown? From where do we resurrect them from their valuative invisibility? The reality is that there are probably many "places" to find them. But I want to deal here with one where many have not looked for them—precisely in the realm of entertainment itself and, more specifically, in the genre of science fiction. Looking here, we find that sophisticated instruction about and advice on how to think about and act in the face of death has permeated many areas of the media landscape in the past and more recent present. The very label we have attached to such stories already makes a negative judgment about the content they express. That is, such stories are located by their content in the realm of "science" with all its inherent biases, but also in opposition to it. It is "fiction"—make-believe science, impossible science, speculative science, imaginative science—really, no science at all. Thus, science fiction's mythic qualities are seen as having essentially no real import or value when measured against the standard of actual scientific enterprises.

In this chapter and the following, it is not my goal to demythologize science as it were, nor to reify the genre of science fiction. Rather, by analyzing two of the most popular programs in this genre, I want to demonstrate how such programs can be reinterpreted and reevaluated in terms of their mythic qualities, particularly as they provide valuable insight, direction, and a sense of communal connection in regard to the experience of death—the different attitude and perspective of death they inspire from our dominant ways of viewing this experience.

Beyond Good and Evil: Deconstructing Death and Time in *The Twilight Zone*

A fundamental premise of modern cosmology is the objectification and quantification of time, which calls into existence, existence itself. It gives us consciousness of the individual self who, located in time, is characterized by two defining moments—our beginning and our end; our birth and our death. When the individual is regarded as the measure of all things, and time the measure of the individual, then it is no surprise that life and death are not equally valued. While life is welcomed with wonder and excitement, death—the end of time, and the end of "being"—is fundamentally that which must be avoided by any means necessary. But what happens when we interrogate these prejudicial valuations?[2] What happens when our discussions move beyond a dogmatic acceptance to an advocacy of such oppositions? What happens when we question our "faith in opposite values" and rip the proverbial rug of absolute certainty out from underneath our feet? When we do so, we find ourselves, indeed, in *The Twilight Zone*.

As Nietzsche deconstructed the binary opposition between good and evil and all other moralistic and valuative foundations, so too *The Twilight Zone* (*TTZ*) disrupts the modern notion of time (and as a consequence, space) as it relates to two sets of binary oppositions—good an evil on the one hand (a question of moral value) and life and death on the other (a question of being and time). While many are apt to view *TTZ* as the collected projections of fear and anxiety in a post-World War II and emerging cold war era that incited the advancement of vast new technologies, *TTZ* is much more. *TTZ*, in its reciprocal and interrelated deconstruction of death and time, serves as a collection of myths that provide guidance about how one might view and experience the inevitability of death and the possibilities that lie within the realm of the world that death brings.

The technologically rendered uncertainty and fear form the basis of most of *TTZ*'s plots and are the basis of the show's rightful placement among the science-fiction genre. However, fear and anxiety are not, I believe, the desired reaction to the uncertainties and realities of human nature constructed and expressed in its stories. Rather, many of the individual episodes, and the show collectively, advance the perspective that life and death and the uncertainties surrounding them—while possibly frightening—should be viewed in terms of the possibilities they incite, the new wonders they may lead to. This reading of *TTZ* can be seen in a brief analysis of both the structure and content of the show, two aspects of which are discussed below.

Metaphysical Speculation as Introduction

In the realm of fictional television, Rod Serling is author, creator, and narrator. Mythically speaking, he is a sublime raconteur of sorts, bearing the responsibility and imbued with the credibility to communicate stories. But he also interprets and elucidates the meaning of these stories as a way of providing guidance to a community about not only how to be "one of the collective," but also simply how "to be"—how to live in the world vis-à-vis all that with which our being is co-constituted. In this role, Serling generally introduces the plot in each of *TTZ* episodes; he also delivers its moral at the conclusion of each. While space does not permit a description of these functions in each of the episodes, there is a singular and standard introduction that begins each of the episodes. And while the actual text of these introductions has changed several times throughout the show's original seven-year history, the meaning communicated in each of them is relatively the same:

> There is a sixth dimension beyond that which is known to man. It is a dimension as
> vast as space and as timeless as infinity. It is the middle ground between light and
> shadow, and it lies between the pit of man's fears and the sunlight of his knowledge.
> This is the dimension of imagination. It is an area that might be called The Twilight
> Zone.[3]

The most significant element of this introduction is the spatial metaphysic used in the two similes, "vast as space" and "timeless as infinity," and the associated metaphors used to further supplement the descriptive introduction.

A simile requires that we not only evaluate the nature of the comparison being made, but the object of comparison itself—that which is ultimately being described. This demands that this analysis begin prior to the invocation of this figure of speech in the sentence where it is used. Here, this object is the setting for the story that follows; each story takes place in this "dimension" which is objectively "real" in that it exists as a place of human action. Yet it only exists descriptively on a metaphysical plane "beyond" the empirical, which does not, however, belie its existential validity. The use of the simile here to describe a setting is significant in that it grounds the story that follows in the realm of being and existence, making the case that the unseen world is nevertheless a real one, and one that has a bearing on the experiences taking place in the life-world. This is what makes the story truly mythical—the existence of two realms, one seen, another invisible, both nonetheless intimately related and valued. In phenomenological terms, the myths here serve to bring this unseen world to the conscious awareness of its viewers.

So what of this dimension? What else helps us to understand this place that we are gaining privileged access to through our identification with the storyteller and our suspension of empirical prejudices? The terms "vast as space" and "timeless as infinity" are two ways of describing the same plane in which the stories here take place—this dimension—yet they each emphasize a different characteristic with varying, but related, implications. The purely spatial term "space" refers here to what we might call "objective" space[4]; space is a container that, because of its unbounded extension, is one which holds all things. It is both a space where all things take place and one where anything *can* take place. In the next descriptive phrase, a temporal comparison is made about the space in which the following episode or experience occurs. The term "infinity" represents a range of possible iterations. This temporal designation is conditioned on the preceding spatial condition, thus signifying this dimension as not only a container and condition for existence and experience, but also as a possibility that any number of qualitatively different kinds of experiences can and may take place. This seems inconsequential, perhaps, yet it is significant in terms of what is accomplished by the precise wording of these descriptive phrases. Time and space here are seen as mutually dependent. Space provides the container and possibility for experience, while time provides the condition for the *kinds* of experience that will take place.

In the Kantian sense, time and space are universal and necessary preconditions—the two fundamental a priori phenomena in which all experience takes place. All phenomena are played out in time and space, and the variations of conceptualizing each form the basis for all manners of cultural expression. In this way, the experiences and actions that take place in *TTZ*, though they exceed the known dimension of the visible world, are nevertheless grounded—constituted by and within the same concepts as are any other form of "reality." Again, the description here within the realm of time and space serves to equalize the physical and the metaphysical world, providing legitimacy for both in their interrelationship. The stories of *TTZ* are not those that are so far out that they exceed the possibility of having existential value in the physical world. This ground must be established if we are to make the case that such programming has any real consequence for those who avail themselves of its stories.

But there is more here in the introduction that helps to clarify and establish the plane in which the show's stories play out. It also posits that the dimension in which the unfolding story takes place is a liminal space between binary oppositions. References to a binary system of opposites are a necessary step in the deconstructive processes undertaken by this introduction, and the show as a whole. The deconstructive turn here is accomplished not only by characterizing the "twilight zone" as a place essentially "between," but also in the terms used to represent the opposing referents.

First, it is a dimension between "light" and "shadow." It is clear that these are not what are typically referred to as spectral opposites. Yet we assume they are intended to be described as such by virtue of their descriptive placement "between" two points (without a delineated frame, the term "between" here would have no meaning). Why is this space not in between "light" and "darkness"? In the language of optics, the shadow is perhaps one of the best representations of the notion of synergy or co-constitution. The shadow is an entity defined only comparatively; only light and dark together constitute the shadow. But this notion of shadow implies not just a comparative definition. The shadow is formed through the penetration or interception of light. Thus, the shadow is not simply the resulting contrast of light and darkness; the shadow encloses both light and darkness. And so when we are in pursuit of the "light"—illumination, visual clarity, enlightenment, clarification, etc.—the shadow is as necessary and valid a source as the sun, a lamp, or the proverbial light bulb that goes off in one's head.

The language of psychology explicates a somewhat different, but related, conception of the shadow. In Jungian terms, the shadow is a representation or reflection of the individual or collective unconscious.[5] It is a hidden persona—one rejected by the self as evil, but which necessarily exists and finds expression in the life-world through a variety of expressive manifestations. Though the shadow in psychological terms generally takes on a negative connotation, it is nevertheless a necessary aspect of the self, without which our "true" self—our "real" identity—could not be recognized by ourselves or others.

The juxtaposition of these differing conceptions of the relationship between light and shadow represents well the purpose—or at least the outcome—of the deconstructive act of identifying light and shadow in dual opposition. While the psychological conception of the shadow is negative, the optical understanding infuses the notion with significance; the darkness, no matter the shade, contains the possibility of illumination and all of those things we receive through light. Both the optical and psychological conception of the shadow, however, allude to another defining characteristic of each, moving us beyond these two explanatory categories: color. Despite the object being reflected, the color of the shadow is always the same—some semblance of gray. The reason for this, optically speaking, is clear. Psychologically speaking, this aspect of the shadow catapults us from the realm of both optics and psychology into the domain of ethics, linguistically constructed in another popular figure of speech—the "gray area."

Characterizing a particular moral issue as a "gray area" signals its ethical indeterminacy between absolute right and wrong, and introduces the instrumental question, "What should be done?" Referring to something as a "gray area" in this regard shifts our focus of judgment. It sublimates absolute judgment, thereby privileging the question of the good, the most profitable, the best course of action. For example, it redirects our judgment of physician-assisted suicide away from whether the act itself is categorically right or wrong to the question of whether we *should* relieve the suffering of one's mother who is dying in excruciating pain with no hope of survival. It leads us to question, as a basis for judgment, whether or not we are indeed preserving life and whether life in this circumstance is really living at all. This shift in focus in the ethical dimension of judgment is directly related, as we shall see shortly, to *TTZ*'s deconstruction of death. However, one remaining colloquial expression involving the shadow is important to identify before making this point.

As far back as the ancient Hebrews, the term *shadow* has been used in reference to death. The phrase, "shadow of death" (Heb. Salmaveth; tsalmaw'-veth, meaning shade of death, i.e., the grave; figuratively meaning calamity), remains in our day a popular way of describing this experience; it generally retains some fidelity to its theological origins. As a description of the phenomenon of death, this saying also implies both a temporal designation and a valuative judgment. "Walking through the valley of the shadow of death" precedes its eventual fulfillment or culmination (in death); the gray indeterminancy of the shadow exists prior to death, characterized as absolute darkness. Despite the psalmist's exhortation to fear no evil, the valley that we walk through on our descent into life's ultimate negation is understandably viewed negatively. The comfort the Bible offers during this time is a traveling companion—God—who is said to accompany us through this shadowy moment, thereby removing some of death's sting.

The theological myth here guides us through the experience of death by positing another absolute who promises a return to the light on the other side of the darkness—the other side of death. *TTZ* provides similar guidance; however, it does so by introducing the ultimate indeterminancy—replacing the darkness of death with the all-encompassing shadow. The Biblical story remains on a linear plane of beginning (light and life), end (darkness and death), and then a new beginning in an absolute and permanent heaven (eternal light and life) or hell (eternal darkness and death). The lesson provided in *TTZ* myths deconstructs this rational conception of time, life, and death by placing the indeterminate shadow in place of the absolute position of darkness and death, thus admonishing us to approach the experience of death with a question mark. It directs us to view death as a realm of possibility where anything can happen. Rather than death leading to an absolute time of either eternal life or death (the eternal nature of such a time denies the very possibility of temporality, a place "outside" of time), it posits that the individual in death exists in a dimension "in" time and "in" space—that is, within the life-world (as opposed to some otherworldly, figurative dimension) these two a priori condition. It seeks to extinguish our fear of death not with the some absolute certainty, but with the possibilities that pervade the realm of uncertainty.

But two other metaphors are prominent in *TTZ*'s introduction that bear on its mythical significance in relation to death. The dimension of *TTZ* myth is not only a place in between light and shadow, it "lies between the pit of man's fears and the sunlight of his knowledge." Exercising some interpretive license here, the replacement of the term "sunlight" with "summit" in a revised version of *TTZ* introduction expresses best the point made by the descriptive metaphors used in this phrase vis-à-vis the previously described similes (though the term *sunlight* still makes the connection). Here, "pit" and "summit" are the two figures that are the locus of the binary opposition which metaphorically describe two aspects of the human psyche and its various expressions. The previously described figures used in *TTZ* introduction expanded the realm of valuative judgment about light and life, darkness and death by replacing one end of a binary opposition with a term signifying indeterminacy and possibility—by showing the valuative terms associated with them to be intimately interrelated. The deconstructive act here in this second set of descriptions is accomplished by using a true set of binaries to metaphorically describe human expression in regard to death and the realm of the unknown.

In this binary system, the "pit," is that which is hidden from view, a location of uncertainty. It is the lowermost point underneath a foundation of a tangible and visible world. Yet pits are largely instrumental in nature, thereby serving both positive and negative ends. A pit is used to hide something, yet it is also a site of discovery, as when an archaeologist uncovers an ancient relic during a dig. And so it is simultaneously a place of concealment and revelation. Nevertheless, our modern visiocentric[6] bias tends to view it as largely negative—with fear—as if opening up the ground might unleash some unknowable horror (the premise of countless sci-fi, horror and apocalyptic narratives).

The second aspect of this binary system opposes the perspective of the first. We can see into the heavens. And though we may not be able to see clearly, or know at all times what we are seeing, we view the move upward to the summit or pinnacle as the best place to find answers. Moving toward a pinnacle suggests an act of progress associated with knowledge; as it grows, the closer we are to reaching that uppermost plane of reality and certainty.

The use of the binary system to metaphorically describe the focus and route of our progress serves again to destroy the oppositional boundaries created, thereby shifting our perspective about the nature of certainty and uncertainty, life and death. It suggests that to reach some "pinnacle," some point of human technological apex, we must needs go through the pit; at least it suggests this as a possibility. It not only expresses that we must confront our fear of what lies beneath, what is unseen and unknown—death and the grave—but that in the pit itself also lies the potential for discovery, not only about our world and the hereafter, but about ourselves in it.

Confronting Life and Death in *The Twilight Zone*

Taken together, *TTZ* introduction provides a clear context for the stories it begins to tell. They are stories not just about individuals, but about any individual member of our society grappling with the anxious pursuit to render the world knowable and certain through scientific exploration. They are stories that help us to engage the shadow of our individual and collective selves, forcing us to see not only the darkness we conceal within the innermost regions of our psyche, but the light of possibility that is there if we cultivate a relationship between them. Certainty and uncertainty, the known and the unknowable, light and darkness, fear and possibility— these stories teach us both explicitly and implicitly how to deal with the pinnacle of these realities—death. So while each particular story may not deal with death at all in the most explicit sense, all the stories deal with what we must face in death. While the introduction of *TTZ* provides this foundation, many of the stories themselves bear out their mythic significance regarding our collective experience of death and dying.

A good number of *TTZ* stories deal with death in a very direct way. That is, not only do they present the normative acts of killing or being killed either purposefully or accidentally, but they center around an individual's confrontation with some aspect of death, dying, or what might be beyond death. On at least two occasions people confront an actual character—Mr. Death—as a way of illustrating our relationship to the experience. For example, in "One for the Angels" Lew Bookman is an ardent pitchman who has spent his entire adult life making deals, using his words to spin a persuasive web which, when done properly, results in the sale of a variety of goods. Despite his appearance and ragamuffin, street-corner pitch stand that any other sixtyish-year-old man would be ashamed of, Bookman remains loyal to his craft, pitching anything and everything to neighbors, children, and any who will listen. But Bookman is dogged by a tall, black-coated man visible only to him. He sees him at every turn he makes. Bookman converses with him, answers his questions, but refuses to recognize—despite all apparent clues—his new traveling companion, of sorts. He is abruptly shaken when he finally realizes that he is talking to Mr. Death himself, the man ordered to take him out of this world precisely at midnight.

But Bookman has unfinished business; he has never made a truly successful pitch, one that, he explains, even the angels would be enamored with. And so Bookman seeks to make the ultimate pitch, a culmination of his life's miserable work, before giving in to Mr. Death's demands. But he has to undertake a rhetorical task that it seems even the most skilled sophistic artist armed with every necessary advantage could not pull of—to make a deal with death—to risk everything, but lose nothing. Though he is successful in convincing Mr. Death to delay his midnight demise until he has accomplished this one great pitch, he puts at risk the life of a little neighborhood girl he is so fond of—Maggie—who Mr. Death must take in exchange for Bookman's temporarily extended life. Bookman's chance to do the one thing he has always wanted to do turns out to be more successful than he could have ever imagined. His pitch is so good that Mr. Death himself stands baffled and amazed, forgetting to take Maggie's life at the appointed time. Mr. Death, stunned by his oversight, and Bookman, now sublimely content with this last feat, exit together, Maggie's life having been spared.

Death comes to us at our appointed time when most of us are not expecting it; only if we are lucky are we given the opportunity to fully prepare. But in either case, death is not to be feared. Though one's earthly stature and life be meager; though we may see ourselves as inconsequential, death gives us the chance to matter—to mean something. Death is not an end to be evaluated by all we have done up to that point. Death is indeed a sacrifice.[7] We walk quietly into the night so that those who remain may live in the joy of our death,[8] our sacrifice. In death we are all martyrs. He who dies with the most toys truly does not win; he who willingly bequeaths his toys (life itself) for others to enjoy—does.

In another instance, Wanda Dunn, a woman old in years living in all but peaceful isolation in "Nothing in the Dark" meets Mr. Death in much the same way as Mr. Bookman. Wanda, too, has been shadowed by the mysterious, but all-too-real, figure for the better part of her elderly years. But she has recognized him from the moment she first saw him, and became passionately intent on evading his presence and desire to snatch away her soul that she is not quite ready to let go of. She figures the only way to evade his poisonous touch is to barricade herself all alone in her dilapidated shack; the dead bolt on her front door protects her from what she sees as this monstrous figure coming to steal, kill, and destroy. She opens the door for no one. The little boy who delivers her groceries must place the bag outside the door and walk away before she opens it. One day she hears the sounds of a gunshot and looks through the peephole in her door to see a policeman lying shot on her front porch. Grudgingly, and afraid that it is indeed death lying at her door, she nevertheless lets the injured man inside.

She and the man converse, his gentle manner giving her comfort that she has not put herself in danger by his entrance. Later, after the man has lain down for a rest, she is startled by a forceful knock at the door. When she does not answer, the man on the other side knocks down the door and comes barreling into the house. Wanda, sure that this is the end, sure that Mr. Death has forced his way in, falls to the ground. When she regains consciousness, the man explains to her that he has come to demolish her house because the land is being redeveloped for a new housing neighborhood. Confused that the man has not hastened her to death's end as she expected, she begins to explain the reasons for her fear. She directs the man's eyes to the police officer lying quietly in the bed. But she soon realizes that the man cannot see him; the police officer is only visible to her. And with that she suddenly realizes that she has been entertaining Mr. Death this whole time. After convincing Wanda that it is time to stop running and gracefully acquiesce, Mr. Death holds out his hand, inviting her to grab hold and begin the long journey. As she grasps hold of his beckoning hand, they engage in quiet, peaceful conversation as he leads her out of the small, darkened room of the house and through the door to the white light–brightened space that lies beyond.

Sometimes we get so accustomed to life and living, that we spend our time running in fear of what we think is impending darkness and destruction. But what if all the while we have been planning our escape in total darkness, we end up only to be *rescued* by death itself by stepping out into an endless expanse that looks like a clean, white slate ready to be filled in with the bright possibilities of new experiences?

And what if death, and old age that hastens it, is only a state of mind? This is what Mr. Whitley comes to understand in "Kick the Can," when he is faced with the proposition of impending death following his remaining years in a nursing home, where he is surrounded by a host of others simply waiting to die. When Mr. Whitley catches a glimpse one day of some neighborhood kids playing "kick the can," a childhood game he remembers all too well, he surmises that though he cannot physically be a child again, he can be child-like and renew his miserable life by playing the games of children. Mr. Whitley's doctor thinks he is deluded by his anxiety; his cohorts in the home think he is just plumb crazy.

But one night he decides to make a go of it. He wakes up his house-mates, begging them to come with him outside to play kick the can. Some of them balk but then follow him out, an air of excitement countenancing their faces. His boyhood friend, however, chastises him for his foolishness and chooses to stay behind. He awakens the doctor to tell him what they are do-ing. When he gets outside he sees Mr. Whitley jumping around playfully in the sprinkler with childlike carelessness. When told to come inside, he runs away with the rest of his friends. Later, Mr. Whitley's old friend comes out to the street. He sees a child playing who has come to the street to fetch the can he and his friends have been playing with. Inquisitively, and with face full of both hope and anxiety, he looks into the boy's eyes and realizes it is indeed his friend. He is a child again. He begs him for a second chance to come and join the game, but boy Whitley says that he had his chance. As his friend runs away back to his game, the man stands there with a look of an-guish fastened on his face with intense regret.

The narrator's voice ends the story:

> Sunnyvale Rest—a dying place for ancient people who have forgotten the fragile magic of youth. A dying place for those who have forgotten that childhood, matur-ity, and old age are curiously intertwined and not separate. A dying place for those who have grown too stiff in their thinking to visit...The Twilight Zone.

TTZ viewers, and sci-fi fans more generally, tend to focus on the two buzzwords of the genre as a guide to interpreting and understanding the pro-grams categorized under its rubric. The mythic elements of such narratives, however, are often in the details. As seen here, the sci-fi focus on the un-known, and its appeals to the depths of our psyche and collective conscience in facing it, offer much in the way of dealing with death, the ultimate unknown. In doing so it instructs us how we should live in relation to the myriad of possibilities that confront us throughout both life and death.

The X-Files, which I turn to in the next chapter, both reiterates and adds to much of the mythic message expressed here in *TTZ*, but does so from a different perspective, utilizing different (and more) symbolic indicators, and being presented in an entirely different structural format.

NOTES

[1]   Joseph Campbell, *The Power of Myth* (New York: Doubleday, 1988).

[2]   For Edmund Husserl, the suspension of received ways of viewing a particular experience was the first necessary process to understanding the lived experience of the phenomenon under investigation. These prejudices, once suspended (perhaps only temporarily), allow us to "see" the same thing in potentially different ways. Thus, I argue here that *The Twilight Zone* accomplishes this in regards to our dominant attitudes about death and dying.

[3]   This introduction was used in the pilot episode of the show.

[4]   Elisabeth Ströker, *Investigations in Philosophy of Space* (Athens, OH: Ohio University Press, 1987).

[5]   Carl Jung, *Man and His Symbols* (Garden City, NY: Doubleday, 1964).

[6]   Eric Kramer, *Postmodernism and Race* (Westport, CT: Praeger, 1997).

[7]   For a deeper explanation of this statement, see Jacques Derrida, *The Gift of Death* (Chicago: University of Chicago Press, 1995).

[8]   Alphonso Lingis, *The Community of Those Who Have Nothing in Common* (Bloomington, IN: Indiana University Press, 1994).

CHAPTER SEVEN

Believing in What's "Out There"

The Myth of The X-Files

The artistic quality and commercial success of *The X-Files* has long been attributed to the fact that it defies any singular reading or interpretation. The times and circumstances that produced the show, the breadth of subjects dealt with over its nine year history—government conspiracies, aliens and UFOs, paranormal phenomenon, and forensic crimesolving, to mention a few—make the imposition of any one frame virtually impossible. However, for all that it offers, *The X-Files*, understood in terms of its mythical qualities, provides us with an interpretive connection to the previously described *The Twilight Zone* in terms of its guidance on matters of the unknown, death, and the life lived in the light of these experiences. To analyze the structural form and content of *The X-Files*, which give rise to its mythic significance, we must understand the domain of *The X-Files* myth as explicated in its originary context (in the pilot episode); the role that death, dying and the dead play throughout; the iconic significance of "alien beings"; and the culmination of the myth in the context of the final episode, fittingly titled, "The Truth."

Symbol and Slogan: The Domain of *The X-Files* Myth

What is the central issue of *The X-Files* myth and what is the focal point of the messages it expresses? These questions can be answered, to a large degree, by looking at its primary guiding symbol and the interpretation of its three most significant slogans—all of which are repeated in visual representations or in verbal articulations throughout *The X-Files* series. While the primary symbol represents mythic polarity—synthesis—each of the three slogans expresses some form of tension: tension between competing ideas, ideals, dreams, goals, means, methods, and characters themselves. The use of both symbol and slogan, then, not only provides a springboard for the ensuing drama exhibited throughout, it also outlines the mythic dimensions of the show; it provides the rationale for its mythic reading.

"X" Marks the Spot

The primary symbol of *The X-Files* is, of course, the "X." The meaning of this symbol is manifest here in three interrelated expressions.

Mathematical Unknown. The symbol itself is the mathematical representation of the unknown—that which needs to be deciphered in order to solve an equation or problem. Symbolically, it is closely akin to the "?" which is the figure of the question; the one (X) always implies the other (?). So, the general question of the unknown takes center stage. In mathematical, symbolic logic systems, however, "X" is not only a symbol of the unknown, a gap to be filled in to solve an equation; it is also known as a "universal quantifier." As such, "X" can stand for any variable; it varies. It can be qualified, such that whatever gap it fills in an equation or proposition may be said to be true in either all or only certain cases. These two mathematical characteristics of "X" in *The X-Files* highlight the degree to which the unknown perpetually exists, and adds to the ambiguity as to the particular truth that the characters search for and/or protect throughout the majority of the show. It also adds to the manner in which the show characterizes truth—as universally unknown, variable, qualified.

Orientation. It is clear that the "X" in the show is also a designation by which to orient oneself. "X" indeed marks the spot, as is seen early in "The Pilot." While traveling to a small Oregon town to investigate the mysterious case of several unexplained vanishings, Mulder and Scully, the primary characters of the show, drive through the woods where some of these disappearances took place when, all of a sudden, the car radio is overcome with static and begins rapidly switching from station to station. A deafening, high-pitch ring pierces their ears. Scully covers hers while Mulder looks toward the sky with anticipation. Suspecting the events are more than coincidence, Mulder quickly pulls over to the side of the road, gets out of the car, and heads to the trunk, from which he pulls out a can of pink spray paint. Scully watches with curiosity as Mulder shakes the can and paints a large "X" on the street at the sight where the incident first occurred.

The "X" not only signals the spot where the incident first occurred, it serves to orient them in confirming a similar incident that takes place later in the episode. The subsequent occasion takes place under virtually the same circumstances. After getting out of the car and seeing the "X" he marked the spot with earlier, Mulder quickly runs back to the car, while Scully peers down once again at the "X" on the road, then follows her partner. So this "X," this question mark, this unknown, is seen as both the beginning and end of the search for an answer not only to the case, but to all other mysteries that would emerge throughout the remainder of the series.

Unity and Synthesis. The "X" in *The X-Files* is generally enclosed by a circle. The mythological connection here is seen, if not before, in the episode "The Gift" in season eight. Mulder has gone underground, hiding from those invisible, conspiratorial forces who would destroy him for what he knows, and for what he may one day truly come to understand. Agent John Doggett, assigned to The X-Files primarily to ascertain the whereabouts of Agent Mulder, receives a tip from Mulder's cell phone records, which placed him in the small town of Squamash, Pennsylvania, only a few months before. His presence there was filled with controversy because, as was later revealed, Mulder went there to find a disease-eating man who could possibly cure Mulder of his deathly illness.

While searching the property around the last known whereabouts of Mulder, Agent Doggett comes across a grave—unsure if Mulder is buried in it or not. There by this unknown grave lies what is commonly referred to in Native American folklore as a medicine wheel. Later depictions of the symbol resemble the more traditional medicine wheel, yet the first time we see it, the picture is identical to *The X-Files* program symbol. The medicine wheel is a Native American folkloric symbol first uncovered on the BigHorn reservation in Montana. The wheel, and the space it occupies, is considered to be sacred, even among contemporary Native American peoples, though the rituals in which it was commonly used are generally no longer practiced. And, though the size and constructive elements of medicine wheels throughout the Americas and elsewhere differ, they generally share three common characteristics: a central stone or cairn; one or more concentric circles of stones; and at least two stone lines emanating outward from the central cairn.

The precise usage and even some of the symbolism of the wheel are mired in controversy; nevertheless, most scholars agree on some of its essential representations—all of which focus on the idea of synthesis and wholeness, including concepts of renewal and rebirth, the union of nature in the calling together the four winds and the approach and passing of the seasons, and planetary orbits. The lines emanating from the center of the wheel, which in some configurations resembles the letter X, also stand for a host of ideas that represented Native American cosmology: the pathway of the spirits among which the living commune, purity, clarity, strength, and love.[1]

This most significant symbol in *The X-Files* mythology provides the foundational element upon which the series' dramas are based; it is the nexus and focal point of the primary message expressed. The remaining mantras all qualify the nature of this foundation, speaking to how the unknown—the enduring question mark—should be confronted by the characters in the show.

"The Truth Is Out There"

The slogan, "The Truth Is Out There," appears in the introduction to "The Pilot" and all subsequent episodes in the series. As it suggests, the slogan begs for the pursuit of truth as something that is attainable. This quest becomes the driving passion and mission of the show's primary character— Agent Fox Mulder. Renowned for his work as an FBI criminal profiler, he is an overachiever, a standout in his educational endeavors at Oxford University, and a distinguished profiler who was on the fasttrack for advancement because of his contribution to catching a well-known serial killer. Mulder, while talking with Scully in their Oregon hotel, their investigative home base in the pilot episode, first explains his discovery of and fascination with the X-Files. He begins by recounting a childhood trauma; without a trace his sister disappeared from their home, no facts or clues provided any insight or hope about ascertaining the circumstances of her apparent abduction. Finding answers to this lingering question drove him to excel in his subsequent educational and professional endeavors, which provided him the prerogative to pursue his own interests at the FBI. Eventually, he stumbled upon a wasteland of unsolved cases, fraught with experiences of the unexplained, the unexplainable—the paranormal. He became fascinated with the stories included in the files and convinced himself that in them were the answers to the questions he sought.

So what particular "interests" is Mulder pursuing? What is the nature of this truth that he seeks through the X-Files cases? In "The Pilot," the domain of "the truth" that Mulder would spend the rest of the show searching for is outlined. Why does the FBI ignore cases of unexplained phenomena? Is the "fantastic" an acceptable realm to look for plausible explanations when science fails? Do extraterrestrials exist? Are aliens abducting humans and playing out a sinister plan to recolonize the planet? Why is the government standing in my way of gaining the information I need to solve these cases? Is there a vast international conspiracy to hide the existence of extraterrestrials? And by the way, who the hell stole all of my evidence?

There are multiple truths that hold out the possibility of a concrete answer and, along the way, some of these "lesser truths" are at least partially revealed. But the fulfillment of these lesser truths imply that something always looms larger. Mulder is not content with just the small stuff. He is searching for *the* truth. And "the truth" here is characterized in two related ways.

Truth as Ends. Many are apt to read this *The X-Files* mantra as an expression of the modern notion of the existence and attainability of absolute truth through rational pursuit. But the slogan itself, as well as the circumstances of the show, belies this interpretation. "The truth," as it is portrayed here, is always left a little ambiguous throughout the show's nine-year existence. The slogan, "The Truth Is Out There" is a play on words that reveals an underlying tension. The truth is out there connotes certainty—the end of the rational road of scientific and philosophical progress. But the truth is also always "out there"—just beyond our grasp, beyond belief, beyond rational understanding. It represents the boundaries of rational explanation, the proverbial line in the sand demarcating explanation from belief, fact from fiction, the known and the unknown. And so the ancient tension works its way into *The X-Files,* the tension that exists by simultaneously insisting that absolute truth is knowable, that it should be pursued as the ultimate end or culmination of human striving on the one hand, and its ephemeral character on the other. The possibility necessitates the pursuit; its seeming invariability frustrates our achievement.

Truth as Human Agency. This slogan not only sets out the parameters of what will be the guiding drama of the show and the central tension at work; it describes the apparent duality of the primary characters engaged in this pursuit. The two characters represent two distinct, but ultimately contiguous, means of pursuing the ends of truth. The first and most obvious reading of the slogan describes the character of Mulder's partner, Dana Scully. Scully, a medical doctor by training, and a scientist by philosophy, adheres to a notion of the truth that *is* out there, that is attainable through scientific inquiry and its methods. Truth, in her view, is only as good as the evidence, the proof that substantiates it with rational explanation and plausibility. All truth is bound by scientific law and she is resistant, at least through most of the show's tenure, to accept anything that traverses the limits of science. The ends of science are inevitable for Scully, who subscribes to its teleology of progress. She entertains metaphysical speculations only as casual luxury, an exercise one might indulge in to brainstorm more probable, "real," credible—rational explanations.

Mulder is different, however, at least in theory. While truth is a real possibility for him, too, it is more an imperative, a motivation that suggests that he himself is the agent of truth. Attaining truth, in his view, cannot be ascribed solely to the domain of science, a naïve faith in its objective role and responsibility in assuming and achieving this task. Because of this, he is willing to look for truth within and beyond that which is certain, probable, provable only by scientific verification; because he personally bears responsibility for finding it, he is and must be willing to look "out there" to find this truth. He necessarily seeks to know the necessary and sufficient conditions of this truth, thereby broadening his understanding beyond the limited cause-effect domain of science and his partner Scully's methodological and epistemological prejudices. This is what draws Mulder to the X-Files, the documentations of experience, the narratives and stories that are clearly beyond but beg for explanation. Gods and monsters permeate his imagination and they lead him, quite successfully at times, to solving specific crimes. Yet his ability to look beyond also allows him to seemingly progress toward the attainment of his ultimate end—to find the truth he so obsessively seeks. This dual outlook on truth and its attainment relates more deeply to the fundamental drive and motivations that help to also dualistically characterize or describe the nature of truth for both Mulder and Scully.

"I Want to Believe"

The second slogan that is a guiding theme throughout the show is seen on a poster hanging in Mulder's office. It appears in the first episode and is always visible whenever this scene is shown. "I Want to Believe," as the positioning of the slogan on the poster suggests, is most closely associated with the possibility of the existence of extraterrestrials. But it thematizes more generally what we associate with Mulder's attitude about his search for the truth. His belief is necessary if he is going to allow the myriad of unexplained possibilities to guide him in his search; certainty and evidentiary proof are a hinderance—a downer, if you will—because that which he encounters along the way is clearly beyond the possibilities and boundaries of scientific law. If such certainty drove him, he would not get very far, being forced to resign to the slow progress that Scully accepts with resolute patience.

This slogan, like the rest, is used, in part, to create a tension between binary opposites in the characters of Mulder and Scully. The truth, in the most literal sense, is out there (it exists) for Scully, her truth being bound only by the limits of scientific possibility, subject only to a progressive teleology. Mulder's search, however, is an expression of intense desire—he wants to, and *must*, believe. But, as "The Truth Is Out There" is a singular statement masking a synthesis of oppositions, so, too, are the two slogans set against themselves. The tensions between scientific certainty and mythic imagination are positioned at odds with one another. Yet throughout the show we are given clear signs that the two collapse into one another. The boundary between science and superstition, fact and fiction, certainty and uncertainty diffuse and permeate one another such that there is little distinction.

The most significant example of the coalescence of science, religion, and metaphysics and Mulder and Scully's characters is seen in the seventh season episodes "The Sixth Extinction" and "The Sixth Extinction II: Amor Fati" (meaning "Love of fate," its religious significance being the love of a destined life)[2], which takes place in the absence of Mulder, who lies trapped by a plague that has increased his brain activity and threatens to kill him. In the first episode, Scully travels to Africa to decipher the cryptic symbols found on a beached craft of unknown origin. Mulder first gained knowledge of the craft and its symbolic message from a scientist working in Africa who claimed that it contained immense power. Scully's task to discover its meaning and power are predicated by Mulder, who has already conjectured the implications of what Scully would find. He says (in a voice-over, not in direct conversation with Scully) that if his presumptions are correct, it would mean that aliens are the biological progenitors of the human race.

When Scully arrives in Africa, she immediately heads to the site, reaches her hand in the wet sands of the beach, and uncovers a small portion of the craft in question, staring at it in amazement. As she considers the rubbed markings made from the surface of the craft, her thoughts turn to Mulder. She expresses to herself that she cannot believe what she is witnessing, it being so far outside the scientific realm she has come to anchor her beliefs. Confused by her discovery, she feels that she is in the wrong place—that it should have been Mulder's destiny to find this artifact and makes sense of its meaning and significance. But it is she that sits there forced to confront what her science would not allow her to believe.

Before understanding the message of the craft's symbols, Scully witnesses its power firsthand when she finds a piece of the craft in the tent where the doctor who originally sent for Mulder's help once resided. The object flies across the room on its own. It conjures spirits, turns the ocean's waters into boiling blood—things all too real for Scully, something she cannot dismiss despite her experience of doing so in the past in other similar instances. She is suddenly joined by another doctor who knows of the craft and its power and reiterates to Scully Mulder's beliefs about the object, saying that it is what theologians have searched for for thousands of years—the answer to everything. Though they have not yet made sense of it, she is stunned by the literal findings expressed by the symbols. "What little we have found," she explains, "has been staggering—passages from the Christian Bible, from pagan religions, from Ancient Sumeria...science and mysticism conjoined." They discover written in the code a description of the human genome, which Scully can only refer to as "the most beautiful work of art." Then they witness the most amazing power of the craft seen yet: it brings back to life animals that were once dead.

When she returns to the United States, she goes directly to Mulder, who is lying uncommunicative in a hospital room. Amid a thousand voices sounding off in his head, Mulder is finally able to isolate one voice—Scully's—which beckons him with intense emotion. "I want you to know where I've been... what I found," Scully whispers to him. "I think that if you know, that you could find a way to hold on. I need you to hold on." The remainder of her message to Mulder reveals that she has not only made a scientific discovery, but a discovery about herself, one that begins to help her reconcile her spiritual beliefs with her scientific grounding. "I found a key—the key—to every question that has ever been asked," she passionately whispers. "It's a puzzle...but the pieces are there for us to put together and I know that they can save you if you can just hold on," she says.

While Mulder and Scully's characters are initially presented as two whose view of the world and its possibilities are vastly different, as they come closer to making sense of their pursuit of the truth, we find that they are not separate entities. They are, rather, two sides of the same coin—the one who seeks the truth among a realm of possibilities too fantastic and beyond the realm of scientific validity; the other who must anchor herself in the certainty of scientific facts. As we approach the culminating episode of the series, we find that their duality has been shifted to synthesis—that they ultimately find the meaning to life, death, and the unknown within themselves, within each other, through the scientific discoveries that enable them to justify their search and their belief in a world of extreme possibilities that ultimately enables them to find a meaning and understanding that satisfies them both. As they come to this understanding, they speak to each other about an element that has been a most significant issue for them both in their endeavors—trust—which became paramount from the beginning of the series.

"Trust No 1"

It is unthinkable that anyone could pursue a dream so big as to find the truth without any assistance—without guidance, insider knowledge, or someone to help put the pieces of the puzzle together along the way. In this regard, those who serve this role for Mulder and Scully are of supreme importance, not only in allowing them to reach their goal, but in terms of the overall mythical construction of *The X-Files*. But as soon as Mulder and Scully realize that their journey through the pit of despair on their way to the pinnacle of the truth is fraught with potentially deadly mines, this final mantra becomes most important.

This warning to "Trust No One" (often abbreviated throughout the show as "Trust No 1") is both an admonition about the sources of knowledge Mulder and Scully rely on in their pursuit of the truth and a description of their comportment to those with whom they come into contact during the course of their investigations. This admonition is first given by a character who emerges in the second episode of the show, and whose name bears that of the episode—"Deep Throat." Deep Throat is a member of the shadow government, a player in the conspiracy to hide the truth about a number of issues regarding extraterrestrial life, biotechnology, and the like. He comes initially to Mulder and helps to provide insight on the circumstances of their investigations, his interests having splintered from his co-conspirators. And so he aids Mulder at great risk and, after only a short time, is killed when they figure out that he has been acting as a source for the man who has begun to cause them some frustration. The curious admonition to "Trust No One"— curious because this would have included people like himself (who Mulder and Scully know has intentionally deceived them on occasion)—are the last words uttered by Deep Throat to Scully as he lay dying.

But many other "Deep Throats" make themselves accessible to Mulder and Scully throughout the show, and their actions all bear the same characteristics: They are always shrouded in secrecy; they all fuel the pursuit of the truth by providing sometimes truthful, and at other times deceptive, information; they each have access to privileged knowledge; they generally appear only to Mulder and Scully either when they are beckoned by them or when the figure sees fit to warn them of an imminent danger or opportunity. Besides the original Deep Throat, two other characters most significantly fulfill this role. "Mr. X" immediately steps in to fulfill the role of the murdered Deep Throat at the end of the first season. The details of his life are shrouded in mystery and surmised only by the depth of his knowledge and his stealthy way of keeping track of the conspirators' seemingly every move. He is summoned by one of them when they tape an X on the window of one of their apartments.

Mr. X's motives and interests are as ambiguous as his character. He first introduces himself to Mulder in "The Host" with a cryptic phone call where he simply says to Mulder, "I think you should know—you have a friend at the FBI," and hangs up the phone when Mulder asks him to reveal himself. On another occasion in episode "731" he saves Mulder's life from the conspirator's assassin. Yet, he reveals to Mulder that he is Deep Throat's protégé and to him only is he loyal. After incidents such as what occur in "Wetwired," where Mr. X manipulates Mulder and Scully toward his own ends, and when Mulder realizes that he once worked for perhaps the most powerful agents of the conspirators, Mulder begins to tire of their relationship. And when, like Deep Throat before him, Mr. X is exposed by the conspirators and is summarily lured into a trap and executed, it is evident that, as his name implies, Mulder and Scully's involvement with him produced far more questions than answers.

The most formidable of Deep Throat characters ultimately becomes Mulder's personal archenemy. Only referred to as the "Cigarette Smoking Man" (CSM) throughout most of the show, he is the public face of the conspiracy run by a group known as "The Syndicate." Besides Mulder and Scully he is the only other major character present in both the first and final episodes of the show. He looms silently in the background in the first episode when Scully, is called in to the FBI director's office and given the assignment to work with agent Mulder to scientifically validate his work on the X-Files. It is his silence that speaks most loudly, establishing his character as one that Mulder and Scully will one day be forced to reckon with. From the beginning, despite his silence, we are compelled to believe that this nameless, haunting figure holds all the cards. This is made especially clear in the final scene of "The Pilot."

After their Oregon hotel room is burned to the ground, the only evidence Mulder and Scully have left is a strange implant taken from Ray Soames's (one of the abductees) naval cavity. When Scully meets with the FBI director toward the end of the episode, she conjectures that the implant is possibly a communication device that allows the aliens to track and abduct their subjects at will. She lays this evidence on the director's desk as some form of proof that Mulder's wild explanations may not be too off base. He looks at it and then dismisses Scully, who walk out of the office passing the CSM on her way out. In the final scene we see the CSM—alone, silent, walking purposefully and ominously down a long corridor, bordered on both sides by rows and rows of shelves with unmarked brown boxes. As if knowing the precise place, he stops and pulls out the drawer to one of the boxes, in which are many vials containing the same device discovered in the abductees. He takes out the metallic object found in Ray Soames's body, puts it in one of the casings and places it among the others, and then slowly turns and walks toward the exit. When he walks out of the door at the end of the hallway, he closes it then runs a keycard through a sensor, locking the door behind him. The sign on the door reads, "In case of fire or emergency, know your exits. PENTAGON evacuation procedure." A map of the Pentagon is visible as the CSM walks out of the building.

It would later be revealed to Mulder that the man believed to be his father once worked with, and came up with, the project that the CSM and his cohort of conspirators continued. Ultimately, the CSM is revealed to be Mulder's father, the result of an illicit union with his mother back during the original days of the project. And so, it is the CSM—the chief among these messenger figures—who Mulder increasingly realizes holds the keys to the real truth he searches for. Mulder's ultimate understanding of his relationship to that truth that the CSM hints at, and leads him toward and away from throughout the series, is not realized until the final episode.

The mythical significance of such characters as these is separate from their individual identities or activities throughout *The X-Files*. Their import lies in the originator of their mythical character, which is patterned after the original figure who symbolically represents their task as human mediators of the truth—Hermes, the wing-footed messenger of Zeus. This prominent player in Greek mythology is the mold from which the various messengers in *The X-Files* were created. Understanding Hermes' character and role in Greek cosmology provides the connection to, and illumination of, the task of Mr. X, the CSM, Deep Throat, and his warning to "Trust No One."

Hermes embodied both the divine and the demonic; he delivered messages from God (Zeus) to the lesser gods and to humans, the lowest of Zeus's creations. But he was also a cunning trickster and master of deception. His present significance here is illuminated by its connection to an important term directly derived from Hermes himself—hermeneutics. As Richard Palmer clearly describes,[3] the term *hermeneutics*, generally interpreted as "interpretation," follows from two Greek words that have their origin with Hermes—the noun form *hermeneia* and its verb form *hermeneuein* both of which describe the process of illumination, of bringing something hidden to the fore, making what was previously unknown and unintelligible recognizable and understood. The nuanced understanding of these two terms that Palmer provides highlights three significant roles of Hermes and therefore all who fulfill his function. The two terms signify three distinct but related tasks: to announce, say or express; to explain; and to translate.

As an announcer, Hermes articulated Zeus's message. It was a proclamation that is always already an interpretation by way of the manner and style in which the announcement was made. It was a signal to its hearers that "this is important, this is the word of God." Throughout *The X-Files* we see this function emphasized by its myriad of messengers. Without providing contextual information, they simply tell Mulder or Scully, "Hey, you will want to take note of this," or "you will want to keep your eyes on what happens with such and such a case." Their proclamations are heeded by virtue of their proximity (or at least supposed proximity) to the truth or those who possess it (making them God). But such actions as these give Scully, in particular, reason for pause; she often warns Mulder that the messenger in such cases is disingenuous, sending them off on some wild goose chase. Of course, on occasion she is right. But most of the time the messages are simply bereft of necessary interpretation that connects it to the larger picture. Thus, the more productive messages from these characters highlight the second function of Hermes, that is, the messages are not only spoken (or written, as is sometimes the case), but are explained.

In one such instance, Mulder and Scully have figured out that the government, with the aid of assylumed Nazi scientists, is engaged in a human-alien cloning project. When Mulder accidentally finds the phone number to the location where members of The Syndicate are meeting in New York City and calls it, he speaks to one of its members, who becomes a reluctant messenger. In their subsequent, and not-so-coincidental meeting, this member of the conspiracy explains the significance of his message on the telephone, as well as the cryptic set of numbers given to them by one of these scientists (ironically named Mr. Mengele) which led to their discovery of an elaborate file of tissue samplings hidden in the confines of a U.S. government hideaway.

More generally, these messenger figures fulfill the third function of Hermes, to mediate between two separate worlds. As language expresses a particular horizon or perspective, it, too, aids in translating from one to the other; the act of translation is a process that presumes explanation and understanding and, in the best of cases, works to fuse horizons, bringing the strange and alien world of others to our understanding. Hermes was credited by the Greeks with the invention of language and writing, the most fundamental and necessary tool of interpretation, translation, and understanding. Language expresses not only thoughts, but mood and emotion. Thus, the ultimate goal of translation is not to simply grammatically represent the words of one language into another, but to capture the essence of the translated language which includes these aspects of motive, desire, intention, etc., to the ultimate end that two separate worlds—that of the author and that of the reader—are joined together, to see the world from a different vantage point or perspective.

This purpose is also fulfilled by the X-File messengers. Mulder and Scully tend to cast doubt upon, criticize, and negate the actions of the government and its conspiracy with The Syndicate, for instance. Yet at times the various messengers seek to help Mulder and Scully understand their perspective that justifies their actions. On occasion they try to persuade Mulder and Scully that they are both after the same thing—the truth. From the conspirators' vantage point—given the vast knowledge they have about the purposes of the alien invaders who wish to recolonize the planet and turn humans into a race of docile slaves—their actions make sense and they try to convince Mulder and Scully of this. On at least one occasion, the CSM actually tries to get Mulder to join them, asserting that his quest would be more easily fulfilled, the truth more easily attained if he left his basement hideaway in the FBI headquarters and joined The Syndicate.

If these messengers express and proclaim knowledge from a higher intelligence, if they are agents of the truth, providing privileged information to those who seek the truth, then why the warning by one of the messengers himself—Deep Throat—to "Trust No One"? While these messengers do often lead Mulder to discovery after discovery, the meaning of this message is that despite the utility of the messengers' word, despite their access to privileged knowledge, ultimately it is the responsibility of the individual—the reader, the recipient of the message—to interpret and make sense of their

world. Though the messengers provide privileged access to truths as yet unknown or undiscovered, the admonition to not trust the messenger—and in
some cases, therefore, his or her message—deconstructs the very idea of
privileged knowledge itself and a privileged being who possesses ultimate
knowledge of the truth. Deep Throat's warning was not altogether meant to
discredit the content of the messages he and his colleagues delivered; it was
meant to remove himself and the others from the picture so as not to be a
distraction from Mulder and Scully's search for answers. If we allow ourselves to be distracted by others whom we set on a pedestal, to be revered
because of their position or the knowledge they hold, we as individuals will
ultimately be diverted from the answers themselves if they do exist and, if
they do not, we are lulled into a false sense of destiny. In either case, overre-
liance on sources outside of our own ability to synthesize our world becomes
futile. The message is essentially that expressed by Buddhist teachings in the
saying, "if you meet the Buddha on the road—kill him!" In the overall
mythic interpretation of *The X-Files* the messenger figures weave for us a
central theme—not only about the existence of truth itself, but of the means
to find it. When we begin to delve into the unknown, to lurk in the shadows
of questions that seem to lead only to more, the question of whom to trust
becomes paramount. And despite the human predilection to look for the answers to these questions among that or those who are beings other than ourselves, we are admonished to disregard the alien for the human—to look to
ourselves and those like us for the meaning of our individual and human existence. This reprivileging of the self as the source of meaning is made more
clear when we take into account the way the primary characters of *The X-
Files* deal with death and dying as a way of finding meaning and later the
relationship to the mythical alien beings in finding meaning in death.

What significance, then, do the primary symbol (X) and the three mantras have in terms of elucidating the mythic message of *The X-Files*? How to
they interpretively relate to and complement each other? If we begin with the
general construct of the unknown, the possible and synthesis (represented by
the X), and string together each of the mantras, we gain some sense of how
this interpretive structure, set forth in the beginning of the series, provides
the central theme of this message. "I want to believe" "the truth is out there,"
yet I can "trust no one" to show or explain to me what this truth is. What we
are left with is an end (truth) that must be pursued as an imperative, the question of how belief relates to that truth, and the understanding of who and how
we are to attain it. The interpretive domain of the show is articulated in its

primary symbol and mantras; the questions that remain allow the possibility of a more focused mythical message to emerge. The manner in which death, dying, and the dead are portrayed throughout *The X-Files* helps to further elaborate, contextualize, and enlighten Mulder and Scully's pursuits, as well as provide the backdrop for its prevailing message.

Death and Dying in *The X-Files*

The process of dying and the deaths of major figures in *The X-Files* play a prominent role in *The X-Files* myth, their experiences played out in both the physical and metaphysical realm. The contexts and circumstances surrounding these experiences, the personal reflections of those intimately engaged in each of them, and the dynamic ecological implications of their occurrences express a coherent perspective that connects these experiences of death, dying, and the dead with the mythical foundations discussed in the previous section. Throughout the series, the greatest insight into the psyche of the major players is revealed largely when they are confronted with their own or that of others. While many of their deepest thoughts are exposed over time in the course of dialogue and in the process of performing their work, it is this moment of death, or its probability, that seems to incite the deepest reflections and emotions. In relation to the previously describe symbol and slogans, the experience of death, in *The X-Files,* offers a more precise definition and understanding of the "truth" that Mulder and others search for; it qualifies what kind of truth exists and suggests that it is the particular form of truth that should be pursued. Additionally, death, here, provides more explicit advice about where to search for this truth.

The Truth of Origin, Justice, and Judgment

Mulder's confrontation with his own impending death provides additional insight about his beliefs, their limits, and his overall worldview that synthesizes the material and metaphysical domain in which we live. In "Anasazi," Mulder uncovers the most important piece of evidence yet in his quest for the truth. He has come into possession of a computer disk that contains the encrypted files that document the government's knowledge and cover-up of UFOs and its conspiracy with alien beings to genetically create a race of human-alien "hybrids." The leaders of this vast conspiracy desperately want to recover the disk and go to great lengths to do so, including burying Mulder alive in a desert pit where he had discovered the remains of alien beings.

When we return to this scene in "The Blessing Way," a man named Albert Hosteen, a former Navajo code talker in WWII who lived there in the desert, aided Mulder and Scully in translating what was on the stolen disk. After learning of Mulder's disappearance, Hosteen worries; in the spirit of his tradition, something only lives as long as the last person who remembers, and he fears that if Mulder is dead, the truth of what he has found will die with him.

Given the importance of his cosmology, Hosteen is comforted when his sons report to him that they found a body buried in the desert. It was, of course, Mulder who, though not yet dead, had the "smell of death" upon him. They take Mulder's body inside a hogan, where they lay him down on a bed of leaves and prepare to perform an ancient Navajo ritual—The Blessing Way—to summon the Holy People, who, according to Hosteen, are now the only ones who can save Mulder from death. But Hosteen fears that Mulder's spirit so longs to join his father (also killed by the government men in an earlier episode) that it may decide it wishes to remain there rather than return to the physical world. Mulder's spiritual dialogue with himself and other spirits during this time prepares the way for the subsequent scenes.

These "holy people" that Hosteen refers to were a gathering of departed souls, those of the most significant people in Mulder's life and his search for the truth. Two of them, Deep Throat and Mulder's father, dialogue with him in this indeterminant place between life and death. Deep Throat chimes in first as Mulder lies there staring up at the stars. Deep Throat begins by telling Mulder that the absence of time is the most startling reality about this new world of the dead that he inhabits; the absence of time denies the possibility of purposeful action and will. He urges Mulder to go back (to the world of the living), admitting to him that "there is truth here," but adding that "there is no justice or judgment." Without these two qualities, truth is a "vast, dead hollow."

With the enlightenment brought on by death, Deep Throat realizes and wants Mulder to be clear about the implications of the choice he must now make—between living or capitulating in death. There are positives and negatives to the choice, he assures him. If he goes along in death to the world Deep Throat and the other dead now inhabit, he will indeed find the truth he has been searching for all along. But to choose to pursue the truth in death means sacrificing judgment and justice. Undoubtedly this point weighs heavily upon Mulder. It would be easy for him to give in—he would have his truth. But he realizes that truth is hollow without judgment and justice—two things that can only be meted out in the realm of the living. Deep throat tries to convey to Mulder that absolute knowledge—gained in death—does not include absolute praxis; in death, one cannot utilize truth to act on the behalf of others. Though this admonition is heeded by Mulder as he returns to the land of the living, it is not until much later that he fully comes to realize the true meaning and significance of these two principles that Deep Throat has encouraged him to continue pursuing.

It is also significant when Deep Throat tells Mulder he must look to not only find this truth, but the justice and judgment that should come with it; reiterating the ancient Gnostic admonition, "know thyself," Deep Throat tries to get Mulder to understand that this truth—the most efficacious kind—lies within himself. But this advice requires some elaboration. Hosteen provides some initial clarification when he tells Mulder later that to find this truth, he must look to that "origin" that is within him. We must look outside the text of *The X-Files* to gain the significance of where Deep Throat and Hosteen tell Mulder he must focus his search for this truth that can be used as a tool for exercising righteous judgment on the behalf of others.

Jean Gebser, in his major work, *Ursprung und Gegenwart* translated into English as *The Ever-Present Origin,*[4] discusses the term "origin" as a mode of being-in-the-world, an orientation to or way of approaching it, making meaning or sense of it. Though this requires a rather complex explanation, the crux of the term "origin" as used by Gebser can be summarized in a word—synthesis. Origin as a mode of being is one of attunement: synthesis and vital awareness among and between the human and natural world, time and space, the physical and metaphysical domains, life and death. For Mulder the admonition is that the truth he seeks must necessarily intersect judgment and justice if it is to have any meaning. It means that finding this kind of truth requires that he look for it among both the living and the dead. It means that he will find it through means of science and rationality as well through the extraordinary means that belie all rational explanation. It means that he must be able to see, to be attuned with his surroundings so that he can recognize what is being communicated without the rational necessities of language and verbal articulation. The death of children, exemplified in the example in the following section, illustrates this necessary attunement, this return to origin within that allows one to recognize the need for and value of justice and judgment beyond truth, a truth that incorporates these two ideals.

The Death of Children and the Limits of Truth

The death of children seems to be particularly meaningful for Mulder. No doubt stimulated by the strange disappearance of his sister years earlier, the tragedies of children seem to weigh heavily upon him. And perhaps more than any other event experienced throughout the show, such circumstances seem both to complement his character as one willing to believe in extreme possibilities yet also to create boundaries about just how much he is willing to believe. The parts of him revealed in the light of a child's death seem to highlight that he indeed has some conviction; something he just is not willing to believe no matter the circumstance, and there are some things that, like Scully, simply must adhere to some firm rule or criteria. It is here that the earlier admonition to seek justice and judgment is realized and exemplified.

One of the best examples of this is seen when Mulder is asked to help with the case of a little girl mysteriously missing from her home in Northern California in the two-part episodes "Sein und Zeit" and "Closure." The reference to Heidegger's major work, *Being and Time*,[5] in the first instance provides a context not only for the circumstances of the episode, but demonstrates the depth of importance and emotion to which Mulder devotes to it. Mulder recalls a similar case some years earlier and seeks out the woman who, in that instance, was convicted of murdering her child when she in fact had not. When Mulder goes to the prison to question her, she reveals that she did not in fact kill her son and that she "sees things." The things she refers to are called "walk-ins," "old souls looking for new homes," as she describes them. They are children who live in "starlight" in a shadowy world where they are, nevertheless, at peace. The woman tells Mulder that his sister is among those she sees. When he asks her point blank whether Samantha (the girl from the current case) is dead, she replies only that she was taken for her own protection against things that were to befall her. But she gives him the assurance that she is alright.

The tips received from the woman, as well as other evidence, ultimately lead to a man who runs a Christmas theme park for children called "Santa's North Pole Village." When they apprehend the suspect, they suddenly take notice of the area in which they are standing and, to their amazement, stare out at what seems to be a multitude of child-size graves scattered around the property. Stunned by what he has seen, Mulder begins "Closure" with a monologue about what he has found and what more he expects to uncover in the horrific scene they have encountered as other agents are busy unearthing the graves.

They said the birds refused to sing and the thermometer fell suddenly as if God himself had his breath stolen away. No one there dared speak aloud, as much in shame as in sorrow. They uncovered the bodies one by one. The eyes of the dead were closed as if waiting for permission to open them. Were they still dreaming of ice cream and monkey bars? Of birthday cake and no future but the afternoon? Or had their innocence been taken along with their lives buried in the cold earth so long ago? These fates seemed too cruel, even for God to allow. Or are the tragic young born again when the world's not looking? I want to believe so badly; in a truth beyond our own, hidden and obscured from all but the most sensitive eyes...

Here Mulder articulates not only his sorrow at the scene surrounding him, but expresses for the first time that with truth there must be justice. The death of children in this tragic way is "too cruel even for God to allow"; it is unjust. Children embody the essence of justice, the protection of those who cannot protect or speak for themselves. Where Mulder's truth was once one of simply finding absolute answers to specific questions, this unjust act, along with the instruction given him earlier, that he must seek justice, will help him find the kind of truth that really has meaning. In the final sentence here Mulder suggests that it takes immeasurable sensitivity, an attunement to origin, oneself, the seen, and the unseen that lie around us, to see that such justice does, in fact, exist.

In the subsequent scene darkness has fallen and Mulder still stands alone in the field, all of the bodies of the children now exhumed from their graves. Suddenly, one of the children becomes visible—transparent like a ghost—and rises from the grave, followed by a host of other children who float in the air, forming a happy circle. With the weight of meaning expressed by his vision, Mulder continues his voice-over reflections:

In the endless procession of souls...in what cannot and will not be destroyed. I want to believe we are unaware of God's eternal recompense and sadness. That we cannot see His truth. That that which is born still lives and cannot be buried in the cold earth. But only waits to be born again at God's behest...where in ancient starlight we lay in repose.

Mulder's words sound like some sort of religious reflection or expression of desire. However, his desire here is not a supplication to God or an expression of the belief in immortality per se. It expresses the desire for justice. That he hopes we are "unaware of God's sadness" is not a statement of belief, but a statement of hope that some justice exists for these powerless souls, whether it come from God or someone else. The injustice suffered by these children is that their lives were snuffed out when they had not even had the chance to live. This is, in Mulder's view, the ultimate wrong that must be somehow righted.

What do we learn from these, but a few, instances of death and dying? Or better yet, what do Mulder and Scully learn that helps to shape not only their individual selves, but the course of their pursuits throughout the series? While many religions and mythic teachings reveal an extraordinary being—a primemover, creator, controller, or puppet master—on the other side of death, the instances of death and dying here in *The X-Files* represent death as a return to origin, ultimately to ourselves. Not religion or God, but we ourselves must be the arbiter of justice; we cannot entrust any other figure, be it god or another human being, to be sensitive to and act on the behalf of justice. Within and among us we find origin from which our lives have their beginning and in this same destination we return to ourselves—the ultimate significance of which is understood in a final figure in *The X-Files,* the alien beings themselves that have haunted Mulder from the beginning.

Alien Being; Being Alien

While the possibility and reality of alien life is prominent throughout in *The X-Files*, the existence of alien beings is an important symbolic aspect of its iconography. Their possibility and presence help to drive the narrative from beginning to end, but they also symbolically represent the nature of, and our orientation to, both death and the unknown by expressing aspects of our xenophobic curiosity, presenting the Other as the object of our ethical concerns, and by suggesting that our very being and identity is bound up with these beings that exist in the realm of "extreme possibility."

The very beginning of *The X-Files* presumes the possibility, and even the probability, of alien life. Mulder wants to believe alien beings exist, that we are not alone in the world—that there exists not only something other than us, but something more than us. The Other—the alien—forces a restructuring of what we know about ourselves and how we view others. Yet we see time and again that when this possibility and Mulder's expectations are actualized, his attitude toward these beings is fear and curiosity, simultaneously. When they come face-to-face with each other, he knows not whether to run for his life or stand still and silent in reverential awe.

When we refer to something or someone as being "alien," we express a sense of personal comportment vis-à-vis its being. It is strange and foreign. It inhabits a different world, literally. Yet in their existence, in many ways, we find the possibility of being—of our own individual and human existence; and this being is conditioned on the inevitability and necessity of death itself. Being—defined by Heiddeger as presence—is only meaningful, and therefore possible, by absence. But absence, too, is a form of presence. In the nothing-ness—the vast emptiness that lies in the depths of the unknown, which death ushers into existence, is the condition for the possibilities of both death and life. As Heiddeger explains, death does not exist phenomenologically; we do not have access to the one who dies, the one who can express his or her ex-perience of it. Yet, the possibilities that exist because of what we do not know about death allow us to reflect on our own individual existence within and among the soon-to-be-dead—reflections whose impetus is found in the possibility brought on by the death of the Other. Thus, our own being, apart from the lives of human beings, finds its existence in death.

In regard to Mulder's confrontation with the alien Other, we see that his curiosity about that which he is so fearful of is driven, in large part, because he sees himself in particular, and human existence in general, in the face of the alien. In "Biogenesis," Mulder finds evidence on an alien craft that con-firms his earlier suspicions that human life is, by definition, alien. Thus, un-derstanding our own being necessitates a relationship with, and reflection upon, the alien, seen as absolute Other. It is this realization that sparks a sense of the ethical dimension, that leads us to consider the nature of our re-lationship to the Other who conditions our own being both by its very exis-tence and what it provides by the certainty of its death. These considerations are much a part of the culminating lessons of *The X-Files* expressed in its final episode.

"The Truth"

The title of the final episode focuses again on the driving force of its narrative—the truth; thus, before watching it, one expects some clo-sure, that is, that the truth that has been sought for nine long seasons will be found. The significance of this final episode in *The X-Files* mythol-ogy hinges again on truth, rehabilitates the notion of the unknown and the anxieties of uncertainty, the interpretive paradoxes brought on by messengers of the truth, and sustains the desire to believe. Mulder finds his truth. Its messengers, most of whom are now dead, serve a different function. Despite Mulder's accomplishment, the truth remains "out there," and we are left with two characters who still assert their desire to believe. The way in which the primary symbol, the three slogans, the experiences of death and dying, and the figure of the alien coalesce in this final episode reveals the ultimate mythical message of the show.

The two-part episode begins with Mulder finding this illusive truth regarding the existence and purpose of alien beings. On the advice of an unknown messenger, he is taken prisoner and delivered to a secret military base where this truth exists. After he breaks away from his captors, he hurriedly scurries through the elaborate maze of tunnels and doors with one purpose in mind. He knows that this is *the* place. It is the place where the elaborate tapestry of nine years of lies was woven in the secret corridors of men without faces into an international conspiracy. It is the place where detailed documentation of elusive secrets is concealed by electronic machines whose central processing units reveal the dark knowledge encoded in secret files protected by encrypted passwords. It is the place where "the truth" resides; God, heaven, and the omniscience of immortals are there waiting for him in a dimly lit room with no indication that this is indeed the light at the end of the tunnel. Mulder finds a computer terminal, where he sits down and immediately enters the "End Game Access Code," unlocking the doorway to the slippery secrets that guard the truth. In only partial words and phrases, the computer screen reads:

> The date set for mobilization of alien forces culminates in the complete...of Civilian and Miltary...was first recorded by...Daniel M. Miller upon...-igence in Roswell, N.M., Ontact with alien forces...Military Officials are instructed. Follow emergency protoc-...-ructions. It is anticipated...-ment will be destroyed...resulting in the trans-...

The truth was out there, as had been promised and believed, and now Mulder has it. But this was only the beginning of the end, and it was quite clear that, as is customary, things are not quite what they seem. As the episode proceeds, we see the return of some of the hermetic messengers who have led Mulder to this time and place, a continued arbitration of the truth, and the tragicomic end of Mulder and Scully's nine-year quest.

Messengers in the Shadows

Though Mulder has found the truth, several of the messenger figures re-emerge from the shadows of their respective deaths. Though dead, they still have a role to play in the world of the living—a sign that Mulder and Scully's search for the truth is still not fully realized. The messages and direction they offer in this last stand have consequences not only for Mulder and others of the living, but for themselves as well. Alex Krycek, dead since "Existence," first appears to save Mulder from one of his captors. "No! You're dead," Mulder says, surprised by Krycek's ghostly, but all-too-real future. "Go," Krycek says, "There's others," he continues hastily before quickly vanishing. Mulder is confused when he turns to find Krycek has disappeared as suddenly as he appeared.

Despite Krycek's warning and assistance, Mulder is apprehended, charged with murder, and confined to a dark interrogation room where he is continually berated by military inquisitors who attempt to brainwash him, forcing him to repeat, "I'm a guilty man. I failed in every respect. I deserve the harshest punishment for my crimes." Scully and Assistant Director Walter Skinner enter his cell to discuss Mulder's predicament. After leaving, Scully returns to take one last look at Mulder. "I don't understand. Why are you helping me?" Mulder whispers to Krycek who has suddenly reappeared, but is visible only to Mulder. "Because you can't do this alone," Krycek answers before again vanishing quickly. What is the final act still left undone? Mulder's escape? The other messenger figures who come after suggest this is not all.

Mulder's subsequent murder trial begins dismally, after which he is returned to his cell, still stunned by the preceding events. "Get up!" Mulder hears from a loud voice in his cell. "Who's that? Who's there?" Mulder questions. Mr. X, dead since "The Unusual Suspects," reveals himself to Mulder and engages him in a short conversation that elaborates his and the other messengers' posthumous role:

Mulder:	What are you doing here?
Mr. X:	That's what I'm here to ask you.
Mulder:	I'm putting the truth on trial.
Mr. X:	What truth? Whose truth? Do you think these men will even hear it?
Mulder:	They're afraid to hear it.

Mr. X:	They're not afraid. They have too much power to be afraid. You're going to learn that, just like I did. You'll die learning it.
Mulder:	I'm not afraid of that.
Mr. X:	There's a truth that even you're afraid to speak now because you know it's futile.
Mulder:	No, because I refuse to accept it.
Mr. X:	Then you're going to need help.
Mulder:	How can you possibly help me?

The imperative of justice again arises; it, Mulder hopes, is the outcome of *truth's* trial. Mr. X contradicts Mulder's naïveté, warning him that the barriers to truth he has encountered are nothing compared with existing power structures that circumvent justice to satisfy their own interests. Mr. X's statement that there is a truth that even Mulder is afraid to speak suggests that Mulder does not fear the truth he has found so much as he realizes his responsibility to fight the powers-that-be toward just ends—a task that seems futile given the scope and intensity of the power that opposes it. Mr. X gives Mulder a slip of paper with the address of someone who can help him. Then, like Krycek, Mr. X vanishes.

Why these messenger figures go to the lengths they do to aid Mulder at this time is more clearly understood when looking at the actual trial that Mulder is subjected to by those whose truth he has uncovered.

The Tragedy of Truth's Trial

After Mulder has unlocked the electronic vault containing the conspirators' secrets, they insist that he suffer the most grave consequences. Under the pretense that he murdered a military officer, they arrange for a military tribunal; his "peers" at the FBI are his inquisitors and jurors. The brainwashing sessions he is made to endure prior to trial, however, demonstrate that they want to punish him for what he found and now knows, not for the murder which he supposedly committed.

The trial takes place in what can truly be called a kangaroo court. The attorney for the FBI calls no witnesses. Assistant Director Skinner has been asked by Mulder to defend him and to do so, he takes the jurors on a journey through the long and winding roads of the past nine years. They recount Mulder and Scully's findings along the way: the abduction of Mulder's sister

by aliens; the knowledge of human-alien cloning; a secret government conspiracy; Scully's abduction by the military; the failed alien invasion; the
creation of a race of "super soldiers"; the miraculous birth of Mulder and
Scully's child; the successful progeny of the aliens; and the extraterrestrial
origins of human life. These truths come flowing out like a flood from witnesses whose testimony seems to be flawless—expressions of what they have
seen to be true. Yet like the case that began it all, and all those since, when
"proof" had been gathered, there was nothing tangible the witnesses could
offer.

Mulder suspected nothing less of the trial. However, he refused to, as
Scully and others had begged him, to reveal the truth he had found on the
computer at the secret military base. For some reason, the truth seemed unspeakable, even if it was spoken to reveal the truth of the vast conspiracy.
Mulder's response to the whole charade seemed to upset the jurors (only one
of whom seemed to actually know the realities of what Mulder had found)
and influence their final verdict—death. When asked if he had any last words
before the jurors' deliberation, Mulder sat for a moment, as if still pondering
what to say and how to say it. He stands, walks closely to the jurors so that
he can look them directly in the eyes:

> If I am a guilty man, my crime is in daring to believe that truth will out and that no
> one lie can live forever. I believe it still. Much as you try to bury it, the truth is out
> there. Greater than your lies, the truth wants to be known. You will know it. It'll
> come to you as it came to me, faster than the speed of light.

With this, the pursuit of the truth, which held out so much promise at the
beginning of the series, has ended in a horrible tragedy. Despite all his successes, they simply do not believe him. He has, indeed failed in every respect, now looking back and realizing the futility of nine years of tragedy,
denial, ridicule, mortal danger, and a life given completely over to what
seems to be a figment of his own imagination. He realizes he has been condemned to death, knowing that though that death will bring absolute knowledge, it extinguishes agency. Mulder's truth—its definition now nuanced by
the concept of the kind of justice Isocrates said long ago was contingent on
practical action and fair judgment—will be destroyed with him, it seems.

Like the messengers' transformation spoken of previously, Mulder's
character at this point has also been transformed. At the beginning, many
messengers assured him that the truth was indeed out there, that he should
keep on pursuing it. Now that he has found it, it is he who becomes the

messenger to a group of men whose knowledge is not complete. Though complicit in the conspiracy, they are the left hand that does not know what the right is doing. Mulder's belief is also beginning to transform. The truth he once believed was out there he has found. It exists. He has accomplished his task. But there must be more. The truth is still "out there," he believes. In the midst of his tragedy, there is still a conflict raging as to whether Mulder's truth still relates to the future alien invasion, or something more ephemeral. He still has some thoughts to wrestle with, some demons to exorcise. The fate Mulder is condemned to does not lead to some solipsistic nihilism; he does not wallow in the hollowness of the truth he has found. Rather, it strengthens his resolve to continue his struggle for justice against all odds.

Still Believing in What's "Out There"

Mulder's truth—justice—still lingers unrealized. With the help of his friends, he escapes his prison where he awaited his execution. Against all advice to flee the country, Mulder heads to the New Mexico desert where he had been hiding out prior to this final episode. When Scully questions his actions, he replies simply, "I'm going to see a man about the truth." This puzzles Scully since he has already claimed knowledge of the truth. When they get close to their destination, Mulder stops the truck and gets out to relieve himself. He is startled by a group of old friends, an odd group of conspiracy theorists he had come to trust. They, like the other messengers spoken of, were dead, but appeared to Mulder in real form, though Mulder continues to not allow himself to believe it.

Their questioning of Mulder's new quest further complicates Mulder's realization of his final task to effect the justice now so intimately intertwined with his knowledge of the truth. His friends urge him to turn back; Mulder says he cannot. "Why risk perfect happiness, Mulder? Why risk your lives?" one of his friends asks. "Because I need to know the truth," Mulder replies. "You already know the truth," his friend vehemently counters. Acknowledging that, Mulder says, "I need to know if I can change it." His friends, always willing to go to whatever lengths—even the death they indeed suffered—to aid Mulder, are ardent that Mulder is pursuing a foolish task. "Change it?" they reply. "For crying out loud. All you're going to do is get yourself killed." This statement is significant. Imbued with the truth that death brings, they admonish Mulder about the risk involved in his quest for justice; they do not, however, ever say that it is impossible. Mulder shoulders the weight of his responsibility; his friends remind him that justice requires more risk than the search for absolute truth.

The final question—the final conflict Mulder must endure—is not about the existence of the truth, but its nature. Is it fixed, permanent, impossible to alter? Can one indeed act on the behalf of others toward just ends, or is the truth always the handmaiden of power? This question looms larger when Mulder finally finds the man he has come to the desert in search of. He climbs into a seemingly deserted and isolated Anasazi pueblo in the middle of the desert. When he walks into one room, a Native American woman sits there. She does not speak English but seems to know exactly what Mulder and Scully have come there for, whom they have come to see. She points them in the direction of a back room. When they enter, they face a figure whose back is turned to them. We know immediately who it must be, seeing the now-infamous smoke rising from the trachea implanted in his throat. He turns, and Mulder and Scully realize that, though they and everyone else thought he was dead, the CSM was there, still alive in the flesh. Mulder wants to believe that he is a ghost like the other messengers, but he is very much alive. It was he that led him to the secret government facility. It was he that led him to the truth. And it was he that provided the information of his whereabouts there in the desert, knowing that Mulder would escape and come looking for him.

Until this point, Mulder hid the realizations of his new quest from Scully, only saying that he had found the truth, but not revealing what that truth was or the implications of his knowledge. The CSM, however, is all too eager to tell Scully, as a way of mocking the seeming futility of Mulder's search. He says to Scully:

CSM: You waste your time. Ask Mulder. He knows the futility of hopes and prayers. He knows the truth now.

CSM: (to Mulder). You have told her the truth, haven't you, Fox? I helped you find it.

Mulder: You didn't help me. You sent me to that government facility knowing exactly what I'd find.

CSM: And now you refuse to speak it. Not to Scully, not to anyone. You've even refused to testify what you learned, even though it would have saved your life? You damned me for my secrets—but now you're afraid to speak the truth.

Why does Mulder protect this truth he has now found? Why is this thing he has searched for so long now so unspeakable? What is the reality behind his fears? These questions, and the CSM's statement that Mulder knows the "futility of hopes and prayers," resurrects the advice of the earlier slogan—"trust no one"—and the earlier admonitions by Deep Throat and Navajo Albert Hosteen—"the truth is within you."

The tragedy of the truth of the impending alien invasion adds weight to the responsibility one assumes to seek justice on the behalf of others. The justice Mulder seeks has consequences not only for himself but for the rest of the world. The impending tragedy is a collective tragedy, one that will affect all; it is this collective responsibility, the imperative shaped by being bound one to another by, if nothing else, a common destiny, that forces Mulder to act, to continue to seek justice after he has already ascertained absolute knowledge in this case.

After all is said and done, the truth remains, "out there." Mulder knows that there is something even greater than the knowledge that he has found—that the final alien attack and destruction of earth will take place in 2012. It is with this final conflict that the mythic significance of *The X-Files* is fully laid bare. And though it is a simple truth, the guidance it provides is rather profound. No matter how much we believe in the existence of truth—that which is the summit of all knowledge, the cure for all our uncertainties, the end of all fears—to find it means death. It is this that Scully's friends appearing to him in the desert warned him of. He had faced death before, as did they, and they knew that this was only a small danger. The real danger is in accepting the capitulating to the reality that truth's permanence brings. In the end, *The X-Files* warns of the futility of the truth. It admonishes us to live what seems to be a contradiction: to constantly pursue the truth, though attaining it will mark the end of living—the nihilism Nietzsche speaks of—which comes when there are no more adventures, no more mountains to climb or valleys to sink into because we already know what each has for us. The truth of *The X-Files* is that a life lived among all of the contradictions, uncertainties, pleasures, and pains is to be desired more than attaining divine perception.

But there is a secondary lesson as well that connects *The X-Files* myth to these truths and death itself. The conspirators find Mulder. They track him down and destroy the pueblo where he found the keeper of the truth. But Mulder and Scully escape, leaving the truth still open. Mulder and Scully retire to a hotel room, reminiscent of the one where their relationship and journey first ensued—in that small Oregon town in "The Pilot." Lying side by side in an embrace strengthened by the passions only their nine years of experience could produce, the final conflict about the truth still rages. They know the truth. But what is left for them now? Mulder's final repose is fraught with a faith that he cannot relinquish, as he reveals his innermost feelings and thoughts that the knowledge this truth brought to him:

> I want to believe that the dead are not lost to us; that they speak to us as part of something greater than us—greater than any alien force. And, if you and I are powerless now, I want to believe if we listen to what's speaking, it can give us the power to save ourselves.

Scully's simple reply: "Maybe there's hope."

In the end, Mulder's hopes, his search for the truth and the justice that must necessarily come with it, are expressed by invoking the experience of death. It is the experience of death that binds together members of the community and the world. Death and the dead are our source of appeal for truth. And it is death that imparts the imperative for the living to seek justice—to save ourselves. When others tell Mulder that "the truth is within you," they mean that it is within us—the community of the living who draw our responsibility and our necessary resolve to seek justice from the experience of death and the dead themselves.

Death is not the end. It is that truth not yet known, but because of that very fact, there remains a host of possibilities. Death does not usher into existence that perfection that absolute truth brings, for in reality, such a perfection would be worse than any hell we could imagine. The uncertainty that death brings assures us of a life beyond full of all the possibilities—the hope—that makes the lives we now lead worth living. And while this comes to us here in the mythic form of *The X-Files* saga, it seems that this reality, this need to preserve the hope that death and the dead brings, secretly lurks within us, but is seeping out in another form that we see in the following chapter.

NOTES

[1]   For more information on medicine wheels, see J. Rod Vickers (1992–93), "Medicine Wheels: A Mystery in Stone," *Alberta Past*, 8, 3, pp.6–7; Matthew Liebmann (2002), Demystifying the Big Horn Medicine Wheel, *Plains Anthropologist*, 47, 180 p. 61; and Karl H. Schlesier (2002), On the Big Horn Medicine Wheel, *Plains Anthropologist*, 47, 183, p. 387.

2   The phrase is referenced by Nietzsche. See Friedrich Nietzsche, *The Gay Science: With a Prelude in Rhymes and an Appendix of Songs,* trans. Walter Kaufman (New York: Random House, 1974).

3   Richard Palmer, *Hermeneutics: Interpretation Theory in Schleiermacher, Dilthey, Heidegger, and Gadamer* (Evanston, IL: Northwestern University Press, 1969).

4   Jean Gebser, *The Ever-Present Origin,* trans. Algis Mickunas (Athens, OH: Ohio University Press, 1985).

5   Martin Heidegger, *Being and Time* (New York: Harper, 1962).

CHAPTER EIGHT

Two Mediums, One Message
Crossing Over *and the Mass Consumption of "Contact"*

Crossing Over with John Edward (*Crossing*) presents a number of conundrums for those seeking to understand and critique its significance among the array of contemporary television programming. It is a talk show. There is a host, an immediate and mediated audience, and their interaction drives the dramatic narratives. Yet it does not conform to the traditional manner of descriptions and critiques regarding the genre. It is not confrontational, does not present any clash of moral values, and it is not explicitly political. While its content is intensely personal, and problematic in many ways, neither its host nor any other invited guests appear to provide "expert" advice per se, as on most daytime talk shows. It is not comedic, celebrity-based in its appeal, or structured in the typical interviewer-interviewee format of the shows that dominate late-night television. Despite these departures, however, it has regularly split time between daytime and late-night slots. Though its content has universal appeal, it is narrowly segmented for audiences, first appearing on the Sci-Fi Channel. However, only the human medium (the host), not the primary subject (death), can be neatly categorized as either science or fiction.

Crossing derives its significance in the vast media landscape by defying the structure, social valence, and audience appeal of the talk-show genre, making its appearance a novelty. In this case we have a human "medium" who portends to link the living with the dead; an alleged conversation between three participants (host, the dead, and the living); the exchange is communicated to copresent listeners and onlookers through an electronic medium which extends and broadens the television studio experience to remote audiences; however, it prevents them from immediate participation in the conversation at hand. Rather than discussing the generic (or nongeneric) contours of *Crossing*, my interest here is more limited and bypasses what is admittedly an important conversation surrounding how it fits in with or departs from other such shows. Thus, rather than providing a close reading of *Crossing,* as I have with programs discussed in previous chapters, I seek here to offer some general explanations about how the host of *Crossing* defies tradition, how and why audiences accept and are continually drawn to the premises and common motivations regarding connecting with the dead, and the significance of the show's influence on death attitudes in the broader American culture.

When the Medium Is Not the Message: A Brief Prolegomenon

Sometimes the medium is not the message—especially when focusing, as I do here, on the manner in which *Crossing* has and may continue to influence societal attitudes about death, dying, and the afterlife. The nature of *Crossing* sets up a contrast and intersection of media interpretations in terms of their social significance. That is, entertainment critics and the news media in general focus on John Edward, the personality of the human medium. If we, however, proceed in concert with celebrated media theorist Marshall McLuhan's thinking, the form in which the content of *Crossing* is mass-produced and electronically mediated is of utmost importance in determining the depth of its message and its scope of influence. How do we account for, and what are the implications of, the simultaneous presence of a human medium on an electronic broadcast medium? To address this question, I seek to integrate each of these media forms to better understand the connection between *Crossing* and American death attitudes in a way that highlights the significance of the audience demographics and psychology, the entertainment nature of the medium of television, while de-emphasizing (though nevertheless including) the nature of the "paranormal" aspect of John Edward's work.

In the following pages I argue first that American audiences have been primed for the acceptance of, belief in, and curiosity surrounding what is popularly referred to as paranormal phenomena. I argue that the basis for this priming lies not in the acceptance or rejection of "science," but in the failure of religion to provide the required assurance and comfort regarding the meaning and nature of death (specifically what happens after). Second, I argue that the significance of *Crossing*'s host, psychic medium John Edward, lies not in his credibility in practicing his craft, but the nature of his interpersonal interaction with members of both his immediate and mediated audience. That is, I proceed from the perspective that insofar as he influences the way in which we view death, dying, and the afterlife, the debate surrounding his clairvoyant validity is relatively irrelevant. Third, and finally, I argue that the real significance of *Crossing* is a combination of these first two arguments in concert with the nature of their expression in television as a mass medium. *Crossing* is important in that it forces the private experience and conversation about death and dying into the public domain, and that participants and viewers in the public sphere provide the much needed impetus to explore death and the validation of our fears surrounding it.

Priming the Paranormal

In most cases it is proper to describe the subject of examination before proceeding with an analysis. This process is reversed here, however. The appearance of *Crossing* in our contemporary media landscape is better understood, in my opinion, after demonstrating the clear but complex history and context in which it developed. Until my more detailed description of *Crossing,* let us proceed with the assumption that a show now exists where a psychic portends to link the living with the dead, and that it is arguably the only such show that has been widely accepted by a television audience in the history of American television programming. *Crossing*—as a phenomenon, not just a television program—did not appear overnight. It was more than two decades in the making, waiting for just the right magical mixture of solidified religious beliefs, disregard for the "truth" of scientific fact as a source of meaning regarding the experience of death, and a widespread and visceral need for validation and hope about reconnecting with those who have "passed on."

Close Encounters: Science, Skeptics, and Television

1978—neither this year, nor the preceding, conjures much in the way of collective national significance. Yet the time marks an important beginning in the still ongoing debate surrounding a host of paranormal phenomena, from ESP and various forms of psychic occurrences to UFOs and belief in alien beings. Many Americans spent their pre-1978 Christmas holiday flocking to sec Stephen Spielberg's *Close Encounters of the Third Kind* George Lucas's *Star Wars* wowed audiences early that year. In the year following, the *New York Times* conducted a formal inquiry about police departments' use of psychics to bolster crime-fighting efforts. Duke University scientist J. B. Rhine mesmerized a group at a Smithsonian Institute gathering, offering scientific support for ESP (but not communicating with the dead, as it turns out). And the Gallup Public Opinion Organization conducted its first-ever poll about Americans' belief in the paranormal. Obviously, there was heightened attention to paranormal phenomena in 1978. But why this year? Claims about the paranormal are nothing new. This date marks the first time that science began to publicly weigh in on the paranormal debate. The result: Many would begin to realize that despite the technological progress of the preceding decades, Americans' faith in scientific knowledge was far weaker than might be expected.

As previously mentioned, the term paranormal is defined vis-à-vis what is considered "normal," that is, scientifically explained and verified phenomena. Thus, the 1978 conversation, which seemed to emerge almost out of nowhere, was largely a scientific debate. But it was also a debate about media, particularly television and film. Specifically, scientists—individually or through collective organizations—cited the entertainment industry for making the paranormal a significant aspect of both fictional and nonfictional programming content, and castigated it for ignoring questions about their on-screen subjects' scientific validity. By doing so, scientists argued, television and film normalized and led to the widespread acceptance of what they saw as phenomena that were pseudoscientific at best, and patently supernatural figments of the imagination at worst. For these scientific critics and myth debunkers, there was a causal link between the nature of paranormal treatment in the media and the country's acceptance of the probability or possibility of paranormal phenomena.

1978 marked the first year that the Committee for the Scientific Investigation of Claims of the Paranormal (CSICOP) was publicly "announced" in the U.S. national news media. The group, whose notable members included the likes of Isaac Asimov, B. F. Skinner, and Carl Sagan, touched off a debate reminiscent of the ancient antagonist philosophers, with Plato on one side and the Sophists on the other. Albeit through different means, the scientists of our day claimed to know the only acceptable means of ascertaining truth. Those who claim paranormal powers were attacked for being mere artists, schooled in the methods of arousing human passions, pleasing crowds, and taking pleasure in exerting some kind of psychic mind control and influence over their followers (viewers); not to wit they profited from their services. Like Plato, members of CSICOP saw paranormal purveyors as

charismatic charlatans who exploited the public's gullibility and need to believe in the supernatural, despite having access to absolute scientific knowledge about these phenomena. Their belief and acceptance of such
phenomenal claims represented, to these scientists, a regression to a presci-
entific world where myth, magic, and fantasy were the modus operandi for
the genesis of meaning. "It's just amazing, this reversion to primitive credulity in the world's most technologically advanced country,"[1] said Paul Kurtz,
who in 1978 headed CSICOP.

Perhaps the most significant expression of scientific criticism of the public's acceptance of paranormal phenomena is seen in a 1978 Federal Communications Commission complaint filed by Kurtz and the committee against
NBC (they have continued to file such suits since their inception). Their
claim at the time: NBC's airing of the special, *Exploring the Unknown*,
which dealt with paranormal phenomena such as psychic healing and communication with the dead, failed to provide equal time under the fairness
doctrine that would allow scientists to weigh in on the phenomena being discussed in the documentary. NBC's defense, of course, was that "it's just
television, stupid," [my words]—"entertainment". The FCC, and the U.S.
Appeals Court that subsequently rejected his appeal, sided with NBC.[2] This
helped to fuel what Kurtz and the committee saw as a sinister conspiracy at
work within the broadcast community. Kurtz spoke of his organization's
frustrations, saying:

> What concerns us is the way these things are being packaged and sold like deodor-
> ants. Before the development of the electronic media, we taught analytical skills in
> the scolls [*sic* schools], we taught people how to read intelligently. Now there's this
> reversion to the spoken instead of written language. Everything is based on pure im-
> ages, pre-verbal and pre-analytical knowledge. Images instead of concepts. And,
> whenever the media deals with the paranormal, the temptation is to take a favorable
> position, even if jocularly.[3]

Kurtz's view here reverses the value given to oral rather than written speech
by Plato, who preferred oral speech because it allowed others to challenge it.
With an electronic medium, however, this possibility of challenge and open
public debate is denied—something Plato could not have anticipated. Thus,
Kurtz rightly argues (and Plato would have likely argued were he a contemporary) that unless the same opportunity for oral (and visual) communication
in the same television medium is afforded to the scientific view of paranormal phenomena, there exists virtually no avenue for public challenge or de-

bate, and therefore, what is presented is assumed by many to be reality, or at least reasonable.

On the face of it, CSICOP's arguments seemed justified given the correlations between media programming and public opinion about paranormal phenomena at the time, some of which are directly related to how we conceive of death and the nature of the afterlife. As can be seen in Figure 8.1,[4] American belief in phenomena such as UFOs, ESP, and aliens was high, reaching its peak (in respect to years prior) in 1978—accepted by the majority of the population (57 percent, 51 percent and 51 percent respectively). Though the percentage of Americans who believed in clairvoyance (24 percent) and spirits (11 percent) seems low compared with the phenomena cited above, they are still significant considering how far they exist outside the realm of scientific possibility.

But what else about 1978 is significant in this regard? Why did this come forth as such an issue of public concern for those in the scientific community then, when as far back as World War II, scientists from a variety of fields actively explored the nature and validity of paranormal phenomena (usually in connection with war strategy)? And why, after years of increasing scientific discovery and technological progress, did Americans seem to rampantly disregard the value of scientific fact and validity? One important indicator is the nature of individuals' religious beliefs and practices at the time, especially since science is often seen as being dualistically opposed to the faith on which religion is based. In Figure 8.1, we see that despite the fact that few Americans at the time actually attended church services regularly (40 percent), and fewer viewed religion as having an increased influence on American life (37 percent), the vast majority said that religion was important to them (84%). Taken as a whole, these measures of religious value are significantly lower than in most years prior. In such a climate, it is perfectly understandable that people were not so much yearning for something to believe in as they were willing to depart from traditional church doctrines and incorporate a wider array of possibilities about the nature of the universe into their worldview and entertain alternative explanations for their experiences in order to derive some meaning for their own lives. The burgeoning electronic medium of television, adding to the already existing visiocentric culture, allowed people to *see* the phenomena on which their beliefs in the paranormal were based. Such visual representations offered some modicum of proof—proof that their religious faith could not provide. This visual proof offered by television—not the need to believe—better explains the increased attitudes of

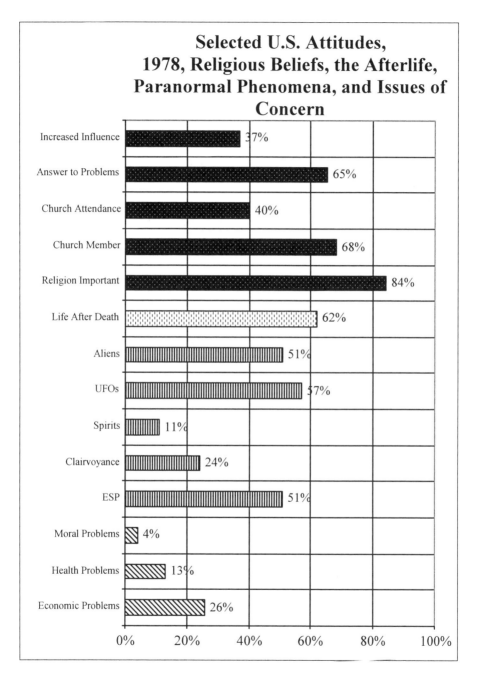

Figure 8.1. Selected U.S. attitudes (in descending order according to line pattern) regarding religious beliefs and practices, belief in the afterlife, paranormal phenomena, and cited issues of concern. Taken from collected results of Gallup Public Opinion Polls, 1978.

paranormal acceptance, not the least of which was at least tacit proof in life after death.

But there is more that helps us understand the times in which belief in the paranormal skyrocketed, touching off the debate between faith(s) and science. Religion is often our anchor when we experience extremely problematic situations. It is a place we run to for shelter, comfort, and the assurance of certainty. However, as we see again in Figure 8.1, Americans in 1978 were quite comfortable with their lives, citing few significant problems that concerned them, either nationally or on a personal level. There was no crisis of morality, no threat of death, and few were insecure about the economic situation providing any risk to their personal or collective existence. Thus, the broadening boundaries of religious belief were not the only variable that helped to bolster belief in, or at least consideration of, paranormal phenomena. Americans also had the luxury of leisure and comfort, allowing them to focus their attention away from the routine affairs of daily life. As Desmond Morris pointed out long ago,[5] when a society has the comfort of not having to devote all of its attention to survival needs, they become free to explore new and different ways of finding both pleasure and personal meaning, as well as to develop and accommodate new interests and tastes.

There was no crisis of meaning in 1978, no significant "need to believe" as the scientific community asserted was the principal cause of the public's willingness to explore the possibilities of the paranormal. They merely ignored, or refused to accept, the fact that the same science that aroused new technological possibilities could not make possible the phenomena not yet explained by science. The indulgences of time, comfort, and relative leisure provided a willingness to explore beyond scientific boundaries—the same lifestyle freedoms that allowed many Americans to become glued to the tube, revel in the wonders of entertainment, and integrate imagistic, electronic realities into their nexus of meaning. Within this cultural context and with this prevailing attitude, the paranormal possibilities of connecting the living with the dead were ready to make their way into regular television programming.

Clairvoyance as Costume

Television audiences have long satisfied their insatiable appetite for entertainment with the caricatured and controversial antics of psychics demonstrating their craft. But unlike the Ms. Cleos of the world, who have been the standard commercial television jokes for years,

John Edward is decidedly different, both with regard to his character and what he purports to do. While most television psychics have entertained audiences by giving them a glimpse of their future, Edward refers to himself as a "psychic medium"; he is a translator, a go-between, a conduit between the living and the dead, bringing the voices of past dead into the present. Those among us who have died are the focus of his retrospective gaze.

But again, this medium—Edward—is not the primary message of *Crossing*. Edward has by no means been immune from criticism and the harsh barbs of skeptics. However, unlike his predecessors (and a few who have come after), Edward has been able to sidestep the scientific validity debate that haunted previous television psychics. The result: The possibilities and curiosities of reconnecting with the dead—more affirmations of our collective desires—emerge as the central message of his show, while Edward's role and significance is diminished. This has been accomplished through the novel intersection between the two primary elements of television—its producer(s) and its audience(s); its host and genre on the one hand, and the attention it gives to desire and wish fulfillment on the other, construct and fulfill the purpose and message of *Crossing*. This is to say, the specific crafting of Edward's on-screen persona and presentation, in addition to the motivations viewers bring to their immediate or mediated experience, constructs additional purposes for the show beyond providing mere entertainment.

Host and Genre: A Different Kind of Television Talk

John Edward began exploring his connections with the dead around age fifteen. After some mentoring in his craft by another psychic colleague, he began conducting private consultations and making public stage appearances where he would relay messages to the living from those on the "other side." His success in these limited arenas sparked the opportunity for a regular television series, which the Sci-Fi Network produced and first aired in July 2000. By the first anniversary of its debut, the show's ratings had increased by 60 percent, making it the network's most successful television program to date. It was after this first-year mark that split runs of the show began airing in syndication, both on the Sci-Fi Channel and other networks in various markets throughout the country. The show filled various time slots, from late morning to prime time and late night.

As a medium and host, Edward's communication between the dead and the living is much more like the dialectic interchange between Plato and his dialogical companions than a simple one-way transmission from those in the hereafter to those still here. He does not so much as talk to the dead as he does hear and sense what they are saying. The dead initiate the conversation, and when Edward responds, it is audibly directed toward members of his audience who "validate," refute, or ignore what Edward senses and expresses. The following is typical of the interchanges that take place; this one is directed toward a woman whose father recently died:

Edward: Is there a joke between them with the celery or something?

Woman: [gasping, laughing] It's onions.

Edward: The chopping of it?

Woman: [smiling] No, they have a nickname in Italy, it means like a running onion.

Edward: So if they show me the vegetable joke, you know what it means?

Woman: [nods, grins]

Edward: He's telling me to acknowledge the wedding, do you understand this?

Woman: [begins crying and shaking] [6]

Edward sees and hears symbols or messages from the dead, interprets them, communicates them outwardly to the audience, and then waits for some member of the audience to recognize and validate the message for themselves. Usually the messages begin generally—a letter in a name, a particular moment in time, or the cause of one's death. As the received message and its target become more focused on a particular individual or group of people, the messages move from the general to the more specific, things that seemingly indicate that only one who was really in contact with the dead could know such details.

Edward has the personality and pull of a televangelist, without the hell-fire and damnation tone. A mystic humanist, he exudes the sensitivity and mild manners one would expect of an authentic psychic, but is assertive enough to convince his audience that he is speaking for the deceased; this assertiveness adds to his ethos. At times, however, he has the persona of a stern parent who demands or at least pleads with his audience members to recognize the dead and the messages they seek to communicate. His quick-tongued auctioneer style of relaying the initial revelations of these messages—"I'm seeing an E, an E, maybe an Ev, is there an Evelyn, someone in the room know the nickname Ev perhaps?—is in stark contrast to his quiet and unassuming way of calming audiences, dealing with their emotional outpourings, and way making himself the silent man in the middle.

This allows him to direct attention to those who matter most in the conversation—the living and the dead. The only time that this sensitive father figure persona seems to wane is when audience members refuse to "honor the dead" (as Edward refers to it) by ignoring and not validating their message expressed through Edward. As an example, one writer describes an example of such a situation, when Edward, focused on a single person for twenty minutes, refused the individual's nonconfirmation of the message he was receiving. "Do not not honor him," Edward said, glaring into the eyes of the man.[7] In general, Edward sublimates his personal ethos as a means of persuasion, rendering his work as seemingly nonpersuasive in intent. By doing so, he allows or asserts that he is out of the picture, that the dead is making the case, begging to be recognized by the living. An audience member's refusal to recognize is an affront not to Edward, but to the dead persons themselves—a much more persuasive message than Edward demanding people accept him.

Crossing is a genre-bender, significant beyond mere novelty among similar programs. It is dubbed science fiction—hence its network placement—because of who Edward is and what he claims to do. Yet its broadcasts have spanned the television spectrum, belying its initial audience segmentation. It draws people—most of whom are women—who do not consider themselves sci-fi fanatics; these viewers are not attracted to the plethora of other such programs aired on the Sci-Fi or other channels that air such television or film content.[8] Produced on a plain, no-frills set, talk is the central content of the show. But many of the genre staples are missing. On its regularly aired programs, average people rather than celebrities are the primary subjects (Edward does do celebrity readings that are aired as specials, or broadcast via his web site). There are no "expert" advisors to supplement interaction between the host and audience. And there is no "side" entertainment such as musical performances and the like.

What one experiences when watching *Crossing* is an unfolding drama with a virtually unpredictable outcome. The antagonist-protagonist duality is set up in the interaction between the dead and the living. The plot unfolds as more and more details from the dead are expressed, translated, and confirmed by a particular member or members of the audience. The conflict occurs within this dynamic of revelation, questioning, and confirmation, as

Edward wrestles with understanding what the dead are trying to communicate and audience members struggle to claim the message as their own. As discussed earlier, resolution is often achieved, but sometimes it is not. It is reached by an audience member's acknowledgment, internalization, and acceptance of the message they received from their dead; such confirmation being expressed either in a cathartic release of emotion or in a resolute acquiescence to the message received.

So, while *Crossing* takes on a talk show format, it provides the drama of typical primetime programming. And while its primary experience may be considered fantasy, the authenticity of the audience (they are not actors) and the unpredictability of call (from the dead) and response (by the living) resemble a reality-television program much more than some fictional sci-fi otherworldliness. So in the end, what is the significance of this genre blurring? How does it buttress not only the show's importance but also the experience of participants in and viewers of the unfolding drama played out between the living and the dead? First, the production of television talk as a dramatic experience allows for the kind of identification and suspension of disbelief of the paranormal. Second, the genre placement of *Crossing* effectively works to explode and upend the hierarchy between the fantasy-reality duality; it exploits the aftermath of the explosion of this relationship, the expansion of paranormal beliefs spoken of earlier. It refocuses our gaze and interpretation of experience. It allows us to suspend metaphysical prejudice in favor of the phenomenological experience played out on the screen. This is to say that experiencing the drama of real people whose lives and experiences of death we can identify with emerges as a paramount theme, while the science versus metaphysics/religion debate surrounding "psychic" phenomena or mediums is either muted in experience or is seen simply as irrelevant.

This becomes clearer if we consider alternative methods that could have been used to produce *Crossing*. As has been the case with former shows of this type, *Crossing* could have been constructed as a test of skill and accuracy, where the medium repeatedly tries to contact the dead of specific people who may appear on the show (the 1970s to 1980s program *That's Incredible* often displayed such examples). In this case, the focus is on the psychic themselves and the validity of their craft. It may have also been set up as a typical séance where the setting is not a television studio but a place where a particular spirit of the dead is suspected to appear or otherwise present themselves (a typical reality "haunting" program, for example). Technological devices may have been set up to "sense" the presence of such spirits as a way of confirming the dialogue taking place between them and the medium. In this case as well, participants and viewers are made to focus on whether certain expectations were or were not met, whether "contact" was indeed made. By focusing attention on audience experience and expression, highlighting the tension that unfolds in the dramatic revelation-confirmation struggle between the living and dead, and diminishing some empirical test of Edward's skill, *Crossing* is able to communicate the message that the ability to contact the dead is of relatively less importance than the desire, emotional struggle, and fulfillment that is expressed by people just like us who share the same desires and need for realization through reconnecting or knowing the possibility of reconnecting with the dead. The show and its audiences necessarily bypass "proof" altogether, and no one seems particularly compelled to address the question begging.

Beyond Belief: Bridging Desire and Fulfillment

If the luxuries of time and comfort had paved the way for the skyrocketed acceptance of the paranormal in the late seventies, the public mood of American television audiences in 2000—when *Crossing* first aired—is characterized by a more attuned belief in and concern for paranormal experiences directly related to death. As shown in Figure 8.2, levels of religious belief and participation seemed to figure little into the public's attention to such issues, such measures remaining relatively static between 1978 and 2000. As well, most Americans remained reasonably comfortable with their lives, citing few problems being of significant concern. However, belief in phenomena directly related to death, and to the purposes that John Edward seeks to accomplish as a psychic medium, was widespread. A vast majority of people expressed belief in the existence of spirits (55 percent), in ESP (part of what allows for a psychic medium to "sense" the presence of those dead spirits) (70 percent), and clairvoyance (55 percent). While belief in phenomena suggesting that the spirits of the deceased remain and can communicate or otherwise interact with the living was significantly lower than that just mentioned, more than one-quarter of the population said they believed that people can communicate with the dead (28 percent), and close to half said they believed in various forms of "hauntings" (42 percent). Additionally, in this decade prior to the airing of *Crossing,* when Americans were

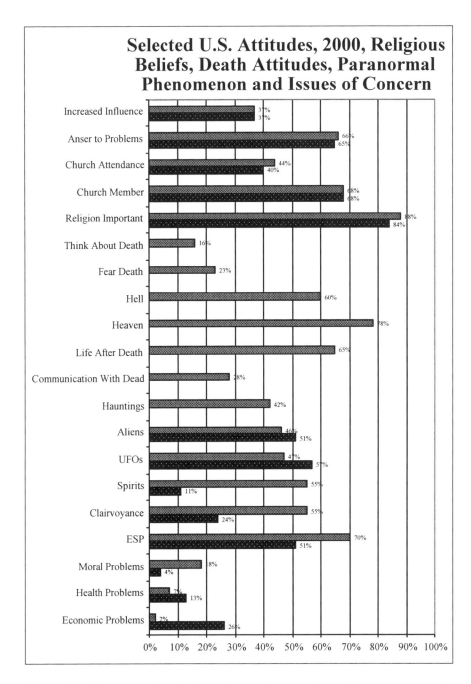

Figure 8.2. Selected attitudes (in descending order according to line pattern) regarding religious beliefs and practices, death, paranormal phenomena, and cited issues of concern. The 2000 data (bottom line) is juxtaposed with corresponding data from 1978 for comparison.

first polled about their beliefs regarding a variety of issues related to death and dying, Americans expressed overwhelming belief in life after death (65 percent), heaven (78%) and hell (60 percent). These beliefs are consistent with the belief in the paranormal cited above. Accordingly, only 23 percent said they feared death, and only 16 percent said they thought about death often or very often.

As I've asserted, John Edward as the medium and host of *Crossing* has less significance than other aspects of the show, its audiences, and the electronic medium through which it is broadcast. What, then, accounts for the extreme popularity and importance of the show in a culture highly given over to religious and paranormal beliefs, and who fear and think little about death? If all forms of belief are in some way an expression of wish fulfillment, then we have a situation where two mountain peeks separated by a great gulf, of sorts, exists. One mountain represents the heights of our desire for the personal immortality that allows us to maintain connections with the dead; the other the belief that it is indeed likely that we can communicate with them. Both of these contribute to a sense of comfort regarding the nature of death and the afterlife. So, what is missing? The actual experience— the affirmation, confirmation, verification. Like doubting Thomas, we want to "see" for ourselves the alleged nail prints in Jesus' hands. This verification is what makes the bridge between desire and belief, belief never being a complete certainty. This explanation accounts for the dual degree of belief in religious doctrine and paranormal phenomena that many religions see as blasphemous.[9] The belief expresses the desire and the possibility; the paranormal act confirms for us that our desires can be realized. And the paranormal provides the possibility that religion cannot, by virtue of its own nature as an expression of faith in the unseen, unknown, and unknowable.

The Human in the Electronic; the Private in Public

By far, the most significant aspect of *Crossing,* in terms of its influence on societal attitudes about death and dying, is the medium in which Edward's work is produced and communicated. Precisely by de-emphasizing the role of the psychic and the paranormal and emphasizing the emotions and discourse of real participants, *Crossing* is able to exact a greater influence by relocating and projecting private experience and expression from the private sphere to the public. The program is as much a rhetorical act as it is a form of entertainment. The very idea regarding the privacy of death is challenged by relocating and refashioning the space of talk about the dead from the consultation room to a studio audience, and beyond to a larger broadcast audience. It sanctions and revalues the expression of grief and emotion in the public domain and thereby contributes to media's role in renewing death as a public spectacle.

Without traversing the contours of the scholarly debate about the public sphere, I will suffice to state my agreement with Richard Sennett's view of what defines the "public" and the public sphere, which he originally set forth in *The Fall of Public Man.* Accordingly, the public sphere is seen as a realm inclusive of all members of a population; in which individuals have access to the emotional and spiritual—as well as rational—contents of others' person through social interaction; where such interaction is cosmopolitan in nature in that it exposes us to difference and uncertainty; and the consequences of which enhances both the individual and the collective.[10] The private sphere does not negate the public, and those who conceal certain aspects of their lives do not necessarily refuse to pay homage to, or in some way participate in, the public sphere. Rather, the sense of privacy merely extracts from the public sphere those things which it believes are better suited for discussion or participation by a limited field consisting primarily of one's own family and close friends. In particular, issues of spirituality, emotion, and belief have come to be seen as the domain of the private, as individuals seek to control what are seen as explosive issues and expressions that are a matter of individual (primarily psychological) concern. The uncertainty that comes with the social interaction among strangers in the public arena is seen as not being viable for enhancing or controlling such "personal" matters which demand emotional stasis. This idea about the domain of private experience is challenged by the very existence of *Crossing* and the particular way in which it is produced.

Consultation Room to TV Screen

Traditionally, both settings for talk germane to *Crossing*—"psychic advice" and grief counseling—take place in what we might generally refer to as a consultation room. The structural difference between the consultation room and the studio makes it possible to traverse the private sphere in which death discourse most often occurs. There are five characteristics of the consultation room that shape not only what occurs there but also the manner in which it occurs. It is a 1) closed space 2) that delimits the number of participants to few people (generally two; client-provider), 3) ensuring privacy and confidentiality, and 4) thereby creating an atmosphere conducive for the most personal of expression and 5) encouraging one's return so that personal development and progress can be monitored. The professional consultation setting often places a client in contact with someone available to the public, that is, one not among one's immediate circle of family and friends. However, the practice of consultation assumes that the provider becomes a member of the client's world rather than vice versa. The provider assumes the role of trust, where the primary goal is to meet clients' expectations. Therefore, providers guarantee that what happens in the consultation room does not leave it. When one goes to such a place to engage with such a person in matters dealing with death and dying—whether a psychic or grief counselor—the setting reinforces the traditional notion that such talk is, by definition, appropriate only within the private sphere.

The function of John Edward on *Crossing* is much the same as the private consultant or counselor. More than trying to show off his psychic skills, he attempts to provide comfort to those grieving and who have unresolved issues with dead loved ones. He seeks to provide a forum in which such issues can be resolved. However, the immediate audience in a studio setting offers a very different kind of process and possibility for doing so. First, in the studio there is no expectation of privacy. Second, the number of participants and onlookers is multiplied. Third, it creates an atmosphere of tension rather than comfort. Fourth, and because of the other three, the role of the expert is diminished, while client issues are resolved, or at least addressed, through interaction with peers. Those who fill *Crossing*'s studio audience make a conscious choice to work out some of their unresolved issues and grief with and among others beyond the person providing expert guidance. Tensions run high not only because each participant is reeling with expectations of making their own contact with the dead—only a few of which will be realized—but because each are vulnerable and exposed. When one of the many participants does make contact, they are forced to reveal to Edward and other participants the circumstances of the deceased's death and the nature of their relationship with them. They are open to the private, but nonetheless real, scrutiny by others in the audience about such circumstances. Often, such circumstances are those that might be readily shared with others in any situation. However, there are times when participants making contact must admit that they shared a source of ongoing conflict with the deceased, that they themselves contributed in some way to their loved one's death, or that their deaths were by unnatural (and sometimes unsavory) causes such as a suicide, murder, or accident in which they were the cause of another's death as well as their own—issues not generally discussed publicly in the company of strangers.

Participants in such an audience expose themselves by invoking a common association with the others, suggesting that they, like them, have not just lost someone to death as we all have, but that they harbor a particular need to renew some connection with the dead. They expose the depth of their emotional pain, satisfaction, and comfort by knowingly putting themselves in a situation where those emotions may be unexpectedly tapped and expressed in ways that cannot always be controlled. Like a person may fly into uncontrollable fits of crying and vocal expression upon seeing the body of a deceased loved one at a funeral, "contact" and the revelation and resolutions that result often push emotional buttons in much the same way. And such expression cannot always be anticipated or contained. Nevertheless, such actions, though potentially "embarrassing" or painful for some and generally eschewed in other public arenas, provide some form of resolution not only for themselves, but other audience members present.

The fulfillment of studio audience members' desire to connect with the dead is, in the end, somewhat of a cross between an enlarged group therapy session and a religious revival; twelve steps are reduced to one, and the Big Blue Book is exchanged for a remote control. In the group therapy session, participants' problems are worked out not through the expertise of the group leader primarily; each participant expresses his or her own experience as a way of providing empathy and comfort to others. In a revival, or any religious service for that matter, the desire that sustains faith and belief is heightened, verified, and encouraged not by some magical display where God lays out all his cards, revealing the certain fact and nature of our immortality; this is accomplished through the mutual persuasion that takes place between those who want to believe.

I am not saying it amounts to some sort of group hysteria. But even if it did, it would still be consistent with the same point I am trying to make here: the significance of *Crossing* has almost nothing to do with whether or not people indeed connect with the dead, or whether Edward helps them to do so; it has everything to do with the nature of the audience and the forum it provides for mutual discussion, experience, and reflection about death, dying, the dead, and the nature of the afterlife. *Crossing* offers opportunities for its immediate and remote audiences beyond our individual and collective desire for confirmation of personal immortality verified in communication with the dead, beyond employing tools of dramatic narrative to evoke audience identification, personal reflection, and emotional catharsis. The most important aspect of *Crossing* in terms of its collective significance in challenging and reshaping our attitudes and way of discussing death in American culture lies in the message of the technological medium, the implications of broadcasting such material in a way that invites and fulfills these various desires.

Private Pain, Public Grief, and the Renewal of Spectacle

There are two audiences, of course, involved in the production of *Crossing*—those in the studio and the millions more who view the broadcast event on their television screens. While the immediate and mediated audiences share some of the same experience, those who are part of one have a different set of expectations for participating, different interests, and different results. Those present in *Crossing*'s studio audience come with expectations and hopes of making contact. They are not guaranteed the experience, however, from Edward or the network. Thus, much of their expectations are necessarily transformed from a participant and pseudo-client to a spectator. Television viewers, however, by virtue of their remote location, are by definition only spectators. They tune in to watch the drama unfold. But their interest and identification with the drama of *Crossing* is deeper than that of, say, the *Jerry Springer Show*. They do not watch in hopes that they will make contact with someone they know; they watch because they, too, seek confirmation, to some degree—not of their own experience, but of the possibilities. Viewers identify with the immediate audience in terms of their underlying needs and desire for fulfillment, but their experience is to *see*—to see whether Edward is "for real," to see whether others can make contact, to see how they react. They want to see the audience, to experience as much as possible their encounters.

Much of *Crossing*'s success belies the nature of the medium in which it is broadcast, however. There is actually little to see. There are no graphic images of the dead making contact. Edward's unassuming manner is of little visual interest, as he does not devolve into primitive exorcist-like convulsions when doing what he does—something we might find entertaining while watching a horror movie or televangelist healing service. One cannot see the dead. So much of the broadcast content is audio in nature, which begs the question why one would choose to "watch" and why broadcasters would choose to use television as the particular medium of communication. It might seem more logical that radio might be a more efficient and appropriate tool. The object of focus for viewers is not Edward, not the dead; it is in hearing what is going on among participants and, more important, seeing people who by all accounts are just like them.

Conclusion

As I now write, *Crossing* is concluding what will be its final season of new episodes, the Sci-Fi Channel having recently announced the show's cancellation. Plummeting ratings no doubt figured prominently in the network's decision. However, the number of variables involved and the relatively short time it has been since the decision was made make it difficult to say just why audiences have decreasingly tuned in. Notwithstanding, the cancellation does not diminish, in my opinion, the significance the show has had over its four-year run. *Crossing* gave us more than the opportunity to witness and evaluate psychic skills involved in trying to communicate with the dead. It has provided a mirror that allows us a clearer reflection of our collective struggle to cope with the circumstances of death and dying. It has provided a barometer measuring how far we have come in recent decades in terms of our attitudes about such issues and our willingness to discuss them in public forums through television and other forms of popular entertainment. In keeping with my earlier premise, *Crossing* gives us a better understanding not of psychics and psychic phenomena, but of who we are.

First, it has demonstrated the incongruent manner in which we view and cling to both science and faith to understand the nature of life, death, and the hereafter. The logic and fundamental principles of empirical science and premodern religious faith are diametrically opposed. Americans' continued belief in, or entertainment of, the paranormal possibilities of communicating with the dead demonstrates the way in which we are changing the contours of each of these arenas to fulfill our own desires. Science and religious doctrine decreasingly dictate to us what we do, what we should do, and who we are. Rather, we are approaching science and faith like a hungry man at a buffet. The traditional prescriptions of science and religion have left us unsatisfied and unfulfilled. Science has rejected the possibility, or at least diminished the probability, of life after death, much less the human ability to communicate with the dead. Religion, on the other hand, insists that we ac-

cept through faith the certainty of personal immortality, while also suggesting that we must wait until some future time to be reunited with our deceased
loved ones. Neither of these approaches seems to allay our curiosities about
the nature of our own fate after death or our desire to connect with those who
have gone on before us. So, while science crushes our hopes by demytholo-
gizing immortality, and religion offers certainty without proof, we as a society continue to blur and extend the boundaries of both in order to find some
modicum of satisfaction, some way of deriving meaning about our own lives
by exploring the possibility that we do live after we die and that in either life
or death we can or will be able to reconnect with the dead.

Second, by exploring the contours of science and faith, desire and fulfillment in the collective forum of a studio audience, *Crossing* has demonstrated the need not only for individual affirmation that contact with the dead
provides, but also the need for human beings to connect with others who are
living. It suggests that contact with others with whom we identify, with those
who share similar questions, fears, desires, and other attitudes associated
with death and dying, is necessary if we are to assuage such fears and find
meaning and fulfillment in death. It asserts that being in the company of others provides greater satisfaction in dealing with grief and loss than the consultation room, where such issues are worked out alone or in the privacy of
religious spaces, the offices of grief counselors, or the quaint living rooms of
psychics. Connecting with others is, in essence, one way of connecting with
the dead, or at least of quelling our fears associated with death itself.

Third, and most important, the projection of these issues in an electronic
broadcast medium asserts that questions surrounding death and dying—never
mind the psychic sideshow—are not only appropriate, but a necessary discussion that should take place within the public sphere. The production and
airing of *Crossing* helps to renew the spectacle of death in American culture,
in the most positive of ways. It challenges the traditional private domain in
which such issues have typically been discussed. It suggests that there is
profit—both commercially, emotionally, and socially—in airing what has
been seen as "dirty laundry" in public. It demonstrates that the grief, pain,
and desires we have about death and the dead can be dealt with in a medium
and manner conducive to entertainment, while at the same time not diminishing the seriousness and gravity of such attitudes and experiences. In fact, it
suggests that dealing with such issues in a public forum increases and intensifies public discourse and debate by making us more aware of our collective
attitudes, needs, and desires and offering public and collective ways of aiding

fellow citizens in becoming more comfortable in dealing with death and dying.

NOTES

[1]   Michael Kernan, June 11, 1978. The Washington Post. "God's Chariot! Science Looks at the New Occult. The New Credulity: A Quest for Meaning and Purpose in Life." Style, F1.

[2]   Committee for Scientific Investigation of Claims of Paranormal v. FCC 198 U.S. App. D.C. 91, 612 F. 2d 586 (1980). The case was rejected, with no formal opinion being offered.

[3]   Ibid.

[4]   Because of the sporadic nature in which these measures of public opinion were taken (that is, not in regular intervals across time), my attempt was to show time-series data for decades, as I did when analyzing death in television programs in chapter 1. Accordingly, decade designations in the chart are not exact year designations for when these surveys took place. The date of survey in each case, if not in the exact year, took place either a year prior to or after the decade designation. Additionally, several items in the chart are not linearly connected because of missing data in intervening years and because some lines connect only two points. In the former case, two separate markers are plotted separately, and in the latter, they are connected by a line between the two years in which survey data was available.

[5]   Desmond Morris, *The Human Zoo* (New York: McGraw-Hill, 1969).

[6]   Chris Ballard, "Oprah of the Other Side." New York Times, July 29, 2001. Section 6, Column 1, Magazine Desk, p. 38.

[7]   Ibid.

[8]   As an example, more people, and those of very different demographics, watch *Crossing* than the USA Network's (owned by the same company as the Sci-Fi Channel) *The Dead Zone,* a fictional series that in many ways mirrors the psychic communication with the dead claimed by Edward.

[9]   That is, while most religions offer some aspect of supernatural experience, those emanating from sources other than one divine entity are often castigated as devilish.

[10]   Richard Sennett, *The Fall of Public Man* (New York: Random House, 1976). See particularly chapters 1, 2, and 13.

CHAPTER NINE

Digital Media Meets Death Culture

The Impact of Time, Space, and Vision

Technology has increasingly become the new god of modern life, exercising its controlling grip on virtually every facet of human existence. This comes as no surprise. But if technology has so transformed our attitudes and ways of living, how might its intrusion into the largely private sphere of death influence and alter our attitudes regarding, and practices surrounding, the experience of death itself? In chapter 3 I argued that the advent of *Six Feet Under* marked a defining break with traditional ways of representing death and dying in television programming. The creation and growth of *Forever Enterprises, Inc.*, marks a similar disruption in regards to the technological mediation of death attitudes and practices. The use of communication technologies within the domain of death is recent.[1] However, the technological transformations well documented in other spheres of life, and the contemporary manner in which these technologies are being offered and utilized by *Forever Enterprises, Inc.* provide a useful foundation and framework for speculating about the influence technology may have on future ways of thinking about, and dealing with, the experience of death in American culture.

The purpose of this and the following chapter is twofold: to describe and analyze the specific manner in which innovations in technological use shape the way we think about, orient ourselves toward, and otherwise interact with each other given the experience and prospects of death and dying; and to speculate more generally about the implications the use of technology in this realm may have on the future of American death culture. What follows is a necessary, two-pronged introduction. The first includes a description of the origins and services offered by *Forever Enterprises, Inc.* (FEI) highlighting the various technological objects utilized in their business enterprise and by its clients. This focuses on the following primary technologies: video, digital storage, and computer networks that enable webcasting and the development of interactive virtual communities. The second portion of the introduction focuses on the way these technologies have impacted general areas of daily life and provides a brief description of the specific terrain of death attitudes and practices I deal with. Each of these two components supply a foundation for my remaining analyses regarding the implications of technology for the future of American death culture.

My analyses are similarly divided into two separate areas. The first area deals with what I call the empirical domain, and deals with the temporal, spatial, and visual implications of technology on death attitudes and practices. The second area focuses on what I call the social realm of influence and includes critiques of the theatrical, relational, political, and commercial implications of technology used in the sphere of death and dying. The first section is included in this chapter, while the second is the topic of discussion in the following.

Old Tools, New Trade: The Story of Forever Enterprises, Inc.

For more than a century, the Hollywood Forever Cemetery was the resting place of the stars. Celebrities and other film industry luminaries made this entertainingly hallowed ground—fittingly situated adjacent to Paramount Studios—their eternal resting place. They lie there dead, but their memories persist in the litany of entertainment programs they have collectively produced and/or starred in. But after years of mismanagement and misuse, the glitz and glamour that surrounded their final repose were overshadowed by decayed mausoleums, overgrown vegetation, and the perilous absence of care. But Tyler Cassity saw more than a collection of fallen stars lying in sunken graves on an abandoned estate when he stepped onto the grounds in 1990. He came there with a vision: not just to restore the former glory of Hollywood's celebrities, but to provide all who wished the opportunity of a lifetime—in death, that is. His desire was to trump Andy Warhol's promise of fifteen minutes with an opportunity for fame that will linger in perpetuity. Thus, FEI was born to bring eternal stardom to the masses.

The late nineteenth century brought us the professionalization and incorporation of the funeral industry as we know it. Its promise of symbolic immortality through embalming technologies that preserve the physical body represents the single technological innovation in over a century, in an industry that has been as standardized and stagnate as death itself. It took Tyler Cassity—a product of this dying industry and witness to a host of HIV deaths shrouded in New York City's own atmosphere of entertainment and reckless abandon—to recognize that the promise of immortality lay less in the preservation of the human body than in the more ephemeral and immaterial realm of personal and collective memory. What better way to incite the possibility for eternal recognition than to put to use the array of new communication technologies long diffused into everyday life? Better technologies made it possible for us to grasp the very concept of "forever" with advances in scientific knowledge; it seemed reasonable that only the newest technologies themselves could project human images and their memory to the limits of this "forever" as we know it. With these ideas in mind, the stated mission of FEI is to transform not only the landscape of death, memory, and memorialization, but to extend the possibilities of personal immortality through personal, theatrically produced narrative and enhanced access and communication aided by several well-known technologies.

Video

The hallmark of FEI's innovative services its their use of video production technologies. This allows clients—with the aid of the company's production specialists—to produce a self-styled documentary of their lives, or that of their deceased family members. With all of the accoutrements afforded any commercial video producer, clients are able to concoct an audiovisual narrative of their life in their own words, and in virtually any manner they see fit. They impart to their clients themselves prior to their own deaths, or their family members and friends following, the ability to create a set of visual images that can be viewed over and over at any moment—an audiovisual collage replete with childhood photographs, clips from home movies capturing life's most significant moments, personal audiovisual musings expressed by family and friends, theme music, and third-party narrations.

These productions are available for viewing not just by and for those who produce them. The documentaries, or *Life Stories*[TM], as FEI dubs them, are viewed on large screens in their "Forever Theater" and on smaller screens at multimedia kiosks located throughout the cemetery. The dead who lie lifeless beneath six feet of earth and a concrete tombstone signifying only the empirical fact of birth and death live; their bodies are seen and voices heard by all who care to pass by and simply press a button. They live, move, and have their being, sharing the same screen space with Jayne Mansfield,

Cecil B. DeMille, Marilyn Monroe, and countless other recognizable celebrities of yesteryear there laid to rest.

Digital Storage and Documentation

The use of video production technologies of course integrates the ability for recording and preservation of audiovisual material. For additional ease of access, and increased probability for collective viewing by individuals among the general public, FEI complements these analog video recordings with digitally encoded visual images and sound for computer archiving. The collection of each individually produced LifeStory is accessed through what FEI describes as a *Library of Lives*. The metaphor generally holds. It is a collection, accessed digitally through a computer terminal located in cyberspace at a particular domain. Like physical library collections digitally transferred, individual video narratives in the collection are accessed via a customized search engine that allows one to look for a person under a given name, or browse the entire collection by date of death, their physical burial location, or by the specific form of media used in a given individual's record. This may include text only or a variable combination of text, photographic images, oral narrative, and, of course, the video itself.

The search mechanism includes a variable two-or-three-step process for accessing any given digital record. The two-step process begins with the top window, culminates with a bottom, and privileges the user who comes to the site looking for someone specifically. The three-step process for the browser progresses from the top window's name search, to a detailed "media" search in the middle window, and concludes with the bottom window. In addition to privileging the browser, the description of the advanced search mechanism as a "media" search allows the browser to choose how they wish to experience the LifeStory they wish to access; they can choose separately to either read text, view visual images, or listen to audio, or integrate them in any combination.

Computer Networks

Time and distance are in today's world a significant obstacle to attending the funeral of a loved one or friend. FEI offers to diminish this barrier by wiring its funeral chapels for worldwide webcasting of funerals and other memorial events. This service is made possible for the provider through the use of a variety of computer hardware, including a live video source such as a video camera, a content distribution server that allows simultaneous access to computer network content for a large number of potential users, an encoding station that translates analog signals into digital, binary code, and a Web server that fetches particular Web content from a given server. Accessing and using the service requires only an Internet-connected computer terminal and streaming audio-video software. These are the basic, general necessities involved in webcasting.

While the required hardware and software needed to provide, access, and use this service is important, the most substantive aspect of this process, in terms of my specific purposes here, is how such a service influences the actual experience of participating in a funeral as a ritual practice. In order to better comprehend this, we must understand the variety of more specific network protocols that have a significant bearing on what a provider such as FEI is able to provide, and how the client or groups of clients access and use the service. This is to say, while I am most interested in what an individual user produces or receives, the parameters of the technology itself are an integral factor. A further discussion of such protocols is provided in the following chapter devoted to the relational implications of experiencing a webcasted funeral.

Aside from this service, FEI also makes use of computer networks to create and sustain a virtual community, of sorts. This community works in concert with the aforementioned LifeStories products stored online in FEI's Library of Lives. The site is rather rudimentary in that it simply allows visitors to post and send textual messages in response to particular audiovisual memorials accessed and viewed in the online environment. The postings are accessible to anyone who pulls up a given LifeStory; however, the nature of this memorial community is interactively restricted, in large part, to simple access. Users are limited in their ability to contact or otherwise connect with other "posters," be they family members or simply other browsers, insofar as posters may remain anonymous by withholding their e-mail addresses from view by others. Additionally, there is little evidence that the same activities and interactions that take place in a more formal virtual community environment, such as the *Six Feet Under* fan community discussed previously, occur here. So, while multiple users may access the site, view a particular LifeStory, and post a response that is accessible to any future user, there seems to be little possibility or practice of response or real-time interaction (this, however, does not preclude the possibility that the site could be made more interactive).

Funeral Home to Death Complex

FEI is more a high-tech death complex than funeral home; technological systems pervade all of the services they provide. That is, it is "hardwired" into its physical, architectural structure and produces an environment so completely different from traditional funeral and burial settings. It is beyond cutting-edge; it has pushed the process of death and burial on to a completely different plane. Those accustomed to participating in funerals and other forms of death rituals realize that such practices are not reducible simply to a collection of products that one provides or receives. The funeral or memorial experience is as much about cultivating a particular environment for the particular event(s) that are to take place. The traditional funeral "home" is, as its designation describes, domestic—a *private* place of family dwelling. Much more than a house, the idea of home expresses and cultivates an atmosphere of familiarity, insulation, intimacy, and ease of interaction.

The funeral home with which we are most familiar seeks to re-create this atmosphere for families who are "out of place" by the experience of death. Funeral directors seek to make their clients "at home" by controlling what is done there, that is, what kinds of activities are customary and appropriate to the physical site itself. Providing maximum comfort to grief-stricken and anxiety-ridden families generally translates into an environment virtually devoid of emotional expression, where people are shielded from the prying eyes of the public or other problems that may arise.[2] Some even go as far as to re-create a particular home environment for families, where a visitation or funeral service might take place among mom's familiar kitchen, or where mourners greet each other from couches reminiscent of the place where conversations with their loved one once took place.[3]

The "death complex" that describes the physical setting and manufactured environment of FEI is altogether different. A complex is an intricate connection of parts that privilege in importance and visibility the whole, rather than the separate entities of which it is comprised. When one passes by a complex—be it a sporting, entertainment, commercial, or other enterprise—what one focuses on is its enormity, its physical size, and the breadth of its reach in the services and activities it provides, what is offered there. It is quintessentially public; it invites the possibility of excitement, a different kind of experience. It stands out from its physical surroundings rather than blending in with an air of normalcy. When we venture inside we find that there is something there for everyone. It is a place that accommodates different kinds of activities, or the same activities are played out in different ways.

We can choose to participate in a single event or activity or all of them; we can mix and match, or spring for the package deal. Whatever the arrangement, the complex is a place that breeds excitement, wonder, spectacle, and unbounded interaction—in a word, entertainment.

In addition to all of the traditional mortuary services—from embalming to funeral transportation to cremation, in addition to the technological apparatus embedded in every aspect of the physical environment—from the Web-wired chapel to the Forever Theater, and the bundles of circuitry and computer chips that animate the cemetery media kiosks—FEI integrates public and private, life and death, isolation and interaction, tradition and innovation through the integration of solemn ritual and stirring entertainment. It is a venues, rather than a simple place where this integration takes place. One could, at a single FEI complex, have a private family viewing, share in a funeral webcasted to participating friends and family overseas, during which they view the video memorial produced by FEI and the family. They could then walk through the cemetery in anticipation of their loved one's burial, stop along the way to get a "living" picture of those with whom their loved one will be surrounded in death. A week or so later, if one cares to return to visit the grave site, they may as well sit comfortably in the Forever theater and catch a glimpse of the life and death of a stranger, while visiting their own loved one's grave. While there they might avail themselves of one of the movie screenings being held there that week, then retire to a blanket for conversation with strangers while taking in a celebrity jazz concert on the cemetery grounds or, perhaps, a theatrical performance or poetry reading—whatever featured public event of the week and might catch one's eye.

One might also participate in its annual Dia de los Muertos (Day of the Dead) celebration, an ancient Aztec ritual that represents a communion between the living and the dead, celebrated in California exclusively on the Hollywood Forever cemetery grounds. Day of the Dead "mocks" death and continues to be one of the most important celebrations in Hispanic culture. An unparalleled feast for the senses, the celebration is known for elaborate costumes, ornate altars, savory foods, and performances of all kinds. "The tradition reminds us that death is as natural as life, and that remembering a loved one does not necessarily need be a somber experience," cemetery operators add about the celebration, which includes a variety of other live performances, as well as local artisans, food vendors, and traditional altars made of everything from flowers and photographs to candy and candles.

Again, the technologies used by FEI are not new; the manner in which the company uses them are, as well as the physical environment transformed by such technologies. In order to speculate about the ramifications such use may have on specific death attitudes and practices, some cues must be taken from the impact technology has heretofore had on our culture in general. Outlining more specifically what I mean when I talk about "death culture" is also necessary.

Intersecting Spheres of Influence

The various spatial and temporal dimensions of our culture are integrally related to the way we utilize and experience various forms of technology. Our attitudes and practices regarding death and dying— death culture—are one expression of these various spheres of experience.

Time, Space, and the Technological Sphere

It is almost cliché at this point to indicate that technology has infiltrated every facet of everyday life. Siegfried Giedion's[4] concept of anonymous history traces the complex of technological developments that are so implicit in mundane social life that they exist virtually unnoticed; our progressive reliance on them has rendered them invisible and has turned them into an essential given of human functioning. Giedion's contribution to understanding "old" technologies and technological systems is complemented by that of Lewis Mumford, Marshall McLuhan, Jean Gebser, and a host of other scholars in the last century, each of whom begins from the same premise: that technologies do not simply provide us with new tools to accomplish specific instrumental tasks; their implementation and use by human beings reshapes our value of the tools themselves, as well as our whole perspective of reality and norms of individual and social conduct. It influences epistemological, moral, and social values and refocuses the gaze on particular areas of social life. The cyborgs of science fiction are only fictive in their empirical reality; their theoretical veracity, however, correctly describes the relationship between technological machines and human conduct. Technologies become so naturalized in their use that they not only direct our bodily movements and sensory faculties; they create and dynamically alter the boundaries within which we can operate.

Contemporary scholarship on "old" technologies assumes the notion of anonymous history, and my analysis of what is now commonly referred to as "new media" proceeds with the same goal: to render transparent the way that technological objects influence human action and social interaction, specifically regarding our attitudes and practices surrounding death and dying. In the following paragraphs I begin this analysis by outlining the spatial and temporal shifts affected by relatively new technological media in our general cultural environment, as a basis for my remaining discussion about the connection between technology and death culture.

Technology has transformed the way in which we conceive of and live both time and space; such transformations express themselves in, among other things, the cultivation of specific objects of desire (and fulfillment), shifting norms of social interactions, and the revaluing of values. Technological time has virtually blurred the line between the world of work and leisure, cultivated a general sense of temporal anxiety, and shifted our orientation toward how we view the past, present, and future. Faxes, e-mail, cell phones, and the like have created an environment in which twenty-four-hour, non-localized communication is possible. Like previous "time-saving" technologies, however, these technologies have simply rendered the possibility of such communication a necessity. Any longtime user of cell phones, for example, has had this experience. The cell phone allows us to make use of what was previously "dead time" in terms of work. The ability to accomplish work-related communications during a morning commute should theoretically decrease the amount of time needed to accomplish them. However, cell phone users often find that one is essentially always at work; they are always available, always capable of accomplishing work-related tasks, and consequently, always expected to do so. As Robert Levine and others[5] have demonstrated, new technologies that allow for greater time efficiency have created a situation in which we are time-anxious, that is, always chasing time, feeling like there is always something more to be done, and that we should be doing it. Americans work now more than ever before, despite the proliferation of time-saving technologies.

More generally, temporal aspects of technological use have focused our temporal orientation to privilege the present. The past we cannot change, and the future we cannot control. In such an environment, our need to fill "now" time is significantly increased such that it becomes a compulsion. The consequence of such a restricted time orientation is that it limits our ability and desire to reflect on the future consequences of present actions. It creates the illusion that if I fail to act now I will miss out on something; but if I do something now and it turns out poorly, I can always deal with that later, when it actually happens. So, along with the blurring of work and leisure, and the diminishment of "spare" time, the temporal orientation effected by new technologies necessarily constricts our sense of both ethics and our deliberative judgment about how to institute the "collective good." We only have to look at the current political election cycle for an example of this, where debates about tax cuts, outsourcing, and international relations are all framed by immediate solutions with little regard for future consequences.

The spatial environment in which we live has also worked to privilege work over leisure, and, in addition, has reconfigured the balance of private and public space. It limits our range of motion and overlays the values of economy and efficiency onto our norms of social interaction. Leisure space has consistently diminished, rendering the majority of social space as work space. This has the added attribute of diminishing public as opposed to private space. The spatial restrictions afforded by new technologies increasingly turn more and more space (in conventional practice, if not by legal conscription) into places where there must be some instrumental reason for occupying it.[6] We parcel out places where only one or a limited range of activities is considered appropriate.

Technologies have, of course, extended our reach beyond traditional spatial boundaries. This, too, has consequently limited our range of movement and our norms of social interaction. We increasingly use our ability to traverse spatial boundaries to bypass interpersonal and social interaction altogether. We communicate socially and professionally according to new rules of electronic etiquette where efficient transfer of information is the primary goal, the diminishment of emotional involvement is paramount, and the sensory restrictions of face-to-face interchange are accepted as new norms of interaction. We increasingly withdraw ourselves from crowded shopping malls in favor of "PurchaseAnything.com," isolate ourselves from coworkers via e-mail to reduce the time of idle office chitchat, send electronic pictures via cell phones to communicate our current location to a friend rather than engage in a few moments of conversation, and exchange our five-block walk for food for the convenience of home delivery. The very technologies we exploit to overcome spatial distance to connect with others often have the opposite effect of reducing our need for the very forms of interaction the technology promised to enhance.

A third consequence of technology on spatial experience is the value we place on certain spaces, and on our spatial environment more generally. Instrumental space is valued in terms of what it allows us to accomplish and profit from. Instrumental work space tends to be seen as something undeserving of our reflection as long as it allows us to accomplish what it is we wish. The relationship between this aspect of spatial experience and the temporal experiences spoken of prior is this: If technology has transformed our orientation of time such that work time becomes more valuable, then the spaces in which such work can be accomplished necessarily increase in value. The result is the continued atomization and dissociation of individuals in the public sphere, examples of which are readily visible in any major city in the United States. and the world, as well as in suburban spaces that have consistently streamlined pedestrian and other social spaces for work, travel to the city, etc.[7]

Defining Death Culture

If we are to demonstrate and speculate about the relationship between technological use and our attitudes and practices of death and dying, we must know precisely what attitudes and practices we refer to. Attempts to offer a general theory of death culture in America have generally led to the simple reduction of the entire complex of death attitudes and practices to the all-purpose category of fear and denial. However, changes in every other area of social life over the past three decades, and the very cosmopolitan nature of the way we orient ourselves to and practice ways of death and dying in America, render this reduction virtually meaningless. Both culture and technology (of any form) are best understood by first grasping the temporal and spatial configurations inherent in any expression; knowing this allows us to describe and analyze more fully the particular expression itself. This is to say, we cannot proceed to understand American death culture by beginning with an epistemological prejudice that reduces it to a set of mere psychological characteristics.

The concept of "death culture" that underlies my analysis of technology in the following sections is ecological, comprised of six related dimensions, each of which is an expression of spatial/temporal configurations. These include: a) our general view of our individual and collective certainty of impending death along the lines of optimism/pessimism; b) our propensity to and value for preparing for this certainty; c) our level of involvement and engagement with individual, social, and collective rituals of death and dying;

and d) the scope within which such practices are played out, whether in private or in public. Thus, in the remaining analysis I am interested in demonstrating how injecting technology into the complex realm of death, dying, and memory changes or is otherwise likely to influence the degree to which we invite or eschew death, how much we are willing and able to prepare for it, how much we are engaged with death rituals and the circumstances of that involvement, and our value of expressing each of these within a public arena of social, communal life. Our understanding of the temporal and spatial dimensions of technological change discussed in the previous section provides the related basis for this analysis. The following sections deal with what I refer to as the empirical domain of technology and death; the theoretical dimensions of time, space, and vision as they connect with death attitudes and practices. Throughout, I refer to narratives from several individuals that I have spoken with who have or do use various aspects of FEI's technological services, including Valerie Lawrence, who produced a video memorial of her mother who died in an accident in 2000, and Giovanni Voltaggio, as well as Melissa Fuhr, both of whom are frequent visitors to the ForeverNetwork online archive of FEI's collection of LifeStories.

Empirical Domains of Death Technology

Technology alters in some way the experience of time, space, and vision; necessarily, the way we confront death and the rituals surrounding it shift accordingly.

The Temporal Domain

The way we exercise memory of the dead, as well as the existence and the nature of how we record them are two of the most prominent areas where the temporal aspects of technology have some bearing.

*To Remember, or Not To...*The de-temporalization of memory by technologically mediated memorials, and its use as an impetus for memory and remembering, is likely to lead to what I call *memory anxiety*. An excerpt of Valerie's story provides an excellent starting point for understanding this possible consequence of technologically rendered memorial objects and occasions. For four years now, Lorene—Valerie's mother—has lain resting at Oakhill Cemetery in St. Louis, Missouri. It is a plot nestled somewhere on the acreage that Valerie customarily returns to to remember her mother. A few pictures pulled from her purse, a pen and diary, and the knowledge of the special woman that lies beneath the earth upon which she sits help her to remember. She looks into the face of her mother plastered on the front of Kodak paper; in the stillness of her quiet contemplation the memories come flooding back. She pens them in the pages of her diary—a private collection of her thoughts that remains sealed until her next visit with mom.

But today, for whatever reason, the scene changes for the first time in the two years since her mother passed. The serene comfort of the cemetery is replaced with the trappings of home; her pen transformed into a computer keyboard, her diary into a digital interface hosted at www.forevernetwork.com. There, in the ephemeral locale of cyberspace, Valerie leaves "a message," as she puts it. The message is clearly for her mother. But unlike those in her diaries, this one sits there waiting—not beckoning for an audience, but nevertheless there to be read by any and all who come looking; those looking for a new experience through the eyes of another, looking for comfort in the arms of an invisible stranger who shares one's suffering, looking to add memory to history.

"Mom, I think about you all the time and I cry because I miss you so much," Valerie opens her message to her mother:

> Comfort does eventually come to me because I begin to pray and thank God for allowing me to have such a wonderful mother in my life. Some people are not as fortunate to have a beautiful, caring, compassionate and loving person as you in their lives, I am so happy I did....Pastor Bonner says that we are just visitors here and we should not become too attached to things of this world and I believe that with all of my heart and soul, going home is not as fearful as it used to be because I know you are there waiting to receive me in your loving arms. I will wait on the Lord to call me and I will be ready when he does. I am trying to live as God would have me live and treat people as God would have me treat them, this way I know I'll see his glowing face and be with you again....I love you and miss you but I'm comforted by the many wonderful memories of you. I'll be seeing you, your daughter Valerie.

Valerie's story here conjures up several points of interest, chief among them the temporal moment of grief and remembrance.

As she was quick to repeat often to me, Valerie typically visits her mother's grave; it is her preferred site in which to remember her mother's life and death. At this particular moment, however, she found herself unable to replicate her usual routine. Memory, grief, and all the other related emotions that come with it can be conjured at any time and may be stimulated at any moment, catching us unawares. On many occasions, such sudden moments of unanticipated memory are fleeting, curtailed by other present obligations on our time. In this case, however, the existence of the digitally-stored memorial of Valerie's mother, and Valerie's access to it, allowed her to extend the available time to remember and grieve again over her mother's death.

Valerie's experience provides a substantive basis for demonstrating the lengths that her experience might be taken to more extremes by others, as use of this technological service becomes more diffused into the cultural landscape. That is, the access to omnipresent technologies may transform the impetus and consequences of her limited experience in much the same way that these technologies have accomplished this in other areas of experience. Temporal anxiety, an obligation to fill time, brought on by the concomitant freeing of time through technological means, provides the possibility for memory anxiety, a compulsion or ever-present sense of obligation to remember and grieve at any moment because one can do so without the usual temporal limitations. The cell phone makes communication and work always possible, leading to a sense of obligation to always be available for work and to create a sense that we should always be working; the digital memorial makes memory and grief more possible (and more intense, as discussed later), and, extended to the same ends as cell phone use, is likely to create a sense that we should always be remembering and, therefore, possibly always grieving.

A colleague and psychologist told me recently that her advice to grieving clients she counsels is to set aside time every day, or as often as it seems necessary, to remember and grieve. Such advice about time and memory is not only common from psychologists and other grief counselors of various stripes, it is embedded in our temporal landscape, our memorial traditions. When the dead became separated from us with the emergence of the suburban cemetery park (discussed in more detail later), the spatial dissociation occasioned a temporal one. That is, a person's grave not only became the place we go to remember; the time set aside for the visitation became time now commonly set aside for the specific purpose of remembering. We have little time for the encumbrances that memory of the dead may stimulate, and so we "make" time to remember when we can afford (emotionally, socially, and economically) to do so.

"What is the significance for you to be able to access a deceased loved one's memorial anytime through the Forever Network?" I asked Giovanni. "Well now, that is a complicated question," he says. "Why? Because if I go online and revisit them and it makes me sad or melancholy, then I could be making my life much more difficult." He adds the caveat, however, that "being able to see them from time to time, in addition to remembering them everyday as I live out my life, is a plus, *if used properly*." The emphasis I have added to the end of Giovanni's reply illustrates the precise point that is most significant here. One has to make a calculated and conscious choice to spend the time and energy to travel to a cemetery to visit or remember a loved one buried there. However, the online video memorials integrated into the Internet web of experience are virtually omnipresent. The temporal constraints of remembering within the cemetery space and other accoutrements as an inducement are removed. Mother's memory in moving images, voices, and all the other visual production bells and whistles are always just a few keystrokes away. Suddenly, one finds oneself forced not with having to make the *choice to* consciously reflect again on a loved one's death, but to make the *choice not to*. It would be like Valerie having her dead mother in the room all of the time and Valerie having to decide whether or not to acknowledge and engage her mother's presence.

To remember or not to remember is not the most significant question in this case; to do one or the other is a personal choice made based solely on one's own emotional capacities, needs, and desires. What is significant is the advent of the choice—one induced by the technology itself. The technology produces an imposition of sorts—if we can call an invitation to remember the dead an imposition—and the invitation to remember demands a response, creating the possibility that memory and remembering may become an obligation that may infringe on other areas of life. Temporal anxiety has led to many stress-related physical and psychological problems for many. The possibility of increased memory anxiety may likely add to the mountain of stress that grieving individuals already deal with.

The Digital Record. Digital storage technologies offer the dead a sense of permanence, identity, and the possibility of inclusion in the historical record. The digital storage technology used to archive, catalog, and extend for public use our memorial record—like any record—serves as proof of life. Record keeping, while used to maintain bureaucratic control, has extended significance for the individual, especially when they are in control of the form of record being produced. Records document and substantiate one's being. To a large degree they call into being one's very existence. In the increasingly bureaucratized and digitized world in which we live, to have no record of one's existence literally means one does not exist, for all intents and purposes. Others document the existence and circumstances of our lives, but we individually also keep track of ourselves by the amount and substance of the records we keep. Those records—the ones we create and keep for ourselves—are the principal tools by which we create, substantiate, and preserve the quality of our identity, especially once we are dead. The drive to sustain being—to be known—is much greater in death when our existence is threatened by extermination and erasure. Throughout life our physical existence, our ability to signify, to speak for ourselves, aids in verifying that we indeed are somebody. Our very corporeality allows us to present ourselves to others. In death, however, all that is left is the record, and that record is what will stand and speak (or not) to lend credence to the fact and circumstances of our existence. When the record goes, so too do we, and to leave no record is much like never having been born at all. It is the record that provides the permanence needed for our continued existence, conditioned by others' sustained recognition of us.

For many, however, mere empirical proof of our existence is not enough; we do not want to be known and remembered as a mere recounting of name, rank, and serial number. It is insufficient that a birth or death certificate define us. Thus, we seek to add quality to the empirical record, leaving more than simple unambiguous facts that can be verified or refuted. This quality allows us to communicate the essence—identity, if you will—of who we are and were. This drive toward continued significance is enhanced when we give others the responsibility to preserve it, when those responsible extend beyond our individual selves or that of a limited circle of family members, and when those records are accessible to the public. History is just this—a story or a related set of narratives that are written or otherwise recorded to signify and preserve for public memory some significant aspect of one's life, or the life of a given group of people.

The primary import and effect of FEI's digital memorial services lies beyond simply creating an object of memory for particular members of a deceased's family or friends; it injects the common stories of ordinary people into the historical record. But what does this mean? What significance for the individual and the public does this insertion have? First, it fulfills our personal narcissistic needs and fantasies to be recognized.[8] Second, it extends the scope of our significance by including our own narratives and perspectives on and about life (and death) into a permanent record accessible to the general public. Such permanence implicitly confers value on the individual's story in the corpus of recorded her-and his-stories. Third, the permanent narrative record serves as evidence for the public's ever-present compulsion to interpret and understand history according to our own needs, purposes, and perspectives. This is to say that inserting my individual narrative into the historical record necessitates that I—my story, my perspective of the past and future—be acknowledged and taken into account in any future reinterpretation or attempt to create meaning of the past, or to guide future experience.

Death, Time and Technology. The temporal aspects of the technologies used by FEI—the extended occasions and obligations for remembering, and the various aspects of digital memorial archives—are likely to have temporally based impacts on our attitudes about death and dying. More specifically, I contend that they will work to rearrange our dominant valuative conceptions of the past and the future; better satisfy our need to create a sense of symbolic immortality; increase the degree to which we live our lives with the continual recognition of death's inevitability; and compel us to prepare more substantively for death's occurrence.

As previously mentioned, our culture generally privileges the present over either the past or the future. The past—history, more precisely—tends to be discounted both because it is seen as having little bearing on present experience, present ways of making meaning and interacting, or present decisions. Additionally, we are generally not the subjects of history itself, nor are most others like us. We are dissociated, disengaged, and otherwise disconnected from a past made up principally of those with whom we cannot identify—at least not to the same degree with which we identify with present people and circumstances. The existence, availability, and access to a historical record—of past stories told by and about those with whom we personally identify—are likely to affect our value of the past and the manner in which we allow it to influence both the present and the future. The more relevant our connection with the past, the more we are likely to retain it not only as an object of memory, but as an instructive guide for how to face present and future situations.

This is especially true when we may increasingly have access to those with whom we closely identify and who, because of their impending death, speak specifically to and about a future that will someday be ours. Imagine being able to access untold numbers of stories of people who not only tell us of their specific past, but who in the present (by virtue of our viewing) are able to speak to us directly about their future death (which is now past at the time of our viewing), as we contemplate the possibility of our future when we will follow in their footsteps. Such possibilities not only are important in how we think about the future, but are important inasmuch as they allow us to be more comfortable in thinking about it.

Related to this possibility enhanced by technological products used and offered by FEI is the fulfillment of our desire for immortality. As Toynbee discussed in great detail,[9] the promise of immortality is one way that human beings reconcile themselves with death. And though extremely rational cultures such as our own dismiss much of the possibility of any real physical, personal immortality, the desire for various other forms of symbolic immortality often suffices. This symbolic immortality—once available to only the most recognizable and influential among us, and in some circumstances, only at the behest of those other than ourselves—is increasingly possible given the technologies that allow for such preservation and production of our own stories. Regarding this matter, Toynbee also notes that failure to believe in the possibility of immortality—in principle or in our ability to attain it—often leads to nihilism. If this is not the extreme consequence, it definitely contributes to our fear and unwillingness to contemplate the future, and death which lies at its end. The increased ability to attain such symbolic immortality, of leaving a permanent record of one's own life and story, is likely to contribute, at least in some way, to our optimism about the future and our impending death. In order to fulfill that desire for immortality, it is necessary to think about our future death, and if this desire can be fulfilled, we are thus more likely to see such contemplation increasingly become both individually and collectively valuable in our society in terms of how we think about death.

With a renewed value for the past and the future, and their reciprocal relationship to the present, it is also more likely that the technologies that make this possible will affect an increased sense in which we live life in the light of death. The ever-presence of death, memory, and history, aided by technology (and our access to it), works to increasingly make these issues and experiences part of our everyday awareness. With renewed possibilities for dealing with this in a manner that is more comfortable than entertaining our fears, and more healthy than simply ignoring it, the greater we will allow ourselves to be consciously affected by death's continual presence. Again, Toynbee and many others since recognize that a "mature" orientation and attitude toward death and dying is determined by the degree to which we consciously allow it to moderate our daily experience. The by-product of such an orientation is not only a renewed sense of how we ourselves live in preparation for, and because of, the fact of death's inevitability; its influence on how we treat others among those with whom we live—ethics—is an added value. As Emmanuel Levinas and Alphonso Lingis explain in great detail, this conscious awareness of our death and the death of others cultivates an ethical imperative unlike any other experience.[10]

The final temporal consequence of technology's injection into the terrain of death and dying is related to, but perhaps more tangible than, the others. That is, it is likely to increase the more systematic ways in which our cultural institutions allow us to prepare and plan for death. This includes the degree to which we inform others in our circle of family, friends, and related agents about what we would like done to and for us (and our possessions) when we die, and the degree to which we document these wishes in accordance with current law and public policy. This includes not only making decisions about bequeathing our material possessions, but includes things such as donating organs or other aspects of our physical bodies, the manner by and place within which we are disposed of, the circumstances of our memorials, etc. Many such methods for preparing for death are currently given only tacit attention by Americans. Fewer than half of Americans have life insurance; significantly fewer than these have prepared wills (the vast majority of people between twenty and fifty have not done so), and the numbers of people who are registered organ donors is relatively miniscule. The Federal Trade Commission and other death care providers increasingly stress the value of preplanning and "pre-need," yet these calls are largely unheeded (though the practice is slowly increasing). While for many these items are seen as luxuries, our failures to plan in this way are in part an expression of our current unwillingness to look ahead and consider the inevitability and possibility of imminent death. A technologically enhanced awareness of forward looking will likely have an impact on such quantifiable signs as these of our temporal attitudes and practices regarding death and dying.

The Spatial Domain

The spatial elements of technology are also likely to alter our experience of remembering the dead, particularly as it relates to the spaces where this exercise takes place.

Remote Memory & the Second Supplanting of Sacred Space. Rather than resurrecting the public communal significance of sacred space (primarily cemeteries), technologically rendered virtual memorials invite the possibility for its impending obsolescence, continuing to diminish the propensity for collective, embodied memorial experiences and public celebrations of life and death. This supplanting of physical, "sacred" space would be a second such transformation made possible by a first, which was much less influenced by communication technologies than it was by the tools that buttressed economic and commercial production. To understand the transformation likely to follow from technological advances in this area, we must understand the first transformation regarding the geography, use, and value of cemetery space.

The first supplanting of cemetery space put the dead largely out of reach of the living, transforming and compartmentalizing our desire to remember. The introduction of digital mechanisms of memory and memorialization may effect a second supplanting of these now singularly sacred spaces, erasing their personal and public significance altogether. Spaces occupied by the dead were once transformed from the public domain to the private. The same modernist impulse that placed vision in a privileged place above all other bodily senses and faculties also bifurcated the natural landscape into sacred and profane spaces. This division corresponds to the same division of public and private spheres of human life; private, sacred space being reserved for personal spiritual reflection and introspection, and public space for all other profanities of experience. As mentioned in the introduction, the "city of the dead" was once an active, living space that integrated the metaphysical presence of the dead with the physical presence of the living, who not only utilized it as a space of worship, but as a place for reunion, celebration, and all other activities of communal public life.

Up until the early/mid-twentieth century in America, the cemetery continued to serve the same public, communal, and spiritual function.[11] Cemeteries most often occupied spaces alongside other public communal institutions such as the church and home. It was not out of the ordinary to find one amid a busy commercial corridor, right next to a public market, shops, or municipal offices. And people were accustomed to picnicking, patronizing, and even politicking amongst scores of their dead family members and others of the community. The first supplanting of sacred space in America coincided with the drive toward rampant industrialization, urbanization, and technological production—all of which were premised on the basic dogma of efficiency and economy. As masses of the living moved from the outskirts to the central city, the dead—the spaces they occupied—were transplanted in the opposite direction. Initially, this transplantation was a logical move given the innovation and diffusion of transportation technologies that provided efficient means of travel to visit our deceased loved ones.

But the same technologies that made it feasible to one's conscience and to technological capability to exhume the dead from their city home to a suburban resting place also worked to disconnect those who would utilize such technologies to maintain their personal and collective relationships with the dead. Industrialization and urbanization, and their by-products of increased technical specialization, meant that people would now have to travel to and eventually move away from their original communities to find work. Millions of people, now hundreds and even thousands of miles away from their dead, found themselves restricted by the very technologies that first freed them to be able to visit their loved ones in their new suburban locations. Automobiles were not yet equipped to travel such distances with much speed, and what once was a hop, skip, and a jump to see grandma's grave became a three-or-four-day affair. The problem—who could afford to take that amount of time away from the requirements of work?

In more recent years urbanization gave way to suburbanization (for the living). One would expect this transformation to effect a reunion of sorts—people now returning to be closer to the suburban homes where their dead were displaced in prior decades. But the earlier cultural and technological transformation had already fully taken hold. If people found themselves now living near a new suburban cemetery "park," it was more than likely that it was inhabited by people they did not know. New suburban dwellers were strangers to their old suburban (dead) neighbors. The effect of each of these transformations and retransformations was to cultivate a vastly different function and significance for cemetery space.

First, it became a specialized place for people to go at a particular time, and for particular reasons. We go to the office to work, the park to play, the cemetery to remember. With distances still being an obstacle, and the rigors of work circumventing our ability to travel them, the cemetery has become a place set aside—made sacred—for the purpose of remembering a dead loved one when we can or need to do so. Our earlier technological displacement already effected the requisite disssociation for such a mental and practical compartmentalization. Second, and related to this, the range of acceptable activities in this new sacred space was greatly curtailed from times past. In today's culture, the motives of anyone not actively burying someone or engaged in "visitation" are suspect. The moneychangers have been forever banished, so to speak.

When the cemetery becomes the primary place for remembering and its objects the very inducement for memory; when our access to such spaces is limited by space and time, and a limited desire to remember (a culture of for-getting),[12] a technological intervention comes as a welcomed panacea for some. The technological services offered by FEI provide the means for re-membering the dead in a way that overcomes the problems of distance and time. They provide a technological product of memory to which one can attach oneself without the necessity for travel. The service is immanent. They also afford a tangible product perhaps more "real" and more conducive to remembering (discussed in the next section in relation to the efficaciousness of visual media), allowing greater access to visual and audible recollections of the dead discussed earlier.

Valerie still returns to the cemetery, the place she prefers to go to re-member her mother. Yet sitting by the grave, she still pulls out her mother's pictures. She may be in the space that her mother now occupies, but she still needs a visual stimulus to aid her memory. I suspect that many, if not most, people have already made the break between the two—preferring any form of visual memorial of the corporeal being they wish to remember to a par-ticular space to which they have long become detached. That is, one can get the essential elements of cemetery experience through a virtually mediated mechanism. Why do we visit the cemetery? It is because that is where our loved ones are; their headstones and the physical space their plot occupies provide an impetus for memory. We go there to experience the presence of someone now gone. Yet technological memorials can provide much the same thing—other than our tangible sense of the actual body that lies buried. However, most people realize that the experience is detached from the physi-cal remains, and their proximity to their location matters little in creating an atmosphere conducive to memory and presencing. In this way, the services of FEI offer the best of both worlds—the ability to transform any space into sacred space, the vision of their faces and the sound of their voices providing the necessary attuning atmosphere for our precious moments of memory and reflection.

But this technological remedy (of sorts) that enables an increased oppor-tunity for remembering and an intensification of the emotional attachment we have with the dead also has important consequences for the renewal of cemetery spaces for personal memory and sacred communal use. At the same time that this technological innovation is being introduced for the purposes of memory and memorializing, an effort is taking place to renew old and de-teriorated cemetery landscapes and to cultivate an increasing sense of com-munity within such spaces. The growth of the Internet as a tool for reconnecting with past generations of family and friends through public access to genealogical information has and continues to lead to the rediscovery of the places where our ancestors are buried, as well as a renewed impetus to search for them. In cases where these newly discovered places still exist, efforts have increased to beautify and preserve them. However, if technical means of digital memory upset such prospects for renewal—which I suspect is more likely—the existence and significance of any form of physical memorial space will be lost not only to the individual who may go there to remember someone in particular, but to the stranger—the public—who might wish to renew it as a more general space of personal and collective commemoration and reflection. This possibility is enhanced by the declining use of physical burial spaces themselves in favor of the growing trends toward cremation as a preferred mode of human disposal.[13] It is difficult to identify what tangible detriment this may have for the American public, except to point out that the declining significance of such spaces due to technological intervention precludes the possibility of their future renewal should we decide at some point their worth is again of great value.

The first supplanting of sacred space was driven by an ideology that placed industry at the center of social life; the second supplanting is driven by communication technologies that privilege individual, isolated use. The first conditioned our emotional detachment from the physical place of the cemetery; the second intensifies our level of disconnection. The first made the cemetery a private, sacred place; the second may render it obsolete. The first transformed it from a place of vibrant public activity to largely a dull environment unfitting of such activity; the second will complete the decline, squeezing the very life out of it and leaving it literally for dead—as a space where we simply dispose of human remains and nothing more. Thus, the tangible, likely effect of technology—especially in the creation and use of virtual memorials—is the manner in which it influences not only how we use sacred, cemetery space, but the concomitant individual and social value we perceive it has in terms of allowing us to engage or otherwise experience the presence of the dead.

The Visual Domain

While there are of course, important spatial and temporal dynamics and implications of FEI's technological services, its entire complex of products and uses for the individual and the public are primarily visual in nature. Videos, webcasts, virtual memorial sites, cemetery multimedia kiosks—they all emphasize vision, seeing, and looking, through displays, monitors, and screens. As much as they construct memorial events, they variously set the stage for a visual event. Should the trend begun by FEI continue, it becomes increasingly necessary to understand the relationship between "death culture" and "visual culture." How do a culture of seeing, the act of viewing, and our interaction with visual, representational objects influence the complex set of attitudes and practices surrounding death and dying? Another way to ask this question is, how will the ways in which we create meaning in death be transformed by the manner in which we synthesize and construct visual meaning? I contend that the visual experience emphasized in the virtual (simulated) memorial is the central component of my previous arguments regarding the possible obsolescence of physical cemetery space. I also argue that the increased emphasis of the visual experience in death and dying provides the possibility that representations of this experience will become increasingly useful as a communicator of personal narratives—a collection of new death mythology—that are more satisfying than death myths represented in religious or popular cultural narratives that circulate throughout television, film, and other media.

The Visual Intensification of Memory. The visual memorial complex erected by FEI creates several dilemmas in terms of its mission to alter traditional methods and landscapes of memorialization; it sets up a conflict between the efficacy of visual experience and the attachment to physical cemetery space. The contradiction lies in two of the company's technological services; on the one hand, the video/virtual memorial diminishes the need for, and attachment we have with, cemetery space as a place of memorializing and otherwise collectively celebrating life and death in the cemetery landscape. On the other hand, the same visual material wired into the company's cemetery kiosks enlivens what is now typically "dead" space, creating a more inviting and attractive impetus for using cemetery space as a place of collective celebration and contemplation. Let us begin by unpacking what the visual memorial experience provides for the individual seeking some space—be it physical or virtual—to remember deceased loved ones.

A trip to the cemetery for our planned moment of remembering has traditionally been a spatial experience. We drive down a winding road that directs us to the general area where our particular loved one is buried. We get out of our vehicle and, if we know where they are buried, we walk directly to that plot, perhaps glancing at the other gravestones on our way. When we get to our loved one's plot, there is a marker, perhaps a head stone, some flowers still lying there if there have been recent visitors. We stand or sit, think and remember; we clean the physical space surrounding it, and each of these actions constructs the essential aspect of our experience of memory which is fluid throughout, as we occupy the space where the dead is buried. No doubt the atmosphere created there integrates what is in our visual field—trees, the landscape, flowers, other gravemarkers, and perhaps other people strolling around looking for their own dead. But it is our connection with that physical space that "makes" the experience; our connection to the lifeless, but still meaningful, physical body that resides there. Despite this connection, however, there is nothing to see. The landscape surrounding us is nothing special, really. What does have significance for us—the body of our loved one—lay shrouded and encased in a box buried beneath the earth. We cannot see their faces, cannot stroke their hands or face; they cannot look at us, and the truth is, most of us would care not to—if not refuse altogether—disinter them for the satisfaction of seeing them. If we did, we still would not see them; what is left are decayed remains that no longer resemble the person we knew and loved.

Anything that enhances our vision in this situation strengthens our experience of remembering, recollecting, contemplating. As we sit there, if we can take a picture out of our wallet or gaze upon a physical object associated with our father or mother, brother, sister, or friend lying there, we feel that our experience was more full, more fulfilling. The act of viewing is a synthesizing experience whereby we not only reflect upon things; our gaze is the experience, it is our meaning. To visualize—particularly that thing which we cannot actually see—intensifies our emotional attachment to that which we are looking upon. It is perhaps one of the best examples of Baudrillard's simulacrum.[14] The physical being we wish to remember is absent and inaccessible to us. It is our viewing of their representation that becomes our experience of interacting with them; the representation becomes real and is the only sense of reality we can have in this particular experience. Thus, we see that visual objects provide what the physical burial space cannot—an opportunity to invoke a presence that is not necessarily more real, but more intense in terms of the strength of the emotional attachment that it offers. It resurrects to a greater similitude the degree of attachment we once had with the person when they were alive.

The point is that these visual objects are things we have access to in places other than the cemetery. And the products offered by FEI provide a wider array of such visual material than what have previously been available.

Their video memorials enhance the visual representation of the deceased with both movement and sound. This allows us not only to remember our loved ones with a greater degree of emotional significance and attachment, it allows us to remember them *how* we want to remember them—alive (this, too, has some important implications which I discuss shortly). If, as funeral directors have been claiming for decades (and we, too, given our propensity to avail ourselves to their services), it is important for our last visual image of the deceased be one that projects their living state, then it stands to reason that the repeated occasions of remembering, beyond the initial memorial, prefer a representation of them that is as lifelike as possible. It also stands to reason that the experience of remembering evoked by the physical cemetery environment can be replicated in other spaces. We are all living evidence of such. Any place may on occasion invoke our memory of the dead and transform the space we occupy at that moment into an atmosphere conducive to thoughtful reflection, an atmosphere where rational time and objective space are suspended in our experience. If the visual products offered by FEI provide a more significant memorial experience, and that experience can be satisfyingly enacted in a home, an office building, park, or any other space—then what real use to we have for the cemetery as a specialized space for such experiences?

However, what if the cemetery space itself incorporates these visual accoutrements? The integration of such material in the kiosks scattered around the cemeteries that FEI operates institutes these memorial objects in the traditional cemetery memorial space. This provides the possibility of transforming the traditional dead space of the cemetery into a living space—one where death, represented by those who reside their, and life, represented by the visual, vocal, and mobile representations of those located there, are integrated one with the other. This scenario provides something that remote memorializing does not. It allows us to keep in view both life and death, the living and the dead, simultaneously. We live in fantasy when we remember the dead in a former state; in a sense, it, too, is a denial of death. The opportunity to experience an emotionally satisfying memorial experience through the act of viewing, coupled with the present reality of death and the dead, seems to make for a more balanced sense of orienting and reconciling ourselves to death and its inevitability.

Life, Death, and the Sublime. Traditionally, religious dogma and spiritual beliefs expressed in various texts formed the basis of our understanding of the meaning of death, the experience of dying, as well as the state of the individual following. However, the increasing use of visual technologies is likely to also increase the degree to which we understand death and the here-after as a visual experience, relying on visual representations as a foundation. I argue that as this trend continues to progress, the audiovisual narratives such as those that FEI provides the possibility for will come to be relied on as a more satisfying form of representation of death and dying than religious dogma or fantastic forms of representation in various media that have tradi-tionally filled and currently fill our media landscape.

Photographic or audiovisual images of the dead are quintessentially sub-lime; they articulate that which cannot be understood, that which is beyond representation. The sublime nature of death makes representation problem-atic in that there is no empirical basis for interpretive judgment. However slight, our interpretation and derivation of meaning from any image rests on some standard of authenticity, some notion of the ideal figure or original to which any representation appeals. This is not so for the qualitative experi-ence of death and dying for the individual, or for the descriptive aspects of the world after death, should there be one. In our attempt to understand what it means to die, we have two sources from which to appeal—imagination and personal narrative. We can essentially make it up out of thin air, or we can do so by availing ourselves of the voices of those who are in the throes of death. Heretofore, imagination has supplemented religious dogma when the latter proves too ephemeral. But for many, religious dogma and imagination are one in the same, if not in their source, then certainly in their consequence. This is to say, for many our need to bring meaning to death is not quite satis-fied by either. The closest we can get to understanding this experience is to know how others like us have experienced it. It is in this way that the visual technologies used and offered by FEI contribute to reshaping our attitudes about death and dying.

The simple act of creating a personal, living, visual record in advance of one's death provides a world of access that has heretofore not been available to most of us. In centuries past, people prepared to die,[15] and part of this preparation was to communicate to one's family and often to the public at large what it was the individual was facing at the time when death was fast approaching. This allowed people to not only take care of "family business," but aided spectators in understanding that particular person's coming death, and one's own death as well. Today most of us have little experience inter-acting with someone whose death is imminent. People around us die sud-denly, or are unable to communicate to us after having begun the process of dying. The places where people generally die are isolated and private, and they themselves are inaccessible to us because of facility operating policy or family prerogatives. Because of many circumstances, we have less access to the dying and therefore less access to their understanding of an experience that we will one day face, leaving us to make sense of death largely on our own or through unsatisfying means.

What FEI offers is a mechanism by which we can have increased access to the stories of the dying, to narrative reflections of others who are like us, if in no other way than that they are or have experienced something that we have not but will. Such stories are valuable, and in many ways necessary if we are to transform our cultural attitudes toward death from one of denial or nonreflection to one in which we are willing and find it personally and collectively helpful to think about death prior to our experience of it.

Conclusion

One of the pieces promoting FEI's technological services asks the question, "If your great-great granddaughter comes to a Forever Theater in the year 2150, what will she find?" She will no doubt think quite differently about death and dying than those of previous generations, unlikely to share our fear and refusal to confront death throughout the course of daily life. Her visit to the theater will be set on quite a different landscape for death and dying than we are accustomed to, and she will be both comforted and instructed about facing her own death by constantly entertaining the thousands of stories others have told about their own experience with death and dying. But we cannot fully answer this question about the future until we understand several other, perhaps more tangible implications of death-related technologies. In the following chapter I move the discussion beyond temporal and spatial issues of technology and death culture, considering very practical effects these technological uses may have on the funeral industry itself, the ways in which we ritualize death in funeral and other memorial services, as well as the political ramifications of the changes that these technologies are likely to induce.

NOTES

[1]   I am speaking here specifically about death in terms of our attitudes and rituals surrounding it, rather than the direct link between technology and issues of physical

mortality.

[2] For a more thorough discussion of the emotional realities related to the funeral experience and how funeral directors generally regulate its expression, see Charlton McIlwain (2003), *Death in Black and White: Death, Ritual, and Family Ecology.*

[3] See CBS broadcast news story, "Funeral Sets That Let Your Dearly Departed Bow Out in Style," CBS Evening News, January 27, 2003.

[4] Siegfried Giedion, *Mechanization Takes Command: A Contribution to Anonymous History* (New York: Oxford University Press, 1948).

[5] See Robert Levine, *The Geography of Time: The Temporal Misadventures of a Social Psychologist, or How Every Culture Keeps Time Just a Little Bit Differently* (New York, New York: Basic Books, 1997).

[6] David Steven Worth, *The Built Environment as Communication: Totality, Alterity, and Dissociation in Urban and Suburban Spaces* (Norman, OK: Doctoral Dissertation, 2003).

[7] Ibid.

[8] Christopher Lasch, *The Culture of Narcissism: American Life in an Age of Diminishing Expectations* (New York: Norton, 1978).

[9] Arnold Toynbee, *Man's Concern with Death*, (St. Louis, MO: McGraw-Hill, 1969).

[10] See Emmanuel Levinas, *Totality and Infinity: An Essay on Exteriority* (Pittsburgh, PA: Duquesne University Press, 1969), and Alphonso Lingis, *The Community of Those Who Have Nothing in Common* (Bloomington, IN: Indiana University Press, 1993).

[11] See Kenneth T. Jackson and Camilo J. Vergara, *Silent Cities: The Evolution of the American Cemetery* (New York: Princeton Architectural Press, 1989).

[12] For Nietzsche, "forgetting" was the primary characteristic of what he called "monological art." It described the artist's view of his work (his own self-reflection) as excluding public witnessing or access. See Friedrich Nietzche, *The Gay Science* (New York: Random House, 1974), 367.

[13] Between 1997 and 2001 the cremation rate in the United States increased by 4 percent. By 2025, cremations are projected to be the preferred method of disposal for almost half of the American population. Confirmed 2001 Statistics: 2001–2025, Cremation Association of North America. Found online at: http://www.cremationassociation.org/html/statistics.html.

[14] Jean Baudrillard, *Simulacra and Simulation* (Ann Arbor: University of Michigan Press, 1994).

[15] Philippe Ariès and David E. Stannard, *Death in America* (Philadelphia: University of Pennsylvania Press, 1975).

CHAPTER TEN

Web Funerals, Virtual Memorials, and the Business of Death

The use of technology in the sphere of death and dying is not only likely to alter many of the attitudes about death and dying prevalent in American culture commensurate with various temporal and spatial dimensions. There are more tangible consequences; they are likely to translate into a very different way in which the business of death gets done, the manner of social interaction we engage in throughout the course of death ritual events, and the political values we afford the dead and their memory in our society.

This final chapter proceeds in the following manner: The relational implications discussed in the following section are most directly related to the funeral webcast services provided by FEI. How a webcast funeral changes the very definition and meaning of a funeral as a social ritual is the important question in this case. In the second section I describe the possible implications of what I have previously referred to as a "virtual" memorial. I address specifically the individual and political manner in which we deal with such mediated memorial objects, as opposed to physical memorials traditionally erected as the place and impetus for public, collective memory. In the third section I deal more generally with how the whole complex of technological services provided by FEI is likely to impact the funeral industry specifically. What changes are they likely to effect within the commercial sphere of death and dying, and what is the value of these alterations? Finally, I conclude by discussing how the emerging metaphor describing the new experience of death vis-à-vis these new technological products—that of theater—may impact the future manner in which we come to both think about and deal with death in American culture.

Relational Dimensions of Death Technology

The introduction of technology into our cultural practices surrounding death and dying, perhaps, have the greatest impact on how we interact with both the dead and those with whom we join in ritualizing their death in some way.

The Remote Funeral

As the term *remote* suggests, the substance and style of death ritual events—funerals in particular—are substantially influenced when participation is technologically mediated.

Digital Protocols. A tacit look, at least, at the idea and structure of protocols that govern the technology is helpful, if not necessary, to fully understand how a webcasted funeral differs from a traditional funeral service, On this particular topic, Alex Galloway begins his book, *Protocol: How Control Exists after Decentralization,* with the following statement of purpose:

> This book is about a diagram, a technology, and a management style. The diagram is the *distributed network,* a structural form without center that resembles a web or meshwork. The technology is the digital *computer,* an abstract machine able to perform the work of any other machine....The management style is *protocol,* the principle of organization native to computers in distributed networks.[1]

While Galloway's description here is essential to understanding the general nature of technological control, it is equally essential to my description of the specific practice of funeral webcasting. The computer in this case is the primary technological tool needed to accomplish this task. The distributed network describes not only what takes place between a provider (FEI) on the one hand, and a user (the one viewing the funeral webcast) on the other, within the technological system of hardware and software; it directs the specific manner in which users necessarily orient themselves to the webcasted event. The management style refers to the manner in which the technology here manages the human faculties (movement, emotion, interaction) of those experiencing this technologically mediated funeral event.

Figure 10.1 illustrates the webcasting process. For sake of illustration, let us say Debra's funeral service is taking place at the Hollywood Forever Cemetery (HFC) in Los Angeles. A video camera set up in the chapel tapes whatever is within view of its lens. The captured sound and images are then routed from the camera to a computer server also located on the site; it digitally encodes the audiovisual data. The server packages the data into packets and then distributes them to a subnetwork of computers, where the data is then decoded and made available to multiple clients (other distribution servers). These clients—let us say one is physically located in Germany, Nigeria, Istanbul, and Canada—then repeat the process, each distributing available packets of data to any number of possible networked clients. Connected to any of these client servers are personal computers equipped with the necessary hardware and software to receive the streaming (real-time) audio/video data (Debra's funeral service). Viewers of the webcast funeral, represented in the figure as A, B, C, and D, each simultaneously view Debra's funeral on individual monitors and screens, as one would view a televised event. For the viewer, Debra's funeral ends when the camera discontinues recording, thereby cutting off the flow of data from the audiovisual source.

Efficient data transmission and the possible scope of delivery are the most significant aspects of the distribution system (the diagram). Debra's funeral holds a great possibility of being efficiently diffused throughout the computer network to end users. The protocols in this particular setup, what is referred to as an "IP Multicast," ensure that packets of data can be distributed to and by any network of servers. What does this mean? There is always the possibility the data transmission process from its source to the receiver/user may be interrupted. Particular computers may be temporarily disconnected from the network, or there may be a problem with the encoding or decoding of the data at any point along the way; any of a number of possible obstacles may arise throughout the process. The network protocols used in this form of webcast, however, allow a server to fetch the data from any number of other servers in the event of such possible malfunctions. Put simply, persons A, B, C, and D can be fairly assured that they will see, more or less in real time, Debra's funeral, with little technical interruption. Each viewer should receive the same audiovisual content, despite their disparate physical locations.

This form of distribution also makes possible the simultaneous observations of Debra's funeral by a virtually unlimited number of potential viewers. Thus, the webcast funeral may not only be worldwide in terms of the distance of its reach, but in terms of the possible audience who may have access to the computer-networked audiovisual event. Webcasting is traditional broadcasting, essentially, using a new medium of transmission. Thus, the audience of Web content is limited only by the number of people who have access to the necessary technology.

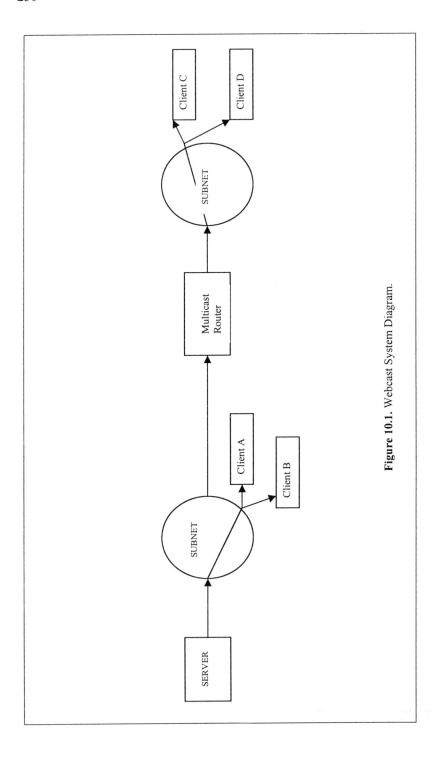

Figure 10.1. Webcast System Diagram.

The technology in this case—the personal computers to which users A through D are attached—serves the primary function of a viewing screen. While the technology extends the viewers' visual capabilities by allowing them to view Debra's funeral from a distance (tele-vision), it simultaneously and consequently limits their vision. Users A through D have access only to what is in the purview of the screen; they see what the camera "sees." The PC monitor on which Debra's funeral is being viewed may be of varying sizes. However, this only enhances the quality of the visual images they receive of the funeral service. The breadth and scope of one's vision is still circumscribed by the camera at the source of the process, something users A through D cannot control.

Thus, the way in which Debra's funeral is experienced by each of the viewers is dually managed both by the funeral service technicians at HFC and the technology itself. What viewers see is dually orchestrated by the camera operators who choose to focus on particular scenes of Debra's funeral. If the camera is focused on the person speaking, the viewers will likely see him or her, and probably Debra's body, which will usually be placed at the front of the chapel. Much of the immediate audience, however, will likely be obstructed from view. If the camera provides a panoramic view of the immediate audience, particular faces among them will likely be largely out of view. The variations could go on and on. The point is that the camera limits the viewer's vision of what is seen, and should A, B, C, or D wish to view particular scenes, or particular people at any given point in time, they have no ability to fulfill their desire. The camera imposes a frame on Debra's funeral, evoking a rhetorical sense of value or meaning of the event as a whole. A camera fixed on Debra's deceased body and casket and the speakers on stage may signal her person, and those speaking on her behalf, as the central defining element of the event. A camera set to view the audience may differently highlight mourners and family members as the predominant focus of attention.

The digital computer itself also controls the orientation of the viewers to Debra's funeral, as well as to each other, especially in the case that A through D are not in separate countries but are viewing Debra's funeral collectively in a single location. In order to view the event, one must face the screen; the screen is the nexus of the funeral experience for the remote viewer. In this case, one's screen-dependence isolates each individual participant, despite the fact of their collective viewing. Let us say that each of them are collectively watching the funeral on a large screen, the visual data being projected from a single source computer—an experience much like watching a movie at a theater. In this scenario, while funeral viewers are not physically separated from each other on separate monitors, the action—the experience—Debra's funeral—is still on the screen. What is happening around the viewer in either case figures relatively little into the overall experience, and what may take place offscreen (or offstage) is necessarily seen as a distraction from the main event. This is important because, as will be seen shortly, at a "live" funeral, *all* of the event takes place onstage.

The technology involved in webcasting and the network protocols that structure it allow those distant to "attend" or view a funeral event. Management is a by-product of its use, and one can begin to see in this brief technical description the implications this mediated event may have for viewers both individually and collectively. The depth of these implications is seen in connection with a discussion of the individual, social, and interactional nature of the traditional funeral itself.

Isolation Ritual. Sociologist Erving Goffman used the term *interaction ritual* to describe the ritualistic components of everyday, face-to-face social interaction. He recognized that human beings interact according to patterned behaviors that, because of their repetition over a long period of time, become a set of codified rules of social conduct. Certain social contexts suggest particular modes of interaction, including our bodily orientation toward others, the content and manner of conversing, nonverbal communications, and the like. These actions take place in "regions" that offer or create a barrier to perceptual cues from others; these cues are what we rely on to shape our initial behavior and subsequent interactions in a given social context. The "stage" is the setting where the nexus of interaction takes place and the setting of such actions generally co-constitute stage behavior. The stage—like the screen spoken of earlier—is the interactional event. That which takes place "offstage" is not meant to be witnessed by others; it is defined by isolation, and the behaviors that take place within its sphere are necessarily intended to be insignificant and disconnected from influencing the acts of others. Goffman puts sit this way:

> ...When a performance is given it is usually given in a highly bounded region, to which boundaries with respect to time are often added. The impression and understanding fostered by the performance will tend to saturate the region and time span so that any individual located in this space-time manifold will be in a position to observe the performance and be guided by the definition of the situation which the performance fosters.[2]

The interaction that is made the focus of attention in any given social situation thus "defines" what the situation is. That is, it answers the essential question: what is this? In the case of funerals, the stage behaviors, the communication and interaction that is placed front and center for viewers' awareness, say what this "doing a funeral" means in any particular case.

Funerals are ritualistic by intent and in practice. They have always existed as an interpretive and emotional occasion that serves to strengthen individual and collective identity, mark one's transition out of one's living social group, and prefigure that transition for the living. They are meant to inspire, instruct, and maintain the structural cohesion of the social group, be it the family, community, or nation. In addition to this basic definition of intent, those who officiate funerals (funeral directors, clergy, etc.) stipulate certain rules for carrying out the event, rules that are generally meant to ensure it takes place efficiently and without incident (the latter being defined principally by the former). On the other hand, with little such guidance, and despite the absence of any hard and fast rules of funeral etiquette, we all seem to know what customary behavior is for this experience—what to say or not to say and to whom we should or should not say it, whom to speak to and when, what to do with our emotions, how to interact with strangers and how to conduct oneself within the immediate presence of the dead. Though these patterns differ widely depending on subculture, one's religious affiliation, or other related customs, a pattern necessarily exists.

Several years ago when conducting research for my first book on this very issue, I spoke with a minister who told me a story about conducting a teleconferenced memorial service. I was shocked and appalled—perhaps I should not have been—of his and the family members' choice to conduct such a service in this manner. My objections, which I questioned him about, focused on the drastic change in the funeral experience given the use of that technology in particular. And while a webcasted funeral has substantively more to offer than one done over a phone line (in some respects), the transformation of the nature of social interaction in such an event is extremely significant, in terms of what a funeral means, its goal as a social ritual, and what individuals receive—primarily emotionally—from such an event. In short, a webcasted funeral transforms an embodied, collective, and interactive ritual into one principally characterized by individualization and isolation.

A funeral is a sensuous experience in which every aspect of the funeral service—the atmosphere of the setting in which it takes place and the interaction that takes place throughout—is considered "onstage." This is to say, the primary significance of the funeral, in terms of it accomplishing its primary purpose as a social ritual, lies in the individual ability—even compulsion—to touch, smell, see, hear, and even taste death. Each of these corporeal faculties and interactions provides the interpretive cues that make a funeral meaningful for the participant. Typically, the deceased is the center of attention at the funeral. People pass by and touch the body; they smell its odor and differentiate it from its former reality. They gaze upon it in wonder, perhaps horror, perhaps with no thought at all at how the dead is dressed, or the makeup that gives him or her a lifelike quality. Some kiss the body, hold its hand for a moment, or lay a precious treasure in his or her hands or by his or her side. Sitting through a eulogy, one not only listens to the voice of the one speaking; we discern the different signs of emotion. We discern through sounds and cues written on others' faces what are cries of sorrow or joy, resolution or emotional vascillation, restraint or expression—each of which are not only indicators of others' experience, but are also cues about how we should respond to the death that we have each come to commemorate.

The import of the funeral experience is not the mere fact that it takes place; it is experienced, and in some respects judged, by the presence of others. This includes the number of people attending, who attends, and the collective actions of the aggregate of individuals, as well as the particular actions of any individual. The collection of others in the same space, at the same time, for the same purpose adds to the quality of recognition we give the deceased; whether one verbally recognizes another's presence or not, it is nevertheless known and felt, and one knows that another is there should he or she need them for anything.

Aside from this, there is also meaning associated with that which may be considered "offstage" behavior at funerals. The funeral, as a performance, is over when attendees are formally dismissed, when the body of the deceased has been removed from their presence, and when all formal condolences have been given to the family members of the deceased. Yet this "ending" serves as a new beginning of regionally fragmented and bounded interactions and conversations among participants. Idol chitchat, the exchange of personal memories of the deceased, gossip, the renewal of old relationships between family members and acquaintances, verbal discussions critiquing the funeral service—all of these are customary forms of interaction that take place following a funeral, but nevertheless still constitute part of its ritual. These "offstage" behaviors provide not only the prescribed definition of the funeral's significance by the onstage performance; they confer meaning for multiple groups of individuals whose funeral experience does not end until they part company—until they are again alone. Thus, the sensual atmosphere and collective attendance and participation, and the onstage and offstage definitions of the situation, point to its fundamental interactive quality.

The webcast funeral essentially defies such interactivity; the individual "player" in the death ritual is transformed and reduced to a mere spectator, a witness, much like a rubbernecker passing by a highway accident. If that which is on-and-offstage defines the funeral experience, and parting company with other participants marks its end, then the funeral spectator who "attends" or participates remotely through a web/screen-related form of interaction essentially has a protracted experience. In essence, one's funeral encounter is always already ended by virtue of the fact of the solitary setting of the viewing experience. One can see what is happening, but that is about it. In all likelihood, one sits isolated with eyes facing the computer screen and perhaps a set of headphones on one's ears. The service begins and ends as though one were simply watching a state-of-the-union address. Afterwards, there is no one else around to converse with about a shared experience. And even in the instance that one collectively attends a funeral webcast with others, the place will have little of the physical accoutrements that add to the mood and atmosphere of the "real" funeral taking place.

I could describe ad infinitum the kinds of things the webcast spectator can or cannot do or otherwise take part in that the person physically attending the event can. But to put it simply, one knows clearly when one is standing on the ball field, and when one is sitting in the bleachers. When we go to hear a famed speaker, we know we would much rather be on the second row than in a separate room watching on CCTV. Similarly, the experience of a webcast funeral is an experience of spectating, rather than "attending." Attending assumes physical presence, generally. And "tele-presence" in this case is a limited proxy since the technology that makes it possible denies the essential element of social connectivity and interactivity.

The ability to webcast funerals and the discussion of its potential are important for two reasons, neither of which includes its present use—which is for the most part at this juncture simply a matter of exceptional convenience. First, its possibility is a barometer of sorts, measuring the degree to which we will continue to value the ritual nature, goals, and significance of funerals in American culture (a culture that has done away with many such rituals and rites of passage). Every new technology reflects or signals the value we attach to what it either allows us to do that could not be done before, or what it disallows. As I mentioned earlier, it introduces a choice where there was not one in the past, and the choice afforded by the new technology expresses much about our values. When it comes to funerals, will what exists now for mere convenience later become the rule rather than the exception? In the short run I think not. Irrespective of this, however, the degree to which webcasting as a service becomes more diffused in ours or any culture will signal, in part, the degree to which we continue to become dissociated from the awareness and experience of death, and from others within the   community with whom we necessarily participate in such rituals.

The import of funeral webcasting as a service lies not in the manner in which it is offered by FEI and used by its clients, which is to say it is in its possibility as a public good rather than as merely a private convenience. Webcasting significantly diminishes the funeral experience for the close group of family and friends who really knew the deceased. If, however, there is collective value in death as a spectacle, in the collective viewing of death-related events of strangers, the wide distributive capabilities of funeral webcasting are important. For this to happen, however, families themselves must increasingly regard the death of a loved one and the rituals they perform to recognize it as a public rather than private affair. It would necessitate public invitation, which, in the case of webcasting, would mean providing as wide an access to the event as the digital communication system allows. This is a political decision, which may be aided by the existence and reliance on what we can only recently refer to as the "virtual memorial."

The Politics of Death Technology

Several years ago Carole Blair and several colleagues suggested that the Vietnam Veterans Memorial was among the first kinds of memorials that could be described as postmodern.[3] Their characterization is not disputed here but presumed in my concluding discussion of the postmodern nature of virtual memorials. However, I would argue that the idea of a virtual memorial is more intensely postmodern than the memorial they describe; that this concept trumps the other in terms of its expressive function, its rhetorical voice, and its political positioning.[4] More specifically, I argue that virtual memorials are more intensely invitational, have more deliberative/rhetorical value, and are more "public" in terms of these former qualities, as well as the expansive nature of the access they afford as a "place" and occasion of memorialization.

My brief arguments here proceed from a somewhat different understanding of the postmodern condition used by Blair, which characterizes it primarily in opposition to modernism and its ideals, in line with Lyotard, Jencks, and others cited in her analysis. Postmodernism is not necessarily a temporally locatable period of time as with Jencks's marking of it in architecture at 3:32 p.m., July 15, 1972, with the destruction of the Pruitt-Igoe housing project in St. Louis, Missouri which was deemed no longer habitable.[5] Nor is it a binary concept delineating an ideological and oppositional break with and progression away from modernity. It is, as Kramer explains, a synthesis of what we might call premodern, modern and postmodern; the disruptive aspect of postmodernism lying with the manner in which the ideals of each discrete system is arranged and utilized. Kramer offers a description of postmodernism as a synairetic, or integral, appreciation of the co-constitutional nature of the postmodern project:

> According to modern perspectivism, there can only be one "best" way. But according to systatic (a)waring, each system has "good" and "bad" aspects....Postmodernism must presume and centralize modernity as the source of its differentiation. Insofar as postmodernism means anything, it is at it differs from modernism. The act of "posting" modernity confers status on it as the source, the semantic place where the diacritical project begins. Postmodernism presupposes modernity as the founding premise of its project. Thus, postmodernism, via its two-valued, diacritical "play," is nothing without modernity. In this way, postmodernists privilege modernity. Aperspectivity does not obsess this way. There is no drive to "deconstruct" anything. Instead, appreciation of differences is promoted without any discursive engineering.[6]

A conception of postmodernity that appreciates both modern and postmodern ideals is necessary to truly understand the postmodern nature of virtual memorials insofar as they are an expression of both modern ideals of technological progress, rationality and individualism and postmodern characteristics of upsetting totalizing metanarratives and other foundations of experience, interpretation, and epistemology, centering previously marginal voices and reconstructing the boundaries between private and public life.

More specifically, virtual memorials are both rhetorical (commemorative and deliberative/political) and fundamentally postmodern given the following characteristics: they collapse the public and private spheres; they revalue the subjects of collective memory; they privilege the magical impulse of technology; and they dislocate memorial space. Each of these characteristics is integrally related to the function of the virtual memorial as an invitation for public memory of all citizens regardless of celebrity, its ability to increase the number and type of voices in the historical record as a basis for political deliberation, and in invoking a sense of public interest regarding death-related issues.

The concept of a virtual memorial does not privilege the public sphere over the private, nor the reverse. The two realms penetrate each other. It necessitates that "private" experience—private grief and other emotional impulses, private knowledge of the deceased, private spiritual beliefs—pervade the public sphere. Similarly, it portends that the private sphere be amenable to the articulation of such private expressions; that individuals beyond the individual avail themselves of the expressions of the Other—those who have died and those who memorialize their deaths. The virtual memorial implicates the public as an arbiter of private experience and vice versa, expressing both the need and desire toward cultural fusion, the sharing of horizons among a cosmopolitan population whose connection and community provides the necessary basis for a single, shared sphere of experience and memory where the fusion of differences abound.[7]

This collapse of public and private afforded by virtual memorials provides for a revaluation of those whom we choose to remember publicly, collectively. By forcing private memories of strangers who have died into the public realm, it implies that these people—non-celebrities—be afforded the same possibility for rememberance as those we generally choose to remember. A theft of memory is exercised by the technology itself, those who provide the possibility for its use as a tool of memorializing, and those who avail themselves of its product. This revaluation is comparable to what took place in New York City in the aftermath of the World Trade Center attacks. Those of us here in the city remember well the hundreds of people whose faces were plastered on any and every hard surface, on every sidewalk, on every corner in the city. The first ones placed in hopes of recovering those who were missing gave way to those that simply acknowledged their loss. They were everywhere, but unlike the mountain of paper material we see plastered similarly for other occasions, we could hardly help but stop and look, to stand there and read the names, look into the eyes, and contemplate the memories of the one whose likeness and story stared us in the face—even though we knew it would lead to tears, to a loss of hope, and the constant reliving of what happened just a short time before.

The state exercised its influence over our collective memories by re-membering the dead as a collective. We who walked the streets remembered them one by one, individually, in as much depth as their makeshift memorials allowed. We were aided by the *New York Times'* "Portraits of Grief," a collection of extended, in-depth biographies of those who died. Those of us who watched the twenty-four-hour news coverage of the event's aftermath were exposed to their lives in a similar way, to the images of their mothers and fathers, sons and daughters who spoke at length about who they were.[8] In this case, the tragedy itself projected the lives of the dead into our gaze. They spoke to us through the voice of others, and our remembrances of them were valued to a community whose personal connections to each other were formed, reformed, and strengthened; a community who expressed intense desire to remember their own. Virtual memorials imply that every person's death is tragic, despite the circumstances. Whether the one who died was known or unknown to us or the world, whether or not they accomplished something spectacular in life, despite their social status, the technology that makes the virtual memorial possible and its use effect an equalization of the subjects of memorialization, suggesting that they should be remembered by loved ones and strangers alike, if for no other reason than that we share a common humanity; in some way we see ourselves in them. It suggests that the experiences of those seen as most insignificant benefit the public at large and compel us to make use of the opportunity to access their lives, avail ourselves of their experiences, and profit from their advice and vision of our future.

The technology that provides the possibility for the virtual memorial is driven by a magical impulse to overcome space and time, to control nature, and to enhance collective identity. Yet its modern use privileges the individualistic and hyper-rational ideals of power, the diffusion of ideologies, efficiency, structure, and permanence. The use of these technologies as a tool of memory repositions the premodern and modern drives, yet does not seek to eliminate either. The magical and mythical expressions of memory and memorialization rely on the rationally configured technology, rendering all forms of awareness visible in expression. A numerical code, mathematics, and all other rational aspects of computer technology, its ability to record and confer permanence and the projection of digital images that work to proffer an objective truth about history and present experience all pervade and are necessary to the experience of remembering that upsets each of them.

The visible, physical structure of the Vietnam Memorial and others like it invites individual and public commemoration expresses a discourse of multivocality and unending variations of interpretation of the memorial itself and the physical environment in which it is placed as a space for political contestation. What happens when the physical architectural accoutrements of a physical monument disappear? Does the virtual memorial erase individual and collective voice and voices? Does it depoliticize memory and history? Is the emotional valence of its rhetoric reduced and rendered ineffectual? The answer to each of these questions is—no. In fact, rather than diminishing these aspects of traditional forms of memorialization, that hinge, in large part, on a physically locatable object of memory, they are intensified. Politics and rhetoric are premised on the expression of divergent interpretations of past and present, deliberations about the future and our fashioning of what is collectively "good" or "best." What could be more political than a technology that seems to speak with many voices in that it offers varying and conflicting modes of use? What could be more efficacious than a plethora of voices who speak of values revolving around a universal rather than constrained experience? What could be more upsetting to political motivations of power and control than a multitude of voices that cannot be easily classified, dealt with, and dismissed?

While the voices that emanate from the wall of the Vietnam Memorial and those who visit it are many and varied, they are nevertheless circumscribed by a limited domain of experience—war, the state, sacrifice, etc. The unity of the experience that provides the basis for the very existence of the memorial itself codifies the range of voices and responses it invites and stimulates. The range of political expressions about the memorial, the event itself and otherwise, thus constrained, can be dealt with, that is, interpreted, understood, and refuted by the state or any other collective expressing a similarity of views about it. The openness of death itself, however—that which provides the experiential object for the subject of the virtual memorial—necessarily expresses an infinite number of possibilities of voices, views, pasts, and futures that, by sheer number, both invite and defy contestation. The voices of the marginal are added to the historical record and the array of voices are allowed to comment about the direction of our collective futures. The difficulty in deciphering, delimiting, and determining the influence of their voices does not remove them from the realm of contestation, it simply makes our public deliberations more arduous, but nevertheless useful.

Commercial Transformations

Two questions remain regarding the manner in which technology may transform the future of American death culture. First, how might it change the business of death, and second, what is the individual and social import of such changes?

No Business like Funeral Business

The funeral industry as a whole has a virtual monopoly on its services, and has for decades. Every state prevents anyone but a licensed funeral director and embalmer from handling and disposing of dead bodies. But the industry's controlling grip over final disposition of the deceased is not only state-sanctioned, it is something that the American public has willingly relinquished control over. I make this point to emphasize that no other aspect of cultural life has impacted our culture's attitudes and practices surrounding death and dying more than the existence and influence of the professional funeral industry. This was, in part, Jessica Mitford's argument some forty years ago, though her arguments centered mainly on the economic and consumer aspects of death and dying. But the funeral industry has not only influenced our compulsion or willingness to spend lavishly on funerals. It has dictated, or at least supported, certain rules of etiquette regarding the appropriate display of emotional expression. It has influenced the time devoted to death ritual events such as wakes, viewings, funerals, interments, and the like. It has prescribed customary modes of interaction at funerals discussed earlier. The breadth and depth of influence the industry has had on our culture in this regard is key to understanding how technology may transform our cultural orientation toward death and dying.

The degree of influence the funeral industry has had on our attitudes and values regarding death and dying has been so great that one can now explain it only as a symbiotic relationship between the commercial industry and the public who purchases its products and services. That is, it is virtually impossible to tell whether the funeral industry decides what we buy, how we conduct funerals and the like, and what we want to spend. The industry claim that it is merely giving people what they desire can no longer be distinguished for criticism, not knowing where one begins and the other ends. How the technological services offered by FEI may influence the industry, then, depends much on the ways in which we the public reorient ourselves toward the business aspect of death and dying.

Industry Impacts

One category of influence I believe FEI will have on the industry is related to the kinds of services offered and the manner in which we the public purchase them. First, I believe that public demand for video memorials will increase and therefore will be broadly diffused in the funeral market. This trend can already be seen in the number of funeral homes (or groups of them) that have begun to offer such services in recent years. More than two hundred companies currently offer the same video production services as FEI, which, itself has found great demand. While the number of sales has varied from 1998 to 2003, the profit margins of FEI have continued to increase. Each of these indicators is offset as well by the fact that FEI which aggressively invested in new operations and capital improvement.[9] These companies other than FEI who provide video services include funeral homes themselves; others (the majority) are traditional video production companies which specialize in these kinds of productions among many others, and all of them began offering their services somewhere between 2000 and the present.

In addition to this, more than five hundred actively used Internet sites have also proliferated the idea of virtual memorials, posting obituaries of the dead, and allowing those who knew him or her to leave a textual message communicating to the family of the deceased and the wider public their sentiment for the deceased. Like the former, these sites have all been generated in this century and most within the past two to three years. Few of these companies, however, currently integrate the two the way that FEI has. That is, few make their video memorial publicly accessible to those who view a site and wish to create their own memorial record for any person who has died. And currently, no cemetery that I know of has integrated these visual memorials into their cemetery landscape. FEI was at the cutting edge of offering each of these technological services individually; the company's real significance as an industry trendsetter in this regard lies in its comprehensive integration of them.

So what we have currently is a moderate level of demand for such services being stymied only by an industry's inability to provide the technical necessities to meet the demand. This is the case for one primary reason. The funeral business has generally been family-oriented and generational in terms of ownership and operation. Those who own and operate most of the funeral homes today have largely not grown up in the same technologically rich professional and cultural environment as the most recent generations of citizens. Thus, the very idea of using technology in these ways is somewhat foreign to many owners/operators, and certainly the technical skills to offer such technological services are largely absent. The degree to which these services become a regular part of death-related services, however, is only a matter of time. The demand is there and growing, and once the generational cycle has had a chance to catch up, it is likely that most funeral home/cemetery operators will not only see the technological value of such services, but will be equipped themselves with, or have access to, those who can provide such services in a financially efficient and profitable manner. Adding to this probability is the continued consolidation and corporatization of the funeral industry. As FEI financial records demonstrate, corporate ownership and multiple, but related, market involvement afford companies not only the financial wherewithal to offer technological services at a rather modest rate (the price of a video by FEI can cost as little as $295); it broadens their reach to be able to access professionals with the necessary skills to provide their services and the financial means to build a technological infrastructure.

The FEI financial records also express a trend that I believe will increasingly impact not only what kinds of technological services may be offered by funeral providers, but the way that the public pays for them. One of FEI's subsidiaries is a life insurance company. The life insurance business is dependent on our ability to think ahead and to plan ahead for death. As indicated earlier, of the significant technological impacts here is its influence on us to do just that, to think about the circumstances of death (including the financial matters) well in advance of death. In many ways, then, the impact of FEI and the technological services they provide ensure their and others' future profitability in an industry struggling of late to maximize profits. One who purchases life insurance has much more money to spend when they or a loved one dies than someone who has to rely only on their available cash on hand at the moment that the death takes place. In addition, because the financial dividends from life insurance are "earmarked," people are likely to feel compelled to use the money they receive from it for the purchase of goods and services related to the deceased, that is, more spending money available to transfer into funeral industry coffers. Thus, the use of technology spurred by FEI will likely buttress what the funeral industry has desperately begun to cultivate among the public in recent years—preplanning.

The remaining ways that technology is being used by FEI are less significant in terms of short-or-long-term profitability. However, I believe the breadth of its import lies in aiding a more general process of resocialization of attitudes and practices toward death and dying. As I mentioned before, I see the practice of funeral webcasting as being only a convenience—and one that few, if any, other funeral homes are currently interested in or likely to adopt as a stable service. Currently, about thirty funeral homes or private Internet companies offer this service. The multimedia kiosks will likely take much time (if they ever do) to become a permanent part of cemetery architectural landscapes. And maintaining a public archive of memorials is also likely to only tacitly be adopted throughout the industry. These services require financial expenditures that are likely to be seen as not being worth the investment. If I can get someone to pay $2,000 to produce a video memorial of their deceased mother or father, why would I as a funeral home operator incur the extra costs to archive each of those visual records and to make them available in multiple media formats?

The socialization changes likely to be engendered by the spirit of FEI's technological enterprise are threefold: they may foster a greater sense of reverence and "playfulness" in regard to death; they may change how we as a culture think about the use of public cemetery spaces; and they will likely place the individual and public interest at the forefront of the commercial and ritual manner in which we deal with the dead.

Life and Death in the New Theater of the Dead

To conclude this discussion about death technology, it is fitting to return to the question posed by FEI in its promotional materials: "If your great-great-granddaughter comes to a Forever Theater in the year 2150, what will she find?" How will our culture be several generations from now if the mission of FEI is realized? How will this fulfillment be realized in our attitudes about death generally and the manner in which we "do" death in American culture? I believe such changes will be expressed in totality by a metaphor: theater. The theater metaphor, of course, signifies much of the tangible aspects of the goods and services provided by FEI. But as a metaphor used to describe the death culture of the future, theater is indicative of the attitudes and practices of death that will follow from these technological integrations. First, death will be seen as a public rather than a private affair. The death of any citizen will be seen as tragic and their memories valued in the larger public sphere rather than being a subject of interest for merely family, friends, and acquaintances as it is now. Similarly, the theater metaphor suggests that the manner in which we memorialize all of our dead will be a more collective endeavor, that our memory of the dead will be bound by and stem from a collective sense of affiliation and interconnection.

Second, theater as a metaphor for future death culture will equalize two dominant modes of emotional response or orientations toward death and dying: fear or seriousness and entertainment. Theater serves two purposes: It provokes emotional responses that we do not usually allow ourselves to feel, that is, it invokes a sense of confrontation and contemplation of who we are and why we behave the way we do; and it allows us an escape, or way of differently viewing ourselves and our world from what is the usual. The theater of death inspired by technology will not likely cause our fear of dying to disappear, but it will allow us to confront that fear, to channel it into individual and collective actions that allow us to allay it to some degree. It will also allow us to see not only the tragedy of death, but also the comedy of it, as well as the fantastical possibilities that death may bring.

Third, technology—especially the visual technologies—provides a text that is always available for interaction not only among living people, but among generations throughout time. As Shakespeare's plays continue to inspire those of us who view them hundreds of years later, as they afford us simultaneous insight into the past, so, too, will the living texts of our technologically rendered personal and collective stories provide such interaction with future generations. These stories provide a continuity of influence that we individually (to however small a degree) and collectively have on future generations who will encounter many of the same things we have encountered throughout our lives and will tread new ground—new realties, new problems, and new needs for public deliberation about the public good.

NOTES

[1]   Alex Galloway, *Protocol: How Control Exists after Decentralization* (Cambridge, MA: MIT Press, 2004).

[2]   Erving Goffman, *Interaction Ritual* (New York: Doubleday, 1963) 106.

[3]   Carole Blair, Marsha Jeppeson, and Enrico Pucci, Jr., *Public Memorializing in Postmodernity: The Vietnam Veterans Memorial as Prototype*, in Critical Questions: Invention, Creativity and the Criticism of Discourse and Media (New York: St. Martin's, 1994) 350–382.

[4]   The very term *virtual memorial* makes it difficult to reference itself as an object of criticism. When I use the term here I refer not to an individual memorial—though that would be enough and appropriate, but to a corpus of such memorials as might be codified in the Forever Network Archive that I have been discussing throughout this chapter.

5   Charles Jencks, *A Post-Modern Reader* (New York: St. Martin's, 1995).

6   Eric Mark Kramer, *Modern/Postmodern: Off the Beaten Path of Antimodernism* (Westport, CT: Praeger) 129–130.

7   Eric Mark Kramer, *The Emerging Monoculture: Assimilation and the "Model Minority,"* (Westport, CT: Praeger, 2003).

8   Janice Hume, *Examining Content—"Portraits of Grief," Reflectors of Values: The New York Times Remembers Victims of September 11. Journalism and Mass Communications Quarterly*, 80: 166–193.

9   Numbers taken from FEI financial disclosure reports, 2003.

SELECTED REFERENCES

Adorno, Theodor, *The Culture Industry: Selected Essays on Mass Culture* (London: Routledge, 1991).

Arìes, Phillipe, and Stannard, David E., *Death in America* (Philadelphia: University of Pennsylvania Press, 1975).

Aristotle, *The Rhetoric*, (*The Complete Works of Aristotle: The Revised Oxford Translation*, trans. Jonathan Barnes, Princeton: Princeton University Press, 1984).

Bagdikian, Ben, *The Media Monopoly*, (Boston, MA: Beacon Press, 1992).

Baudrillard, Jean, *Simulacra and Simulation* (Ann Arbor: University of Michigan Press, 1994).

Baym, Nancy, *Tune In, Log On: Soaps, Fandom, and Online Community* (Newbury Park, CA: Sage, 2000).

Blair, Carole, Jeppeson, Marsha, and Pucci, Enrico Jr., *Public Memorializing in Postmodernity: The Vietnam Veterans Memorial as Prototype*, in Critical Questions: Invention, Creativity and the Criticism of Discourse and Media (New York: St. Martin's, 1994) 350–382.

Butler, Judith, *Excitable Speech: A Politics of the Performative*, (New York: Routledge. 1997).

Campbell, Joseph, *The Power of Myth* (New York: Doubleday, 1988).

Comstock, George, *The Evolution of American Television* (Newbury Park, CA: Sage, 1989).

Crayford, Tim, Hooper, Richard and Evans, Sarah, "Death Rates of Characters in Soap Operas on British Television: Is a Government Health Warning Required?" *British Medical Journal* 315(7123): 1997, 1649–1652.

Derrida, Jacques, *The Gift of Death* (Chicago, IL: University of Chicago Press, 1995).

Gadamer, Hans Georg, *Truth and Method* (New York: Seabury Press, 1975).

Galloway, Alex, *Protocol: How Control Exists after Decentralization* (Cambridge, MA: MIT Press, 2004).

Gallup, George Jr., *Adventures in Immortality* (New York: McGraw–Hill, 1982).

Gebser, Jean, *The Ever–Present Origin* (Athens, OH: Ohio University Press, 1985).

Gelband, Hellen, "Professional Education in Palliative and End–of–Life Care for Physicians, Nurses and Social Worlers," in *Improving Palliative Care for Cancer*, eds. Kathleen Foley and Hellen Gelband (Washington, DC: National Academy Press, 2001), 277–310. and Association of American Medical Colleges 2000–2001 report, "Number of U.S. Medical Schools Teaching Selected Topics," extracted from the report by the Liaison Committee on Medical Education Part II Annual Medical School Questionnaire for 2000–2001.

Giedion, Siegfried, *Mechanization Takes Command: A Contribution to Anonymous History* (New York: Oxford University Press, 1948).

Goffman, Erving, *Interaction Ritual: Essays on Face–to–Face Behavior* (Garden City, New York: Anchor Books, 1967).

Gorer, Geoffrey, "The Pornography of Death," *Encounters*, 1955, 50.

Hamilton, James, *Channeling Violence*, (Princeton, NJ: Princeton University Press, 1998).

Heidegger, Martin, *Being and Time* (New York: Harper, 1962).

Hume, Janice, *Examining Content—"Portraits of Grief," Reflectors of Values: The New York Times Remembers Victims of September 11. Journalism and Mass Communications Quarterly*, 80: 166–193.

Jackson, Kenneth T., and Vergara, Camilo J., *Silent Cities: The Evolution of the American Cemetery* (New York: Princeton Architectural Press, 1989).

Jencks, Charles, *A Post–Modern Reader*, (New York: St. Martin's, 1995).

Jenkins, Henry, *Textual Poachers: Television Fans and Participatory Culture* (New York: Routledge, 1992) 86.

Jung, Carl, *Man and His Symbols* (Garden City, New York: Doubleday, 1964).

Kant, Immanuel, *Critique of Practical Reason* (New York: Liberal Arts Press, 1956), quoted in Lamont, p. 162.

Kramer, Eric M., *Modern/Postmodern: Off the Beaten Path of Antimodernism* (Westport, CT: Praeger, 1997).

_____, *Postmodernism and Race* (Westport, CT: Praeger, 1997).

_____, *The Emerging Monoculture: Assimilation and the "Model Minority,"* (Westport, CT: Praeger, 2003).

Lamont, Corliss, *The Illusion of Immortality* (1935; Fifth Edition: Continuum, 1990).

Lasch, Christopher, *The Culture of Narcissism: American Life in an Age of Diminishing Expectations* (New York: Norton, 1978).

Levinas, Emmanuel, *Totality and Infinity: An Essay on Exteriority* (Pittsburgh, PA: Duquesne University Press, 1969.

Levine, Robert, *The Geography of Time: The Temporal Misadventures of a Social Psychologist, or How Every Culture Keeps Time Just a Little Bit Differently* (New York: Basic Books, 1997).

Light, Andrew. *Reel Arguments* (Boulder, CO: Westview, 2003)

Lingis, Alphonso, *The Community of Those Who Have Nothing in Common* (Bloomington, IN: Indiana University Press, 1994).

Mattelart, Armand, *Mapping World Communication: War Progress and Culture,* (Minneapolis: University of Minnesota Press, 1994).

McIlwain, Charlton D., *Death in Black and White: Death, Ritual, and Family Ecology,* (Creskill, NJ: Hampton Press, 2003).

Moeller, Susan D., *Compassion Fatigue: How the Media Sell Disease, Famine, War and Death* (New York:: Routledge, 1999).

Morris, Desmond, *The Human Zoo,* (1969; New York: Kodansha International, 1996).

Mumford, Lewis, *The City in History: Its Origins, Its Transformations, and its Prospects* (New York: Harcourt, Brace & World, 1961), 6–10.

Nietzsche, Friedrich, *The Gay Science: With a Prelude in Rhymes and an Appendix of Songs,* trans. Walter Kaufman (New York: Random House, 1974).

Palmer, Richard, *Hermeneutics: Interpretation Theory in Schleiermacher, Dilthey, Heidegger, and Gadamer* (Evanston, IL: Northwestern University Press, 1969).

Plato, "The Republic: Book X," in *The Essential Plato*, trans. Benjamin Jowett (The Book–of–the–Month–Club, Inc., 1999), 416.

_____"Phaedo," in *The Essential Plato*, trans. Benjamin Jowett (The Book–of–the–Month–Club, Inc., 1999), 605.

Potter, W. James, *The 11 Myths of Media Violence,* (Newbury Park, CA: Sage, 2003).

Sennett, Richard, *The Fall of Public Man,* (New York: Random House, 1976).

Spinoza, Benedictus de, *The Ethics and Selected Letters* (Indianapolis, IN: Hackett Publishing, 1982).

Ströker, Elisabeth, *Investigations in Philosophy of Space* (Athens, OH: Ohio University Press, 1987).

Toynbee, Arnold, *Man's Concern with Death* (St. Louis, MO: McGraw–Hill, 1969).

Joseph Turow, *Playing Doctor: Television, Storytelling & Medical Power* (New York: Oxford University Press, 1999), xi–xii.

Worth, David Steven, *The Built Environment as Communication: Totality, Alterity, and Dissociation in Urban and Suburban Spaces* (Norman, OK: Doctoral Dissertation, 2003).

INDEX